Building Your Mouseless Development Environment

Matthieu Cneude

Contents

Contents

Contents

Contents

Acknowledgments

To my mom, who always encouraged me and supported me in everything I wanted to do in my life, including writing. What she did for me can't be described in words.

The biggest thanks for my girlfriend Antje, who always supported me in my weirdest dreams, in the bright and dark moments, without judgments. Antje, thanks for being on my side. We need more people like you in this world.

Thanks to Jan Mollowitz[1] and Martin Ohmann[2], who pushed me to try most of the tools I describe in this book. I thought it would be a waste of my time; I was terribly wrong.

I'm not a native English speaker, so I needed some serious proofreading. The proofreaders of this book didn't only help me to improve it: they provided great suggestions and kind encouragements I definitely needed. Thanks to (in no particular order): Tim Collins[3], Dr. Robert Koss, Zack Teska[4], Greg Wagner, Nick Rokosz[5], Colin Roberts[6], Ariel Don, Ben Reedy[7], Joe Gurr[8], Dan Jacobson[9], and Nick Allgood.

Thanks to Abel Pérez Martínez[10] for his precious feedback.

I used one of the free illustration[11] created by Lukasz Adam for the cover of this book. Thanks for providing such amazing visuals!

To all my friends, to everybody who support my work in any way, and to all the kind, peaceful, and merciful people in this world: thanks a lot!

And finally, thank you, dear reader, for picking up this book. I hope you'll enjoy it!

---

[1] https://github.com/phux

[2] https://github.com/martinohmann

[3] https://crumbhole.com

[4] https://github.com/zerodahero

[5] https://nickrokosz.com/

[6] https://github.com/colinjroberts

[7] https://github.com/breed808

[8] https://joegurr.com

[9] https://www.danj.ca

[10] https://abelperezmartinez.blogspot.com

[11] https://lukaszadam.com/illustrations

Welcome, Mouseless Developers

With this book we'll embark, together, in a creative journey where we'll build an efficient and Mouseless Development Environment. We'll go from the void of an empty hard disk to a complete system you can mostly use with a keyboard. We'll install everything manually at the beginning, and we'll become an omniscient entity able to summon the whole development environment with one command at the end.

There are huge benefits to install a complete system by ourselves: we'll learn a tonne along the way. It's good to use tools to achieve our goals, but it's even better to know a little about how they work. It will also allow us more flexibility to modify whatever we want according to our needs.

Knowledge brings flexibility, and flexibility brings efficiency.

Our secret weapon? The command-line. We'll use it for almost everything we'll do throughout this book, because it's simply the most powerful tool we can use. It's consistent, it doesn't get out of fashion, it doesn't get in our way, it doesn't dramatically change when new versions are available. It will make your life easier and it will give you tremendous power. Who doesn't want that?

If you need more arguments to convince you that the command-line is what you need to level up to a higher plane of existence (at least), here we go:

1. As developers, we often have to deal with Linux-based systems on servers (or containers) where only the command-line is available.
2. Command-Line Interfaces (CLIs) don't have any graphical interfaces. To use these programs, we have no choice: we need the shell.
3. The shell gives you the ultimate power we all seek: automation. It's difficult to automate the movements of your mouse on a graphical interface; it's easier when you deal with plain text, like the command-line.

Keep the acronym "CLI" in mind: we'll use it often throughout the book.

I'll explain everything for you to understand what we're doing, why we're doing it, and how you can personalize your system according to *your* needs. To *your* workflow. To *your* personality. The goal: acquiring the knowledge you need by practicing and experimenting. Then, you'll be able to transfer this knowledge on any development environment you want, even if it's based on another Linux distribution, or if you want to use a more standard IDE instead of Neovim, for example. You can even use most of the tools described in this book on macOS too.

Now, a bummer: we won't dive deep into everything we'll talk about, or this book would become way too long for us to survive it; both the poor writer and the poor readers. Instead, it will focus on showing how the different tools described in this book can work together.

That said, each chapter of the book concludes on a list of resources you can read to satisfy your infinite curiosity.

Who Should Read This Book?

Everyone can read this book, but not everybody will get the most value out of it. So, should you read this book?

If you're a beginner in software development, this book is for you. I try to explain everything you need to know to understand what we're doing. Yet, it can be a bit tough on you because it's a lot of information to swallow at once. My advice: go slowly, don't hesitate to try things out, to experiment, to play with the command-line. This book will be truly rewarding if you put the effort and some patience.

If you're a seasoned developer but you don't use the command-line often, you're at the right place. This book is for you if you want to know more about Linux, the shell, and if a Mouseless Development Environment sparks your infinite curiosity. Personally, when I discovered it, the spark looked more like an enlightenment! You think I'm exaggerating? Yes, I am. But still.

If you already use the command-line intensively and the tools I describe in this book, you might not learn much from it. I'm sorry. It breaks my heart more than yours. That said, Building Your Mouseless Development Environment can help you fill the gaps in your knowledge. Buying the book can be a good way to support my work, too; if you like my blog[1], my GitHub[2], my style, or my limited charisma. You can still offer this book to some poor souls who still work on Windows, too. It's not that I judge you, Windows developers; I was in your situation for decades. It's just that the grass is greener and tastier on the Linux side of the fence.

What Is a Mouseless Development Environment?

The obvious goal of a Mouseless Development Environment is to use less of the mouse. It doesn't mean that you can throw your mice through your windows. First, because you might kill somebody, second because it's not nice to pollute, and third because the mouse is still useful in many cases. I'm not dogmatic.

---

[1] https://thevaluable.dev

[2] https://github.com/Phantas0s

Using the mouse is great for some endeavors, like graphical manipulation, video editing, or musical creation. I wouldn't draw in a terminal like I wouldn't write a book with a brush; it wasn't meant for that.

I'm sure you noticed but software engineers deal with a lot of text: we spend our time writing code and (hopefully) documentation. It's for this kind of job that our keyboard and our commands really shine. Text never goes out of trend: you can write scripts to parse them and to automate anything you want, thanks to the Holy Shell. Repeat after me: glory to the Holy Shell!

A Mouseless Development Environment lets you keep your hands on the keyboard most of the time, which is a blessing by itself. It's very comfy not to move your hands to reach your mouse, then your keyboard, then your mouse, in an infinite recursion of pain. Even if you think that it doesn't bother you, you'll see the truth by simply trying not to use it. I thought it wasn't a problem for a long time, but trying to stay on the keyboard definitely changed my way of working.

What Do You Need to Follow Along?

To follow this book, you need to have a *place* to install the whole system and its tools: Arch Linux, URxvt, Neovim, Zsh, tmux, and so on. If you have an empty hard disk, that's a very good container for that. You can also use a virtual machine if you want to see first how it looks, or if you just want to follow the book for learning purposes, without the intention to use the final Mouseless Development Environment.

The good news: even if you finish the book on a virtual machine, you'll have a complete installer for the Mouseless Development Environment somewhere on GitHub. It's something we'll build together, too. You can use it on any standard computer you want, even on a MacBook Pro; tested and approved. If you fall in love with your new shiny environment, as I did, you'll be able to install it quickly on a new computer.

You can create virtual machines using Virtualbox[1]. A virtual machine is a simulated computer using the resources of your physical computer. You can install anything you want on it, without your physical computer to know about it. Both systems (host and virtual machine) are decoupled as much as possible. In general, virtual machines are great to try different OS or Linux distributions without too much hassle.

If you install the Mouseless Development Environment on a physical computer, I recommend you to find a way to be able to read this book while installing everything. You can use another computer, a tablet, or a reader for example.

---

[1] https://www.virtualbox.org/

Creating Your Own Cheatsheets

Since a Mouseless Development Environment focuses on using the keyboard when it's appropriate, we'll see many shortcuts (or keystrokes) in this book. We'll go through each tool step by step to understand why and how to use these keystrokes, for you to remember them easily.

Still, you need to be able to go back to these keystrokes if you forget them while using your system. You can of course download ready-made cheatsheets from the Internet, but in my experience they are not very useful for beginners. You risk ending up in an ocean of keystrokes, not really knowing what are the most important ones, suffocating under too many possibilities.

That's why I would advise you to write your own cheatsheets while going through the book. Write one for each tool. If you need to be convinced, here some arguments:

1. Writing will help you to remember the different keystrokes. You can also write some comments, categorize them, and even add some personal mnemonics. You can draw something funny near your keystroke. Humour is a great tool to memorize. In short, you'll make these keystrokes *yours*.
2. You can organize them in a way which makes sense to you.
3. When you'll come back to them, you'll feel they are some extension of your brain, not 10923810938 unknown keystrokes downloaded from a random, cold, and sad Internet corner.

I followed this technique when I learnt to build my own Mouseless Development Environment, and I believe that's one of the reasons why I never found Neovim or anything else to have a high learning curve. I was then able to get things done in this mouseless system very quickly. Believe me, it's not because I'm a genius; I'm a very standard human.

Similarly, you should also write down the different commands you'll see in this book, for the same reasons.

Experimenting Is Key

To learn, you need to practice and experiment. It's a bit more work than passively watching a Youtube video, but it's more effective too. Write your own cheatsheet, comment your configuration files and bash scripts, and don't hesitate to play around with everything. The goal is not to memorize but to understand how it works. Try to modify a command and see what options you can use, for example.

In two words: be curious.

The more you'll learn about the shell in general, the easier it will be for you to learn what you can put on top and how it works.

Styling Conventions

There are only a few special styling conventions in this book. You'll know, while reading the book, what to execute in the shell, and what to write in what config files.

Sometimes, `<something>` will pop up in some commands you need to execute. That is, an expression surrounded with the characters `<` and `>`. For example, `fdisk <your_hard_disk>`, or `su <user_name>`. These are variables you, and only you, know the values of. No worries: I'll tell you each time how you can find the information you need to replace them with a good value.

You might also see arrows at the beginning of specific lines in code blocks. For example:

```
echo "LANG=<language_code>_<country_code>.<character_encoding>" >
 ↪  /etc/locale.conf
```

It means that even if the command appears on two lines in the book, it should be written on one line.

Choose Your Tools

You can replace any tool we'll see in this book with another one or your liking, but I would suggest you to follow the entire book first to understand how they can work together. Then, you can modify any configuration file or replace any tool you want because, instead of copying and pasting the configuration of a random person on the Internet, you'll have built your whole system by yourself. You'll have a great control over it.

We'll use Neovim for every editing task from the start. If you don't want to learn how it works, you can use Nano instead or anything else you prefer.

In a Nutshell

What did we learn in this chapter?

- If you're not already using the command-line and a Mouseless Development Environment daily, you'll learn many things from this book. Otherwise, you can still try to fill some gaps in your knowledge.
- Create your own cheatsheets to maximize your learning. Make the useful information your own.
- Don't be afraid to experiment with the different commands and the tools we'll see throughout the book.

In the next chapter, we'll discuss about some important basics about Linux-based systems.

Part I - Linux

A General Linux Overview

This chapter is a high level overview of a Linux-based system. Don't worry if you don't remember everything: we'll come back to these concepts in later chapters.

Let's first see some generalities about the system we'll build. More specifically we'll answer these questions:

- What's Linux?
- What's a Linux distribution?
- What are repositories?
- What's the shell?

I know. It might look very boring for seasoned Linux users. Who knows? Maybe you'll learn two or three things from it. Of course, you're free to skip this chapter if you want to.

Diving Inside Linux

Linux is an Operating System (OS) like Windows or macOS. The heart of any OS is a program called the *kernel*. It's the interface between you (and the applications you use) and the hardware of your computer. Thanks to the kernel, the programs running on your system can communicate with the hard disk or the memory, for example.

For you to speak with the kernel around a good cup of tea, you need another interface: the *shell*. For example, you can create a file using the shell, which is in fact you, the user, asking the kernel politely to create something on the hard disk. The kernel might accept your request or deny it ruthlessly.

The shell is an interpreter, which means that it can read *commands* and perform actions depending on them, like running a program or creating a file. You can write these commands yourself using a standard input. The most obvious standard input is a keyboard, but you can use a script too, a file containing commands to execute. We'll come back to that later in this book.

There are many shells out there you can use, like Bash or Zsh. We'll use Zsh to install Arch Linux, and then we'll continue with Bash for a while.

To use the shell, guess what? We need another interface. In computing, we heavily rely on layers of abstractions, and we use interfaces to communicate between these layers. This time, a *terminal emulator*, or *terminal*, will allow you to access the shell. Again, we'll come back to that later, and explain more in detail what it is.

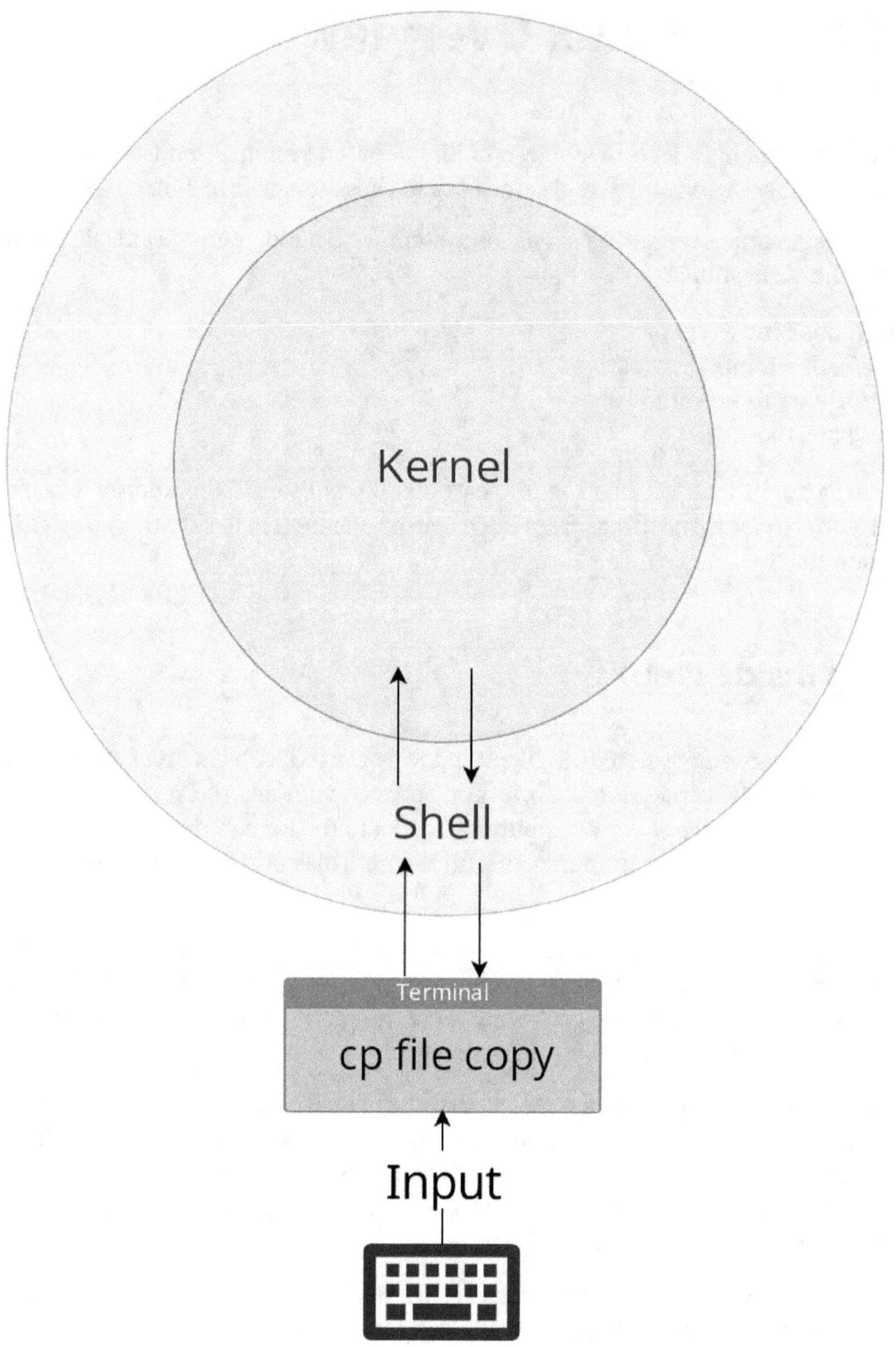

You'll see throughout the book and in many other places the sentences "execute in a shell", "execute in a terminal", "run in a shell", or "run in a terminal". These sentences are all synonym. This means that you need to:

1. Type the command the book provides into a terminal.
2. Press the `ENTER` key to interpret the command.

Then, our friend the shell will return an *exit code*, not directly visible, and possibly an *output* which will be displayed in the terminal by default.

The shell should be your friend. She should be your best buddy, because she can do a lot for you. Yes, the shell is a feminine character in my world, but your shell can be anything you want. The sky's the limit.

The Linux Filesystem

The directories in a Linux-based system are all children of a special directory called *root directory*. In the filesystem, it will seem hidden at first, known only under the name `/`. Don't be fooled! It's the most important directory because it contains every other one. A directory to rule them all!

Direct children of the root directory have specific purposes we'll see all along the book.

How does a path to a file (or filepath) in a Linux-based system look? For example: `/etc/zsh`. The first `/` is our powerful root directory, supporting everything else as Atlas supported the world. The directory `etc` is a direct child of the root directory, and the directory `zsh` is itself a child of `etc`. Every `/` which is not the first character of the filepath is a *directory separator*. It's here to indicate a new level of directory. Confusing? I told you the root directory tried to hide!

If, in a terminal, you run the command `cd /etc`, you'll move from the directory you were to the directory `/etc`. It will become your *working directory*, also known as the *current directory*. Each time you move from directory to directory, your working directory changes too. You can think of it as the place you are, and you can jump from place to place. To display what your current directory is, you can run the command `pwd` (for `p`rint `w`orking `d`irectory) in a terminal.

There are many special directories in a Linux-based system. Here are two you'll encounter very often:

- `.` – Represents your working directory.
- `..` – Represents the direct parent of your working directory.

If you run `cd .`, you'll jump from the directory you're in to the directory you're in. Was it useless? Absolutely! Now, if you run `cd ..`, you'll move to the parent directory of the working directory. Similarly, if you run in a shell `cp ./cat_picture ./file`, you'll `c`o`p`y the file named `cat_picture` in your working directory and "move" it to your working directory. At the end, you'll have two identical files in your working directory with different names.

Linux Distributions

If you install an OS like Windows or macOS, it will include installing the kernel, a shell, and many other programs too. For example, the Windows installer will provide a desktop environment, a bundle of programs sharing the same graphical interface. It includes the desktop where you can place shortcuts of your programs, often a status bar with a truckload of stuff in it, a wallpaper, and all of these things. The OS doesn't let you choose what programs and what desktop you want to install.

A Linux distribution, commonly called *distro*, is a Linux kernel, a shell, and many programs too. The difference: there are 200+ Linux distros you can choose from. For example, the distro Ubuntu will install some version of the Linux kernel, the shell Bash, a desktop environment called Unity, and many other programs, like some Amazon ads. Who doesn't want Amazon ads in a development environment? Everybody? Thanks, Ubuntu.

Sometimes, when people use the word "Linux", it's often not very clear what they are speaking about: a Linux distro? The kernel? The Linux philosophy? What's important to remember is this: there are not many differences between Linux distributions. You can roughly summarize them as follows:

- The set of applications a Linux distro installs on your system.
- The set of applications available in the repositories.
- The philosophy attached to the distro, especially the way you can update the Linux kernel, the shell, and all the programs installed.
- The package manager used to install packages.

Some distros are built on top of other ones. For example, Ubuntu is built on top of another distro called Debian; both will have many similarities.

Arch Linux is a distribution too, but it only installs a very minimal Linux-based system. You'll have the kernel, the shell, a set of programs commonly used in the shell, and a package manager. No desktop environment, no Amazon thingy, not even a graphical environment to display Graphical User Interfaces (GUIs). We'll install all of that ourselves, and at the same time we'll see how these layers work together. By understanding this, you'll be able to install anything you want and personalize everything following your craziest desires.

Packages and Repositories

We were speaking about programs and applications. In the Linux world you'll also often see the term *package*. A package is a compressed archive bundling every file for a given application. This archive has metadata to know how to install the application itself. These packages are stored in some locations called *repositories*. To download and install packages, we'll use a *package manager*.

Different Linux distros often use different repositories and package managers. For example, Ubuntu uses APT as a package manager, and Arch Linux uses Pacman (for `Pac` kage `Man` ager).

Why Arch Linux?

Why will we install Arch Linux in this book, and not another distro?

First, Arch Linux users have often the reputation to be arrogant individuals, pointing the finger to everybody who doesn't use Arch Linux. They always have a great pleasure to mention that they use Arch Linux in any discussion, even if it's about the price of the cheese at your favorite supermarket. I wanted to invite you in this very closed club. My pleasure!

Additionally to the fact fact that installing Arch Linux can teach a great deal about Linux-based systems in general, using it in our daily work has many advantages too.

The Glory of Rolling Distributions

As we saw above, the different Linux distros out there have different ways to manage everything installed on your system, from the Linux kernel to the packages installed.

Arch Linux is a rolling distribution; the packages are kept up-to-date as much as possible. You can be pretty confident that you'll have access to the latest versions of your favorite applications. The small downside: you'll have to update your system pretty often, every week or every other week. Trust me, that's a small price to pay for having the most up-to-date system possible.

If you listen to the urban legend that Arch Linux is "very unstable" because of that, don't believe it. Some friends run Arch Linux for years (otherwise they wouldn't be my friends of course!) and I do, too. We never had any problems doing so. I used Windows from Windows 98 to Windows 7, macOS, and some other Linux distributions like Ubuntu. My conclusion: Arch Linux is the most stable system I've ever had.

The Arch Linux Community

The Arch Linux community is great. Arch Linux folks have solid knowledge in many areas, and they have very useful tips too. The best place to fall in admiration for the Arch Linux community is the Arch Linux wiki[1]. It's simply the best resource you'll find regarding Linux, even if you use another distro.

Official Repositories and the Arch User Repositories (AUR)

The official repositories of Arch Linux provide many packages. I'm not exaggerating: you'll find most of the applications you need in there. Even if you don't, you'll have access to the Arch User Repository too, an unofficial repository where you'll find everything and anything. No need to install, compile, and update manually the obscure applications you use. An AUR helper can do that for you in one command.

The Fabulous Manual

Almost every CLI out there has at least a `man` ual page describing what it is, how it works, and what it can do. This documentation is often very complete: I advise you to look at it as soon as you need some explanations.

Here's how to access the manual:

```
man <command>
```

For example, you can run `man cd` in a shell to read the manual page of the command `cd`. If you're a beginner, it might be a bit difficult to read at first. When you better understand some concepts distilled in this book, you'll find `man` less cryptic.

Keep in mind: you don't have to read everything. Often, reading the description is enough to understand what a CLI can do for you. If you're searching for specific *options*, `man` can be very helpful too. A command-line option is often a single letter prefixed by a minus `-`, or a word prefixed by a double minus `--`. Adding options will modify the behavior of a command.

A command often has some kind of option to display some concise help, often something like `--help` or `-h`. The output is often shorter and more condensed than the man page for the same command. To understand what I mean, try to run:

---

[1] https://wiki.archlinux.org/

```
ls --help
```

Manuals are often divided into sections. To look at a specific section, you can run the following:

```
man <section> <command>
```

I won't go into more detail here. If you want to know more about man (including this idea of sections), you should read the man page of man by running in a terminal:

```
man man
```

It's inception directly in your shell!

Troubleshooting

General Recommendations

Manually installing everything following a book can lead to some problems. Heck, using a computer lead to some problems. In my experience, using an automatic installer for a Linux distro can lead to some problems, too. In short: we can have problems.

If you run into unexpected errors and weird behaviors, you should take a look at these resources:

1. The Arch Wiki[1] is, as we just saw, the best resource for almost everything, except the meaning of life. If you search on the Internet something related to Linux, you'll very often end up on it.
2. The official Arch Linux website[2] is the place to go when you have problems updating your system. It describes the manual interventions you need to do from time to time. Everything is always explained clearly.
3. The Arch Linux forum[3] is a good place to go if you have any question. Be sure that your problem is related to Arch Linux and that you've done some research before posting there.

---

[1] https://wiki.archlinux.org/

[2] https://www.archlinux.org/

[3] https://bbs.archlinux.org/

Using VMWare Software

You'll need to install additional packages if you run this system on any VMWare product. I won't go into the details here, but you can look at this page on the Arch Wiki[1] if you have any problem down the road.

In a Nutshell

What did we learn in this chapter?

- The kernel is the heart of an Operating System (OS). You can communicate with the kernel using the shell, which will read and interprets commands you type into a terminal emulator.
- In the Linux filesystem, every directory is a child of the root directory, named `/` . A filepath looks like this: `/etc/kernel` , where the first `/` is the root directory and the subsequent `/` are directory separators.
- A package is an installer for an application. They are located in repositories you can access using the Internet. You need a package manager to install the application contained in a package.
- Linux distros are not that different from each others. Mostly, they have different philosophies on handling packages, different package managers, and different repositories. They come bundled with different applications, too.

The next chapter will be a short but important one: we'll see how to have good typing techniques. This is mandatory if you really want to be efficient with a keyboard.

Going Deeper

- Manual pages for Arch Linux packages[2]

---

[1] https://wiki.archlinux.org/index.php/VMware

[2] https://man.archlinux.org/

The Power Is In Your Fingers

You remember Frodo? He saved Middle Earth by throwing a ring into a volcano. He was quite small, but how important!

This chapter is quite small too, and like Frodo, very important.

You're reading right now a book to build a Mouseless Development Environment, so it's pretty obvious I'll advocate to use your keyboard as much as you can. The goal is simple: you should move your hands as little as possible from this magical device.

Knowing how to type properly is a stepping stone to master a keyboard driven workflow. You can practice the following techniques while reading the book. When you begin to replace your typing techniques, stick to it as much as you can. Don't come back to your old (and bad) habits.

The benefits are huge. Massive. Colossal!

- You'll feel much more comfy while developing the next trendy application which will make you rich. What a secret pleasure to have our hands on the keyboard!
- The room for progression (speed and accuracy) will increase drastically.

If you look at pianists playing, you'll notice that they never look at their hands. They don't want to spend brain power on those kinds of detail; their hands follow their will as fast as possible.

The analogy holds very well for us, computer addicts. When you are in a state of flow, focused on your craft, you don't want to be interrupted every five minutes by moving your hand to the mouse or by looking at your fingers. You don't want to think about all of that. You want to create, nothing else.

Let's see how we can achieve that.

Efficient Typing: The Two Rules

It's satisfying to see your typing techniques improving day after days, months after months, and even years after years. These techniques are easy to learn but difficult to master.

The first rule you need to be aware of: placing your hands correctly. The keys `a`, `s`, `d`, `f` and `j`, `k`, `l`, `a` `;` are called the *row keys*. They are the starting points for your hands. From there, you'll be able to grab any other key as efficiently as possible, as illustrated by this image[1].

You'll notice that there are little bumps on the keys f and j on your keyboard: they are indicators for you to know where you need to put your indexes. When they are at the good position, simply place the other fingers on the other row keys.

The second rule you need to train for: try not looking at your keyboard while you're typing. Of course, if you don't remember where a key is, look at it, but only after trying blindly where you think it is. We want to train your muscle memory here.

I was only typing with two fingers before trying to follow these two rules. It felt really weird to use these new techniques at first; now, I wouldn't type differently. It's efficient, it's comfortable, it's great!

The First Week

When you decide to use the two rules we saw above, you need to try to follow them *all the time*. We need 100% commitment here. If you surprise yourself using your bad techniques again, which will happen, don't worry: simply come back to the good ones. This is part of the learning process, not a horrible failure cursing your whole family on five generations.

The first three days are the most difficult. You'll alternate between good and bad technique without even noticing it. You'll do mistakes. You'll be slower. That's great! It's how you'll learn.

Fortunately, at the end of the week, the amount of mistakes you'll make will decrease, and the need to watch the keyboard will slowly disappear.

The Second Week

You'll notice during the second week the amount of mistakes decreasing even more, and you won't dare look at your keyboard while typing. At the end of the week, you'll see your typing speed improving already. The good feelings of reward will begin to please your brain. That's what we all want.

---

[1] https://matthieucneude.com/hand_keyboard_points.png

Speed and Accuracy

During your two weeks of initial training, you shouldn't focus on speed or accuracy. Just type, as much as you can, and don't worry about anything else yet. Not even about the mistakes you're making.

Only then, when you feel comfortable enough, you can shift your focus on speed and accuracy: how fast you can type while making as few mistakes as possible.

Keyboard Layout

You noticed that I'm only covering the US international keyboard layout here. If you use another one, the principles are the same. The row keys are at the same position too; only the keys themselves change.

In A Nutshell

What did we learn in this chapter?

- We need to focus on our work, not on our hands. Learning the good typing techniques will help you tremendously in this regard.
- The first rule: place your hands correctly on your keyboard, using the row keys.
- The second rule: don't look at your hands while typing. Even if you don't remember where a key is, don't look at it before trying to get it without looking.
- Only train for speed and accuracy when you're used to these new typing techniques.

In the next chapter, we'll begin to prepare our hard disk for installing Arch Linux.

Going Deeper

As always, to learn as fast as possible, you need to practice. This book ask you to type many commands, so you'll have many occasions to learn these good typing techniques.

You can also use typing software to have concrete data about your speed and accuracy. Here are my favorites:

- Type Racer[1]
- Online Typing Test WPM[2]
- Speed Coder[3]

---

[1] https://play.typeracer.com/

[2] https://www.keyhero.com/

[3] http://www.speedcoder.net/

Preparing Your System for Arch Linux

It's time to get our hands dirty! In this chapter, we'll prepare our system for Arch Linux for us to feel at home. More precisely, we'll answer these questions:

- How to burn an Arch Linux ISO on a USB key?
- How to configure the Arch Linux live system?
- How to partition a hard disk using fdisk?
- How to create and mount new filesystems?

This is the very beginning of the journey, so I'll try to explain most things in detail. Ready for the challenge? Let's go!

Prerequisites

To install our new Mouseless Development Environment, we'll need the following:

1. A computer with a 64-bit CPU (not older than 10 years).
2. Internet access via Ethernet *and* Wifi is recommended, in case one or the other doesn't work on the Arch Linux live system.
3. An empty hard disk, or a hard disk you'll wipe out (at least 20 GB to feel comfy).
4. A USB key (at least 1 GB).
5. A second computer, a tablet, or any other device allowing you to read this book while installing everything.
6. Internet access on your second device is highly recommended, in case you have a problem in the first chapters.

As we mentioned already, the computer can be a virtual machine or a physical one.

Burning the Arch Linux ISO

If you wonder what the heck an ISO is, it's a file representing a physical disk. We can burn ISO files on a real disk, which means copying everything from the ISO to the disk.

To install Arch Linux, we need to start (or *boot*) our computer using the Arch Linux live system, and install the OS from there. Here's how to do that:

1. Download the Arch Linux ISO[1]. Find your country, click on the first link, and download `archlinux-<the_last_release_date>-x86_64.iso`.
2. Verify that the ISO is the official one, and has not been modified by horrible hackers. You need to generate the MD5 hash of the ISO and compare it with the one provided on the download page. To get this hash, you can use the following commands:

   - On Windows: `CertUtil -hashfile <path_to_ISO_file> MD5`
   - On Linux: `md5sum <path_to_ISO_file>`

3. Burn the ISO on a USB key. You can use:

   - On Windows: rufus[2].
   - On Ubuntu: Startup Disk Creator.
   - On another Linux distro: UNetbootin[3].

4. Change the boot order to read USB devices before your hard disk. You can do that by using your BIOS interface.
5. Plug your USB key and start your computer.

For the fourth point, you can normally access the BIOS interface by hitting a specific key when your computer starts. If you're lucky, it might be displayed at startup long enough for you to see it. It's often `ESC` , `DEL` or `F10` . Every computer is different on this point, so I can't really help you more.

When you found a way to access your BIOS' interface, search for any option concerning the boot. You can normally change the boot order of the devices: the goal is to put your USB device before your hard disk. When you're done with that, there will be some options to save your changes and restart your computer.

If you did everything correctly, your computer will boot from your USB key, and you'll see a menu inviting you to install Arch Linux. Let's do it!

Configuring the Arch Linux Live System

Your screen will then spit out many green "OK" messages telling you what systemd is starting. We'll talk about systemd later in this book. Then, you'll end up in a shell prompt. It will look like this:

```
root@archiso ~ #
```

---

[1] https://www.archlinux.org/download/

[2] https://rufus.ie/

[3] https://unetbootin.github.io/

A prompt is a set of characters indicating that you can execute commands. Here, it indicates what user you are (`root`) and the hostname `archiso` . The hostname is the name of your system as it will appear on a network.

Welcome to the Arch Linux live system! What's a live system? For now, nothing has been installed on your hard disk; instead, the system you have access to is running from your computer's memory (RAM). Many distros provide a live system for you to test it even before installing anything.

It also means that everything you're doing in the live system won't survive if you shut down or restart your computer, except if you deliberately write something on your hard disk. For example, any program you'll install on the live system won't be installed on your hard disk.

The shell we're using now is called the "Z shell", or Zsh. It's similar to the most famous shell, Bash. We'll dig more into Zsh later in this book, too. Here are some functionalities you can use with the shell:

- You can enter any command in a shell prompt and execute it by hitting `ENTER` .
- The shell can save the command history:

    - You can quickly access executed commands with the keys `ARROW UP` and `ARROW DOWN` .
    - You can search through the history with `CTRL+r` .

- You can use Zsh auto completion by hitting `TAB` .
- To stop a running command, you can use the keystroke `CTRL+c` . Be careful with it: patience is sometimes safer. Think about what your command is doing before interrupting it, and consider the price you might have to pay by stopping it before it's done.

You are now the *root user*. You can create different users on a Linux system, but the root user is special. It has almost all power a user can have. Don't confuse the root user and the root directory `/` we saw in the previous chapter. A filesystem and a bunch of users are different things, even if they have both root as their name.

By being the root user, you're in fact the demigod (or demigoddess!) of the "archiso" live system. Why only demi? Because a user can't control directly the kernel. The kernel is the real master around here.

Keyboard Layout

By default, you'll end up with the American keyboard layout on the Arch Linux live system. If you're not comfortable with it, you can change it. Here are the two commands you can use to do so:

1. `ls /usr/share/kbd/keymaps/**/*.map.gz` – List all layout available.

2. `ls /usr/share/kbd/keymaps/**/*.map.gz | grep "<your_language_code>"`
   - Filter all layout with grep.

For example, if I want to use a French keyboard layout, I can do this:

```
ls /usr/share/kbd/keymaps/**/*.map.gz | grep "fr"
```

The result will look like the following:

```
/usr/share/kbd/keymaps/i386/azerty/fr-latin1.map.gz
/usr/share/kbd/keymaps/i386/azerty/fr-latin9.map.gz
/usr/share/kbd/keymaps/i386/azerty/fr.map.gz
/usr/share/kbd/keymaps/i386/azerty/fr-pc.map.gz
/usr/share/kbd/keymaps/i386/bepo/fr-bepo-latin9.map.gz
/usr/share/kbd/keymaps/i386/bepo/fr-bepo.map.gz
/usr/share/kbd/keymaps/i386/dvorak/dvorak-ca-fr.map.gz
/usr/share/kbd/keymaps/i386/dvorak/dvorak-fr.map.gz
/usr/share/kbd/keymaps/i386/qwertz/fr_CH-latin1.map.gz
/usr/share/kbd/keymaps/i386/qwertz/fr_CH.map.gz
/usr/share/kbd/keymaps/mac/all/mac-fr_CH-latin1.map.gz
/usr/share/kbd/keymaps/mac/all/mac-fr.map.gz
/usr/share/kbd/keymaps/sun/sunt5-fr-latin1.map.gz
```

You can then choose your layout by using the filename without the file extension
`map.gz` :

```
loadkeys <filename>
```

For example, I would run the command `loadkeys fr-latin1` for a French keyboard
layout.

Write this keymap somewhere, you'll need it again in the next chapter.

Connecting to the Internet

What would we be without Internet? Nothing more than unconscious amoebas lost
in a chain of misconceptions we call reality. Without Internet, I wouldn't even be able
to write the previous sentence!

To connect to this infinite amount of knowledge and cat pictures, we need some network device. The command `ip link` will show you the truth about them. Let's try
to run it in the terminal:

```
ip link
```

Something like this will be output:

```
1: lo: <LOOPBACK,UP,LOWER_UP> mtu 65536 qdisc noqueue state UNKNOWN
   ↪   mode DEFAULT group default qlen 1000
       link/loopback 00:00:00:00:00:00 brd 00:00:00:00:00:00
2: enp0s25: <NO-CARRIER,BROADCAST,MULTICAST,UP> mtu 1500 qdisc
   ↪   fq_codel state DOWN mode DEFAULT group default qlen 1000
       link/ether f0:de:f1:84:f3:a6 brd ff:ff:ff:ff:ff:ff
3: wlp3s0: <BROADCAST,MULTICAST,UP,LOWER_UP> mtu 1500 qdisc mq state
   ↪   UP mode DORMANT group default qlen 1000
       link/ether 08:11:96:0a:12:b4 brd ff:ff:ff:ff:ff:ff
```

Don't worry about the first result `lo`. The second one `enp0s25` is my network device for Ethernet cable; it often begins with an 'e'. The third one `wlp3s0` is for the Wi-Fi; this one often begin with a "w". We don't have the same computer, so it's more than likely we won't have the same network devices either.

If you want to connect to Internet using a cable, simply plug it. For the Wi-Fi, you can run the following:

```
iwctl
```

A new shiny prompt will appear. It works similarly to the shell prompt you had before. Here are the commands you can use:

1. `device list` – List all your Wi-Fi devices.
2. `station <device> get-networks` – Replace `<device>` with the name of one of yours, to get a list of networks you can connect to with this particular device.
3. `station <device> connnect "<network>"` – Replace `<device>` and `<network>` by the device you want to use with the network you want to connect to.
4. If a password is required, enter it.
5. `station <device> show` – Show you if you're indeed connected.
6. `exit` – Exit `iwctl`.

If it failed, you might get the friendly message `Operation failed`. Don't worry and try again: even demigods fail, sometimes. Demigoddesses too. Another reason why we're only "demi" here, and not the full version.

Let's now verify that you're really connected. Millions of people use this command all around the word as we speak, to verify their Internet connection:

```
ping -c 5 thevaluable.dev
```

It will send 5 requests to the address `thevaluable.dev` and display the following:

```
64 bytes from v22017064675050008.supersrv.de (185.183.156.38):
↪   icmp_seq=1 ttl=58 time=32.6 ms
64 bytes from v22017064675050008.supersrv.de (185.183.156.38):
↪   icmp_seq=2 ttl=58 time=32.6 ms
64 bytes from v22017064675050008.supersrv.de (185.183.156.38):
↪   icmp_seq=3 ttl=58 time=32.1 ms
64 bytes from v22017064675050008.supersrv.de (185.183.156.38):
↪   icmp_seq=4 ttl=58 time=32.9 ms
64 bytes from v22017064675050008.supersrv.de (185.183.156.38):
↪   icmp_seq=5 ttl=58 time=32.2 ms
```

If you've got something similar, you're connected to the infinite Internet! Lucky you.

If it doesn't work, try:

```
ping -c 5 185.183.156.38
```

If this last command works, this means that you can't resolve addresses like `thevaluable.dev` to its IP address `185.183.156.38`. In that case, try to run a DHCP client:

```
dhcpcd &
```

What's `thevaluable.dev`? It's my blog, to show you how to do some subtle product placement in your own book.

System Clock

Let's now use one of the oldest protocols on the Internet. Anxious? Don't worry, Internet is the only stuff which never breaks in the computing world. Not like enterprise Java code.

Run this command:

```
timedatectl set-ntp true
```

We synchronized our system clock with the Network Time Protocol. That's all. Next!

BIOS or UEFI?

You remember the interface you used to change the boot order of your devices, to boot your USB key before another device?

This was the interface of some *firmware*, a piece of software tightly linked to a piece of hardware. In this precise case, this firmware is called a *BIOS* (for B asic I nput O utput S ystem) and it's directly embedded in a chip in your motherboard. The BIOS is the first piece of software running when you're booting (starting) your computer.

This BIOS verifies that your hardware works properly. It also makes available an interface for you to configure some basics, like the order of the booting devices. It will also run the *bootloader*, another program which is used to boot an operating system, like Arch Linux.

That said, the BIOS is now considered deprecated for a better alternative, called *UEFI* (for U nified E xtensible F irmware I nterface). BIOS and UEFI are two different types of firmware, but confusion arises when the UEFI pretends to be a BIOS, sometimes using the term "BIOS" on its own interface! It's often an ironic attempt not to confuse people who are used to having a BIOS.

Long story short, because the firmware of your motherboard starts the bootloader of Arch Linux, we need to know if you have a BIOS or a UEFI on your computer. To verify that, simply run in the shell:

```
ls /sys/firmware/efi/efivars
```

If you see the error `no such file or directory` , this means that your computer has a BIOS. If it outputs a bunch of files, you have a UEFI. You need to remember what kind of firmware you have to install Arch Linux properly. My advice: write it somewhere, on a piece of paper for example. We'll need this information later to create our boot partition and install the bootloader itself.

We've just learned the first piece of software which runs on our computer. You know what we should do? Create a diagram we'll complete as we go, to describe the boot process of a Linux-based system:

Boot Process

Motherboard firmware	???	???	???	???	???
BIOS or UEFI	???	???	???	???	???

This process is followed by all Linux distros out there. The box under the arrow indicates the program (or group of programs) used during this process, sometimes specific to Arch Linux.

Partitioning the Hard Disk

Enough explanations. Let's do some serious stuff now. First, let's run the following in the shell:

```
lsblk
```

This command will display your *block devices*. A block device is a file which represents a physical device. Confused? How can a device, such as a hard disk, be represented as a file?

A Linux-based system tries hard to have a consistent way for you, the applications running on your system, the kernel, and the hardware, to interact with each other. In other words, Linux offers a consistent *interface* between you and your physical system, and between the programs running and your physical computer.

Indeed, to facilitate this deep and intimate relationships, there is an important principle to understand on a Linux system: **everything is a file**. You don't need to ask yourself how to read a program or write to a device, like your hard disk: the answer will always be via a file.

For example, you can try to run the following in your shell:

```
cat /proc/stat
```

The output will give you the CPU status at the precise time you read the file. That's what I mean when I speak about an interface between you (or some running programs) and a device (your CPU in that case).

We'll come back to this idea over and over: it's central to any Linux-based system. For now, if you look at the output of our command `lsblk` , you'll see something similar to this:

```
NAME       MAJ:MIN RM    SIZE RO TYPE MOUNTPOINT
sda          8:0    0  465.8G  0 disk
  sda1       8:1    0    200M  0 part /boot
  sda2       8:2    0     16G  0 part [SWAP]
  sda3       8:3    0  389.6G  0 part /
```

- `sda` is a file representing my hard disk (`TYPE` `disk`).
- `sda1` to `sda4` are partitions of the hard disk (`TYPE` `part` for partition). A partition is a virtual division of a physical hard drive.

If your hard disk is empty, you shouldn't see any partition.

You can see the files representing your hard disk in the `/dev` directory ("dev" for "device").

Wiping Your Hard Disk

If your hard disk is not empty, you need to delete everything on it. All its data will be lost, forever. It can take a long time depending on the size and the type (mechanical or SSD) of the hard disk. As an example, for a mechanical disk of 1 TB, it took me 4 hours to entirely wipe it.

If you're good with that, run the following in your shell:

```
dd if=/dev/zero of=<your_hard_disk> status=progress
```

You need to replace `<your_hard_disk>` with yours.

For example, considering the output above when I run the command `lsblk` , the name of my hard disk is `/dev/sda` .

As a result, to wipe it, I need to run `dd if=/dev/zero of=/dev/sda status=progress` .

If you have multiple hard disks, be sure to select the good one! The command `dd` is merciless; its sweet little nickname is "Disk Destroyer". It won't ask you anything and will wipe out everything you give. You don't want to mess up with `dd` !

The command copies everything from the file `/dev/zero` to any file representing your hard disk (for me, `/dev/sda`) . The file `/dev/zero` is a file containing an infinity of zeros; new zeros will be created each time you try to read from it. In our precise example, your hard disk will be filled with zeros till it's full. At this point, the command `dd` will stop and your disk will be "clean".

You can also use `/dev/urandom` instead of `/dev/zero` : it will fill your hard disk with random numbers instead of zeros. It takes even more time, so use this solution only if you don't want anybody to be able to restore the removed data of your hard disk.

Using fdisk

It's time to virtually break our hard disk in pieces! We need to partition it for Arch Linux to come and make its nest. To do so, we'll use a simple and powerful Command Line Interface (CLI) called `fdisk` .

The first time I installed Arch Linux, `fdisk` felt very mysterious to me. It took me a long time to partition my disk, and I couldn't repeat the process afterward without going through the same pain. The horrible truth is: `fdisk` is, in fact, quite easy to use.

First, we need a *partition table*. This table is read by the OS to know what are the partitions on the disk. Then, we'll create three partitions:

1. A *boot partition*, where the bootloader (to start the OS) will be installed.
2. A *swap partition*, a place on your hard disk used as memory when your RAM is full. It's not perfect since the RAM is quicker than a hard disk, but it's better than nothing.
3. A *root partition*, where everything else will be stored: Arch Linux files, your cat pictures, your secret poetry, and so on.

Don't confuse the root partition with the root directory or the root user we saw earlier. These concepts are different.

Let's now run the following command in your terminal:

```
fdisk <device_name>
```

For example, I can see that my disk is called `sda` when I run `lsblk` , so I should run the command `fdisk /dev/sda` . From there, a new prompt will appear. It will look like this:

```
Command (m for help):
```

You can execute special one-letter commands in fdisk. Nothing will be written on your hard disk when doing so, except if you use the command `w` (for `w`rite). So if you do a mistake, don't panic: you can abort everything with `CTRL+c` if you didn't write anything yet.

Let's now create a GPT partition table. Let's execute the following command in fdisk's prompt:

```
g
```

It can be surprising to use one-letter commands, but it's how fdisk works.

Boot Partition

Now that we've chosen our partition table, let's create the boot partition. Enter the following command:

```
n
```

At this point, `fdisk` will ask you the partition number. The default is normally `1`, so just hit `ENTER`.

As CLIs go, fdisk is very curious. It loves asking questions. It will then ask you the first sector of the disk where the partition should begin. By default, it's the beginning of the disk, and that's what we want: simply hit `ENTER` again.

The last question will ask you what should be the last sectors for the partition. It's not obvious, but you can enter the size you want for your partition here. For the boot partition, 512 MB is enough, so let's type:

```
+512M
```

You'll come back to fdisk's prompt after that. The whole operation should look like this, including the creation of the partition table:

```
Command (m for help): g
Created a new GPT disklabel (GUID: <some_GUID>).

Command (m for help): n
Partition number (1-128, default 1):
First sector (2048-71567838, default 2048):
Last sector, +sectors or +size{K,M,G,T,P} (2048-71567838, default
  ↪   71567838): +512M

Created a new partition 1 of type `Linux filesystem` and of size
  ↪   512MiB.

Command (m for help):
```

Now, we need to change the type of the boot partition, depending on your boot firmware (UEFI or BIOS). To do so, enter the following command:

```
t
```

To list all the partition types possible, you can use the command `L` . To quit the list, use `q` .

UEFI Boot Mode

If you have a UEFI, we want the boot partition to be of type `EFI System` . It's normally the first one in the list, so you should enter:

```
1
```

Here's how the whole operation should look:

```
Command (m for help): t
Selected partition 1
Partition type (type L to list all types): 1
Changed type of partition 'Linux filesystem' to 'EFI System'
```

BIOS Boot Mode

If you have a BIOS, we want the boot partition to be of type `BIOS boot` . It's normally the fourth in the list, so you should enter:

```
4
```

Here's how the whole operation should look:

```
Command (m for help): t
Selected partition 1
Partition type (type L to list all types): 4
Changed type of partition 'Linux filesystem' to 'BIOS boot'
```

Root and Swap Partition

We have now configured the boot partition. Don't forget: we still didn't write anything on the hard disk, so if you quit fdisk now, you'll need to do everything again from the beginning.

You should still see fdisk's prompt at this point. We can now create a SWAP partition. If you have more than 8 GB of RAM and you don't do anything which takes a lot of memory (like video editing, for example), you can skip the creation of a SWAP partition entirely. That being said, I always like to create one of 8 GB, because "you never know".

Let's create a new partition with the command:

```
n
```

When asking the partition number (normally 2 by default), just hit ENTER .

When fdisk asks you the first sector of the partition on the disk, the default is just after the end of the last partition. This is again what we want, so simply press ENTER .

Then, we can enter the size of the partition. It needs to be bigger than 512 MB. I want 8 GB, so I enter:

```
+8G
```

When it's done, you're back to the fdisk's prompt. Let's move forward by creating the root partition. Execute the following:

```
n
```

Then, it's even easier: hit `ENTER` for every question fdisk asks. For the size of the partition, it will take all the space left on the disk by default. When you're back at the prompt, enter the following command:

```
p
```

You should see something like that:

```
Device            Start        End    Sectors   Size  Type
/dev/sda1          2048    1050623    1048576   512M  BIOS  boot
/dev/sda2       1050624   17827839    1677726    8G   Linux filesystem
/dev/sda3      17827840  195352513  193569729   923G  Linux filesystem
```

If you have a UEFI, the only difference will be the type of the first partition: it will be `EFI System` instead of `BIOS boot` .

Again, the device name, start, end, and sectors columns can have different values on your system. The things we have in common: the number of partition created, their sizes (except for the last one), and their types.

It's time to write our changes on the hard disk. Enter the following command to write the partitions:

```
w
```

That's it! You can now quit `fdisk` using the command `q` . When you're back in the shell prompt, you can run the command `lsblk` again to see the newly created partitions.

Formatting the Partitions

The partition table and the partitions themselves are now created, but it's not enough for Arch Linux to use them. Each partition needs to be formatted with a specific filesystem.

Basically, a filesystem groups the data on a disk in files and directories. Using the filesystem, the OS can then display the content of a disk as we're used to. Different OS support different filesystems; for example, Windows primarily supports the `NTFS` filesystem.

I won't describe every filesystem available here, it would be too cumbersome and quite boring. We'll simply format our partitions using the filesystems we want, thanks to the CLI `mkfs` (`mk` for `m a k e`, `fs` for `f ile s ystem`).

The UEFI Boot partition

If you have a UEFI, we need first to format the boot partition using the filesystem `FAT32` . Let's run in the shell:

```
mkfs.fat -F32 <your_boot_partition>
```

For example, my boot partition is `/dev/sda1` , so I run: `mkfs.fat -F32 /dev/sda1` .

Root and Swap Filesystems

If you have a BIOS, no need to create a filesystem for your boot partition. It will be done automatically later. For the Swap partition, you need to run the following commands no matter which firmware you have, BIOS or UEFI:

```
mkswap <your_swap_partition>
swapon <your_swap_partition>
```

For example, my swap partition is `/dev/sda2` , so I replace `<your_swap_partition>` from the above commands with `/dev/sda2` .

Let's create next an `Ext4` filesystem for the root partition with the command:

```
mkfs.ext4 <your_root_partition>
```

You root partition is normally the last partition listed when you run `lsblk` . It's also the biggest partition you have.

This operation can take some time. You don't have to input anything, just let `mkfs` running.

Our partitions are now formatted! Glory and joy!

Mounting the Filesystems

If you run `lsblk` again, you'll see an empty `MOUNTPOINT` column. What's that?

For example, if I run `lsblk` on my current system, where Arch Linux is already running, I get this:

```
NAME      MAJ:MIN RM   SIZE RO TYPE MOUNTPOINT
sda         8:0     0 465.8G  0 disk
  sda1      8:1     0   200M  0 part /boot
  sda2      8:2     0    16G  0 part [SWAP]
  sda3      8:3     0 389.6G  0 part /
```

A mountpoint is a directory where we can access the filesystem of a precise partition. For example, you can see that the mountpoint of `/dev/sda1` is `/boot` . What does it mean?

- If I list (read) the files in the directory `/boot` , the files on the partition `/dev/sda1` will be listed.
- If I create (write) a file in the directory `/boot` , the files on the partition `/dev/sda1` will be written.

We've created partitions but we can't access them yet. To do so, we need to mount our partitions on precise directories.

Mounting the Root Partition

First, let's mount our root partition `/mnt` . Your root partition is normally the last partition of your disk and the biggest one. Let's run the following in the shell:

```
mount <your_root_partition> /mnt
```

If you run the command `ls /mnt` , you'll see that your partition is totally empty, except for a `lost+found` directory. A Linux based system uses this directory on every partition to recover bits of corrupted data if needed.

UEFI and The Boot Partition

If you have a UEFI, you need to mount the boot partition on a new directory. Let's first create this directory:

```
mkdir -p /mnt/boot/efi
```

`mkdir` stands for "make (`mk`) a directory (`dir`)". What about the option `-p` ? Try to run `mkdir --help` in your shell. You'll see the argument `-p` and a brief explanation: `no error if existing, make parent directories as needed`.

The CLI mkdir only creates the directory `efi` by default. If the directory `boot` doesn't exist, it returns an error. The option `-p` automatically creates the directory `efi` and its p arent if it doesn't exist. It doesn't return any error if the directory exists already.

Let's now mount our boot partition on our newly created directory:

```
mount <your_boot_partition> /mnt/boot/efi
```

You can run `lsblk` to see if your mountpoints are correct.

Continuing The Installation

We've built, throughout this chapter, a comfy nest for Arch Linux to come and change your life.

If you want to continue your installation later and stop your computer, you'll have to go through the part Mounting the Filesystems again, after loading the Arch Linux live system from your USB key and connecting to the internet using iwctl. For now, we don't have any way to automatically mount the partitions or connect to Internet when the computer is starting.

It's not that big of a deal. If your brain is about to explode, make yourself a good cup of tea, do some Yoga, go into the forest singing with the squirrels, and come back when you're ready to install the one and unique Arch Linux.

Troubleshooting Your Internet Access

It never happened to me but it's possible that the Arch Linux live system doesn't have the drivers for some of your hardware. In that case, just try to install Arch Linux as described in the book, it's likely that the correct drivers will be installed at that point.

It's more problematic if the Arch Linux live system doesn't have the drivers for your Ethernet or your wireless hardware (for the Wifi). You need Internet to install Arch Linux, so here are some resources you can dig into to try to make it work:

- Arch Wiki – Network Configuration / Wireless[1]
- Arch Wiki – Network Configuration / Wireless Troubleshooting[2]
- Arch Wiki – Android tethering[3]

Problematic drivers is not the only problem you might have concerning your Internet access. Some wireless cards on laptops have a hardware switch you need to turn on. You can verify quickly if this is the problem poisoning your life by following the instructions you'll find on the Glorious Arch Wiki[4], before you begin to hammer your computer with rage and despair.

In a Nutshell

What did we learn in this chapter?

- A prompt invites you to run commands.
- An ISO is a file which represents a whole disk (CD–ROM, hard drive...).
- The Arch Linux live system (like any Linux live system) doesn't run from your hard disk but from your RAM.
- A BIOS is a piece of firmware on your motherboard. Modern motherboards implement a different piece of firmware called UEFI.
- You can display information about your network devices using the CLI `ip` .
- You can make requests on a network with the CLI `ping` . Very handy to test your Internet connection!
- You can copy any content to any destination with the command `dd` .
- You can manage your partitions using `fdisk` .
- You can create new filesystems using `mkfs` .
- You need to mount your partitions on directories to access them, using the command `mount` .

In the next chapter, we'll install the basic packages we need: the Linux Kernel and some basic tools.

---

[1] https://wiki.archlinux.org/index.php/Network_configuration/Wireless

[2] https://wiki.archlinux.org/index.php/Network_configuration/Wireless#Troubleshooting

[3] https://wiki.archlinux.org/index.php/android_tethering

[4] https://wiki.archlinux.org/index.php/Network_configuration/Wireless#Rfkill_caveat

Going Deeper

Taking the habit to read the manual of the CLIs you use will bring you an insane amount of knowledge regarding Linux-based systems. For example, you can read the description of fdisk by running `man fdisk`.

Don't worry if you don't understand everything, just try to get into the habit of looking at the manual. You'll understand more and more what you're reading there as you go through this book. You don't have to read everything; often, only the description is enough at first. Don't put too much pressure on yourself.

Installing Arch Linux

This time, we'll do it: we'll install Arch Linux! In this chapter, we'll see:

- What are the basic packages you can install to have a running installation on Arch Linux.
- How to automatically mount our partitions when the system starts.
- How to change the root directory of our system with arch-chroot.
- How to add a password for the root user.
- How to change the timezone.
- How to generate new locales and choose the ones we want to use.
- How to name our shiny new system.
- How to install the GRUB Bootloader.
- What are stream redirections (including pipes).
- What are the difference between an input and an argument when using CLIs.

If you have any problems, I recommend you look at the official installation guide from the Arch Wiki[1]. It's not as detailed and beginner friendly as this book, but it's THE reference to install Arch Linux nonetheless.

We have a lot to do in this chapter. I hope you're ready! Let's install the first layer of our crazy Mouseless Development Environment.

Installing the Base Packages

Let's run the following command in our shell:

```
pacstrap /mnt base base-devel linux linux-firmware
```

Here, we use the script `pacstrap` to install on the root partition (mounted on `/mnt`) the packages:

- `base` – A meta-package including many "basic" packages like `bash` , `pacman` , or `systemd` . You can see the whole list here[2].
- `base-devel` – A group of packages, mostly including tools to build other packages or to compile programs. You can see the whole list of packages included here[3].

---

[1] https://wiki.archlinux.org/index.php/Installation_guide

[2] https://www.archlinux.org/packages/core/any/base/

[3] https://www.archlinux.org/groups/x86_64/base-devel/

- `linux` – The Linux kernel.
- `linux-firmware` – A bunch of firmware for different hardware. That's one of the biggest difficulties an OS needs to solve: trying to be compatible with every possible piece of hardware available.

We saw earlier that the BIOS (or the UEFI) is firmware directly embedded in the motherboard (on a ROM chip, or R ead O nly M emory). That said, not all firmware is embedded in a piece of hardware. The firmware from the package `linux-firware` are loaded from the kernel and linked to the correct hardware, if it exists. If it was directly in a chip on the hardware itself, it would be more difficult to update.

When the installation of the basic system is done, we can move forward and configure some basics.

Mounting Partitions Automatically

We mounted our partitions manually with the command `mount` in the last chapter. The problem: each time we start our system, we need to mount them manually again. How do we automate this operation?

The file fstab (f ile s ystem tab le) is a configuration file which maps the different partitions to different mountpoints. This file is read at startup to automatically mount these partitions.

To generate fstab, simply run in a terminal:

```
genfstab -U /mnt >> /mnt/etc/fstab
```

If you look at the file by running in the shell `cat /mnt/etc/fstab` , you might be surprised to see that the root partition is mounted to the directory `/` . We already talked about this root directory in the first chapter of this book. Every directory in our system will be its direct children, grandchildren, great-grandchildren, and so on. As a result, it makes sense that the root partition is directly mounted to the root directory.

I know you might be thinking: "Why the hell did we mount our root partition to `/mnt` in the previous chapter?"

We need to remember that we are on the Arch Linux live system, a whole OS which runs from the RAM of your computer, not from the hard disk. Consequently, the root directory of this live system is not on the hard disk, either. To install and configure our system on the hard disk, we'll need to swap the root directory from the one we're using right now to a directory on the hard disk itself. We've chosen `/mnt` , but we could have chosen any other directory.

Changing The Root Directory

To change the root directory, we need to use the shell script `arch-chroot`. After doing so, every program we'll run (or the ones already running) will use our root partition mounted on `/mnt` as the root directory. A good example is the package manager: it will install its program on your hard disk, instead of on the RAM where the live environment is running.

I know, it's confusing. Let's move forward, and you'll understand what I'm talking about. Learning by doing is often the best way to go.

Let's dive into the new world of our freshly installed Arch Linux. Run in the shell:

```
arch-chroot /mnt
```

At that point, you should see a new prompt in your shell. If you run `ls /`, you'll see every child of the new root directory on your hard disk. These directories were created when you ran `pacstrap` to install Arch Linux at the beginning of this chapter.

Using `arch-chroot` can be very useful to fix a system you can't even start anymore. In that case, you could:

1. Use the Arch Linux live system from a USB key to mount the root partition to the directory `/mnt`, exactly as we did in the previous chapter.
2. Run `arch-chroot /mnt` and try to fix your system from there. You are still running the Arch Linux live system, but you're using the filesystem of your root partition on your hard disk. Since everything is a file on a Linux-based system, in theory, you can debug everything you want.

This is a very handy way to troubleshoot problems without reinstalling your whole system.

The Root User's Password

For now, our system is very basic and primitive, but it's a solid foundation to install everything we want on top. It's a bit like terraforming Mars, but from the comfort of your favorite chair.

That's nice and all but you want to be sure that you're the only one terraforming your system. Imagine if a group of crazy hackers take over the outrageously powerful root user and begin to do some harm to your poor system. It wouldn't be funny.

That's why we need to create a password for our root user. I would suggest setting a password strong enough: don't use `0000` , your birth date, or the name of your favorite cat.

Here's how to create this password:

1. Run the shell command `passwd` .
2. Type the password.
3. Confirm the password.

Nothing will be displayed on your screen when you type your password. It's to avoid letting anybody looking over your shoulder copy it. Even if you don't see anything, the inputs from your keyboard are registered.

Through Time and Space: Configuring the Timezone

It's time to configure the timezone you're living in. Let's run in a shell:

```
timedatectl list-timezones
```

A CLI called `less` will automatically run when you enter this command. It's a pager which can group and display content in pages. Here are some basic commands to use it:

- To move around, you can use the arrow keys or `hjkl` . What sort of human could possibly use `hjkl` , you might wonder? We'll talk about that later. So much suspense, I know!
- If you want to move faster, you can use `CTRL+d` (for Down) or `CTRL+u` (for UP).
- If you want to quit, press `q` .

You can also search for your timezone by using `grep` , as follows:

```
timedatectl list-timezones | grep "continent"
```

The CLI `grep` is a very powerful tool. In the example above, it will output only the lines where the pattern `continent` is matched. For example: `timedatectl list-timezones | grep "Europe"` will display only the line containing the string "Europe". Very handy if you only want to display the European timezones!

When you've found your timezone, run in a terminal:

```
timedatectl set-timezone "<your_timezone>"
```

For example, I'm living in Berlin, so I would set my timezone as follows:

```
timedatectl set-timezone "Europe/Berlin"
```

Choose Your Locale

Enough with time and space, let's talk about cultures and civilizations.

A locale is a set of parameters that define different parameters like language, region, or currency. Many applications on your system, including the shell, use these locales.

The format of a locale is `<language_code>_<country_code>`. For example:

- For the French language in France, it's `fr_FR`.
- For the French language in Belgium, it's `fr_BE`.
- For the English language in the US, it's `en_US`.

That's not all. The complete format looks like this:

```
<language_code>_<country_code>.<character_encoding>@<modifier>
```

The file `/etc/locale.gen` contains all the locale you need. To display all of them, try to run:

```
cat /etc/locale.gen
```

Doing so, you'll only be able to read the last ones. It's where a program like less can be very useful. Run in your shell:

```
less /etc/locale.gen
```

As an aside, we saw in the first chapter that each directory directly under the root directory `/` has a specific meaning. The directory `/etc` is where all the global configurations - for every user - of the different applications installed on your system are stored.

We can generate locales from the file `locale.gen`. As you can see, there is a comment `#` before each of the locale in the file itself. If you uncomment some of them, you'll be able to generate the data corresponding to these locales.

To uncomment the locales we want, we would use an editor to edit `locale.gen`. We can also add the desired locales at the end of the file.

When you've found the locale you want, you can replace `<your_locale>` in the following command with the locale chosen, and run the whole command in a shell:

```
echo "<your_locale>" >> /etc/locale.gen
```

For example, if I want to have my system in US English, I can run:

```
echo "en_US.UTF-8 UTF-8" >> /etc/locale.gen
```

When you're done, we need to generate the data of the locale. Run in your shell:

```
locale-gen
```

The locales are now generated! However, we didn't tell the system what locale it should use. To do so, we need to write something like

`LANG=<language_code>_<country_code>.<character_encoding>` in the file `/etc/locale.conf`.

To write the file, run:

```
echo "LANG=<language_code>_<country_code>.<character_encoding>" >
 ↪ /etc/locale.conf
```

For example, in my case, I would execute the following in my shell:

```
echo "LANG=en_US.UTF-8" > /etc/locale.conf
```

Then, you can verify that the file was written correctly by running:

```
cat /etc/locale.conf
```

If you changed your keyboard layout in the previous chapter, you need to save it in the file `/etc/vconsole.conf` as follows (don't forget to change `<your_keymap>`):

```
echo "KEYMAP=<your_keymap>" >> /etc/vconsole.conf
```

For example, if I want to use the keyboard layout `fr-latin1` , I need to run this command:

```
echo "KEYMAP=fr-latin1" >> /etc/vconsole.conf
```

That's all for the cultural touch.

Naming Your New World

What will you call your new system? Did you prepare yourself for that? Don't be ashamed of your system when you speak about it; choose a glorious and attractive name.

When you're ready to commit to a name, you can run the following command. Don't forget to replace `<crazy_name_for_your_beautiful_system>` with the name you want:

```
echo "<crazy_name_for_your_beautiful_system>" > /etc/hostname
```

My system is called `tartarus` , because it sounds cool and it's below hell. I didn't think enough about my name, I know. Don't discuss my choice, or I won't speak to you anymore.

Here's what I would do for my own system: `echo "tartarus" > /etc/hostname` , with tears of joy in my eyes.

GRUB, The Linux Bootloader

We're now at an important step of our installation. After installing the bootloader, you'll be able to reboot your computer, boot onto your hard disk, and make your first step on your new system.

A bootloader is the first software that runs from your hard disk when your computer starts. It loads the OS kernel and allows the init process to load everything else; we'll talk more about this later.

The bootloader we'll use is called GRUB (for `Gr` and `U` nified `B` ootloader). We can now fill another gap in the diagram of our booting process:

Boot Process

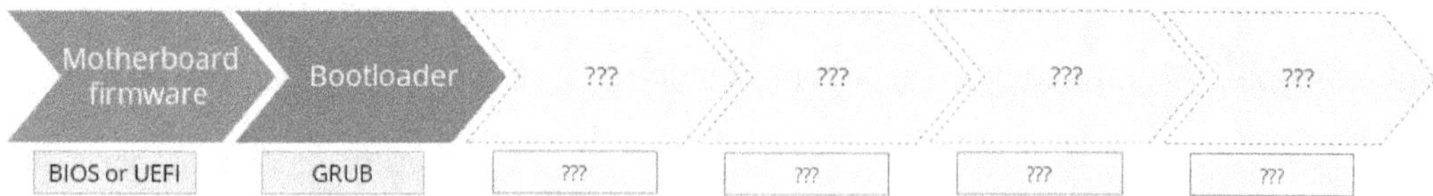

To install GRUB, we'll use for the first time the official package manager of Arch Linux, Pacman. To install packages, you can run in a terminal as the root user:

```
pacman -S <package_name>
```

You'll need to replace `<package_name>` with the name of the package you want to install. You can install more than one package if you specify more than one name.

Bootloader With a UEFI

If you have a UEFI, you'll need to first install `grub` and `efibootmgr` (for EFI Boot Manager). It can be done in one shell command:

```
pacman -S grub efibootmgr
```

Then, let's install GRUB with this command:

```
grub-install --target=x86_64-efi --bootloader-id=GRUB
 ↳   --efi-directory=/boot/efi
```

By setting the option `efi-directory` to the directory `/boot/efi` , we tell our friend GRUB that the bootloader should be installed on your BIOS partition. Indeed, `/boot/efi` should be the mountpoint of your boot partition, as we did in the last chapter.

Bootloader With a BIOS

If you don't have a UEFI but a BIOS, you just need to install GRUB with the following command:

```
pacman -S grub
```

Then, you need to specify the hard disk where the bootloader should be installed:

```
grub-install <your_hard_disk>
```

For example, I would run `grub-install /dev/sda` if my hard disk is named `/dev/sda` . As a reminder, you can use the command `lsblk` to display your block devices.

Creating The GRUB Configuration (BIOS and UEFI)

Finally, we need to generate some configuration for GRUB (for BIOS and UEFI). In a terminal, run:

```
grub-mkconfig -o /boot/grub/grub.cfg
```

GRUB is now part of your life.

Enabling the Network Manager

We have Internet right now because we configured it on the Arch Linux live system, but when we restart our computer and boot on Arch Linux from the hard disk, our RAM will be cleaned up and the live system will be gone. I know you'll be saddened by this lost, but time does heal all wounds.

Let's install a program called `networkmanager` , allowing us to access The Great Internet:

```
pacman -S networkmanager
```

Then, we need to enable the service `NetworkManager` by executing the command:

```
systemctl enable NetworkManager.service
```

What's `systemctl` ? It's linked to the init process I mentioned above. We'll come back to that later.

Diving in the Shell

If you're not familiar with the shell, we saw in these first two chapters several commands which might look pretty weird. Many of them are essential for a good shell experience, so let's come back to them and explain how they work and what's their purpose. I recommend you experiment and play with these commands to learn how they work, too.

Command-Line 101

The commands you'll use often are on top. You can learn more about them by consulting the manual.

- `man <command>` - Display the page of the manual for a command. You can read the manual of the manual with the command `man man`.
- `ls` - List the content of a directory. You can use the option `-l` (for `l`isting) to get more details.
- `grep <pattern> <input>` - Take an input, and output the lines matching the pattern. It's very useful to filter any input, like the content of a file.
- `cat <input>` - Con`cat`enate an input. It's often used to output the content of a file.
- `less <input>` - Pager to navigate easily long input.
- `ip <object>` - Display some information about your network devices. `<object>` can be `address` or `link` for example; for a list of objects, run `ip`.
- `ping <host>` - Send requests to a network host. Useful to test your internet connection.
- `dd if=<source> of=<destination>` - Copy everything from a file to another. Note that the syntax of this command is peculiar.
- `fdisk <block_device>` - Can display or manipulate disk partition tables.
- `mount <device> <directory>` - Mount a device to a directory.
- `timedatectl` - Control the system time and date.

When you see that `mk` (make) is part of the command's name, it will often create something. For example: `mkfs` (create a filesystem), `mkswap` (create a linux swap area), or `mkdir` (create a directory).

When you see that `ls` (list) is part of the command's name, it will often list something. For example: `ls` (list files and directories) or `lsblk` (list block devices).

A Good Complement to the Manual

If the manual is too daunting for you or if you have difficulties to understand it, you can also consult tldr-pages. It will give you a very short description of the CLI and nice examples.

To install it, simply run:

```
sudo pacman -S tldr
```

Then, like the manual, you can use it as follows:

```
tldr <CLI>
```

This tool was brought to you by one of my awesome proofreaders.

Input Output Redirections

Let's look closer at this command:

```
echo "en_US.UTF-8 UTF-8" >> /etc/locale.gen
```

If you wonder what `echo` does, it simply outputs the string of characters given as argument; here, it outputs "en_US.UTF-8 UTF-8".

The sign `>>` is more interesting: together with `>` , they are called I/O (I nput/ O utput) redirections. By default, when you execute a command, the standard output is the shell you're in. If we use `>` or `>>` , we can *redirect* this output to a file or another *stream*. We'll see this idea of stream later in the book.

In short, the command above will redirect the output of `echo` to a file. If I was crazy enough to formulate the command in plain English, it would look like that: "I want to write `en_US.UTF-8 UTF-8` in the file `/etc/locale.gen` ".

What's the difference between `>` and `>>` , you might ask? That's a very good and important question indeed:

- `>` will first **delete** the file you want to write in, recreate a file with the same name (but empty), and write in it.
- `>>` will simply write at the end of the file without deleting anything.

In short, use `>` if you want to overwrite all the content of a file with your output, and `>>` if you want to *append* an output to a file.

You can try it by yourself in a shell. Run these commands in this order:

1. `touch test` – Create a new file named "test".
2. `echo "hello" > test` – Write "hello" into the file "test".
3. `cat test` – Display the content of the file "test", showing "hello".
4. `echo "bye" > test` – Overwrite the file "test". If you run `cat test`, you won't see "hello" anymore, but "bye".
5. `echo "good morning!" >> test` – Append the string "good morning" at the end of the file. Again, if you run `cat test`, you'll see "bye" on the first line of output and "good morning!" on the second one.

The command `touch` … touch a file. This means that the file is created if it doesn't exist. If it does exist, its last modification date is updated with the current one.

When you're done fooling around, delete your file with `rm test` (for *r e m* ove).

Pipes

Pipes allow us to redirect a CLI's output to another CLI's input. Let's look at this command:

```
timedatectl list-timezones | grep "continent"
```

Here we pass the output of the command `timedatectl list-timezones` to the input of the command `grep "continent"`, thanks to the pipe `|`. The role of grep is then to filter this input and output the result.

Input and Arguments

Let's take two commands we used already: `cat` and `echo`. There is a main difference between these two:

- `cat` concatenates its *input* and output the result.
- `echo` output its *argument*.

Since a pipe redirects an output to an input, you can't redirect an output to the command echo, because it doesn't take any input. Let's try the following:

```
echo "hello" | cat
```

Here's what's happening:

1. `echo` outputs 'hello'.
2. `cat` gets 'hello' as input.
3. `cat` con cat enates the input `hello`.

4. `cat` outputs the concatenation.

By the way, if you didn't know, concatenation is the process of joining two strings together. The concatenation of the string "lin" and "ux" is "linux".

Now, let's try this:

```
echo "hello" | echo
```

Nothing is output. Why? Because `echo` doesn't take any input, but an argument. A pipe redirects an output to an input, so it doesn't work. If my superpower allowing me to read minds still works, you might ask yourself: "how do I know what CLI takes some input, and what CLI takes arguments?"

To answer this question, try to run in your terminal:

```
cat
```

From there you'll be able to give any input you want, using your keyboard. Each time you hit ENTER , you give the input to cat, which outputs it. To stop giving input, press CTRL+d . Another example:

```
grep "hello"
```

You can again give any input to grep, which will output your line only if the pattern you try to match ("hello") is in your input string.

Now, if you run `echo` without argument, it doesn't take any input; instead, it doesn't output anything. This is a good way to know if a command take an input or an argument.

You can give a filepath as input, too, to feed the CLI with the contents of the file.

Is there a way to pass an input to `echo` using a pipe? Yes, by converting an input to an argument. The CLI `xarg` does exactly that. You can try to run in a terminal:

```
echo "hello" | xargs echo
```

This silly command will output "hello" as expected. That said, always think twice before using `xargs` : there is often a CLI out there which can directly take an input instead of an argument and do what you wanted to do.

Rebooting The System

We've completed the very basic installation of Arch Linux! Additionally, we saw some powerful CLIs and some very useful concepts surrounding the shell. You can congratulate and applaud yourself with vigor and strength!

We don't have many applications on our system to play with for now, but we're not here to play. We're serious and boring people. Let's restart our computer and boot onto our hard disk this time, to meet our new friend the Mouseless Development Environment. It's very mouseless right now, for sure.

First, let's exit the arch-chroot environment. Hit the keystroke CTRL+d or run in a terminal:

```
exit
```

Then, let's reboot our computer with the command:

```
reboot
```

Don't forget to change the boot order in the interface of your BIOS (or UEFI), to boot onto the hard disk this time, and not onto your USB key.

You'll first see the GRUB interface, then you'll discover the login screen in all its beauty and simplicity. It's simple but effective: type root as user name (it's our only user for now), and type the password you chose earlier. You'll end up in a new shell: say goodbye to Zsh (for now), and give your respects to the famous and powerful Bash.

Troubleshooting Pacman

When you install packages with Pacman, you might bump into 404 errors when retrieving them. In that case, the best solution is to update all your system with the following command:

```
pacman -Syu
```

You can add the name of the package(s) you wanted to install as argument. We'll speak more about Pacman in a later chapter; if you have any other problem with it, the Arch wiki[1] is again the best reference to answer your troubles.

---

[1] https://wiki.archlinux.org/index.php/Pacman#Troubleshooting

In a Nutshell

What did we learn in this chapter?

- How to install the basic packages for Arch Linux.
- How to generate the fstab file, to automatically mount our partitions when starting the system.
- How to change the root directory with `arch-chroot`, and how it can be very useful to debug a system you can't start anymore.
- How to install the GRUB bootloader.
- What a pipe is, how to redirect outputs, and the difference between an input and an argument.
- Common CLIs we'll use again, and again, and again.

In the next chapter, we'll boot on our new OS, Arch Linux.

Going Deeper

- Arch Wiki - Locale[1]
- Arch Wiki - chroot[2]
- Arch Wiki - UEFI[3]
- Arch Wiki - GRUB[4]
- Arch Wiki - fstab[5]
- Arch Wiki - Man page[6]
- tldr-pages[7]

---

[1] https://wiki.archlinux.org/index.php/Locale

[2] https://wiki.archlinux.org/index.php/Chroot

[3] https://wiki.archlinux.org/index.php/Unified_Extensible_Firmware_Interface

[4] https://wiki.archlinux.org/index.php/GRUB

[5] https://wiki.archlinux.org/index.php/Fstab

[6] https://wiki.archlinux.org/index.php/Man_page

[7] https://github.com/tldr-pages/tldr

Welcome To Linux

"That's one small step for [a] man, one giant leap for mankind", said the genius who installed Arch Linux successfully for the first time in history. Now, it's your turn to be the genius and to do your first steps in your new Mouseless Development Environment.

We have the Bash shell for now and a few CLIs we can use. What about graphical interfaces? We won't be able to display them before the next chapter, so let's forget about them.

Here's what we'll do in this chapter:

- We'll first verify that we have Internet. It's useful nowadays.
- We'll see what systemd is.
- We'll discuss about the concept of processes in a Linux-based system.
- We'll create a new user you'll be able to incarnate. Being the demigod (or demigoddess?) root user is quite demanding, and I feel you exhausted by so many responsibilities.
- We'll give a new power to our user: the ability to take possession of the root user the time of a command with `sudo`.
- We'll do our first steps in Neovim. It's a magnificent tool to terraform your new mouseless world, if you can handle such power.

Connecting to The Internet, Third Round

Do you have access to the Internet? We saw in the last chapter how we can verify that. If you don't remember how, that's fine; it's a lot to take at once. The solution is just below.

Using a Cable

If you're connected to Internet with a good old cable, it should work fine already. To verify that, you can run in your terminal:

```
ping -c 5 www.google.com
```

The output should be similar to this:

```
64 bytes from 8.8.8.8: icmp_seq=1 ttl=119 time=39.2 ms
64 bytes from 8.8.8.8: icmp_seq=2 ttl=119 time=38.7 ms
64 bytes from 8.8.8.8: icmp_seq=3 ttl=119 time=40.4 ms
64 bytes from 8.8.8.8: icmp_seq=4 ttl=119 time=39.0 ms
64 bytes from 8.8.8.8: icmp_seq=4 ttl=119 time=38.0 ms
```

Using the Wi-Fi

If you want to use your Wi-Fi, let's first run in a shell:

```
nmtui
```

Then, follow these three steps:

1. Select `Activate a connection`.
2. Choose your Wi-Fi network.
3. Enter a password if needed.

We need now to verify that it worked. Again, try to run the following in your shell:

```
ping -c 5 www.google.com
```

The output should look like this:

```
64 bytes from 8.8.8.8: icmp_seq=1 ttl=119 time=39.2 ms
64 bytes from 8.8.8.8: icmp_seq=2 ttl=119 time=38.7 ms
64 bytes from 8.8.8.8: icmp_seq=3 ttl=119 time=40.4 ms
64 bytes from 8.8.8.8: icmp_seq=4 ttl=119 time=39.0 ms
64 bytes from 8.8.8.8: icmp_seq=4 ttl=119 time=38.0 ms
```

If it didn't work, try these two commands:

```
systemctl enable NetworkManager.service
systemctl start NetworkManager.service
```

This should solve your problems.

Installing the Manuals

Now that we have Internet access, we can install packages from repositories. Let's install the most important CLI and its holy pages:

```
pacman -S man man-pages
```

You can now access the infinite knowledge of the manual by using `man <command>`, as we saw already.

Processes

You remember this command we executed in the last chapter?

```
systemctl start NetworkManager.service
```

Let's look at it more closely: what's systemctl? What's its purpose?

The Init Process: systemd

The command `systemctl` allows you to interact with systemd. To understand what systemd is, let's first speak briefly about processes.

An instance of a running program is called a process. Your terminal, for example, is running right now, so it's a process.

Every process has a unique process ID, abbreviated to *PID*. You can imagine the different processes running on your system as part of a tree: a process can start some child process, and these possible children can start other processes. If a parent process terminates, every child of this process also terminates.

Like the filesystem, the process tree has a root, called the init process. Its job? Creating the processes our system depends on. Many Linux distros use the init process called *systemd*, and its PID is always 1, the one process which rules them all.

As a result, every single process on our system is a child of the systemd process. To display this process tree, you can run the command `pstree` in a terminal. Don't forget that you can pipe it to `less`, to be able to look at it more easily.

Here's the first branches on the tree I get on my system:

```
systemd-+-NetworkManager---2*[{NetworkManager}]
        |-dbus-daemon
        |-login---bash---pstree
```

This means that the processes `NetworkManager` , `dbus-daemon` and `login` have `systemd` as parent process. The process `bash` has `login` as parent process, and `pstree` has `bash` as parent process.

The init process systemd is the first process launched after the kernel was initialized by the bootloader. Great! We can add another piece of our puzzle:

Boot Process

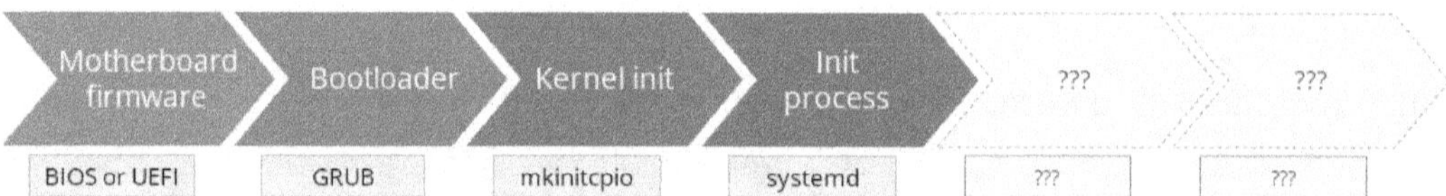

After some various kernel modules are loaded thanks to the bootloader, systemd starts the rest of the system. When we think of an OS, we can all agree that it's highly dynamic nowadays: processes need to be started when we need them, plugged devices (like USB keys) need to be recognized when we plug them, and so on. systemd is an attempt to manage all these changes happening on your system at runtime.

How does it work, you might ask? systemd manages dependencies called "units". There are 11 different type of units in total. Yet, I don't want to bore you to death, so we won't cover all of them here. Most units can be configured with configuration files, and they can be "enabled" or "disabled" as follows:

```
systemctl enable <unit>.<unit_type>
systemctl disable <unit>.<unit_type>
```

If a unit is enabled, systemd will read its config during boot time and, depending on the unit type, it might start it if necessary. In that case, a new process will join your process tree!

To go back to our command `systemctl start NetworkManager.service` , it enables the unit `NetworkManager` , which is of type `service` , and systemd will start it at boot time. If you're curious, you can look at its configuration by running:

```
cat /usr/lib/systemd/system/NetworkManager.service
```

At boot time, systemd can start programs which will continue to run in the background. They are often *daemons*: they'll run on your system in the background till they're killed.

Speaking about killing, you can kill any process on your system with the command `kill`. It's really useful when one of your process doesn't want to stop, or when it consumes too many resources.

A program which has the letter `d` at the end of its filename is an idiomatic way to specificy that it's a daemon. For example: `dhcpcd`, `urxvtd`, or even `systemd` itself are all daemons. Don't confuse a daemon with a demon: the first are useful programs who run without you noticing them (most of the time), the second is a horrible creature from hell you'll surely notice.

You can also start or stop a systemd unit manually for the current session. For example, you could run:

```
systemctl stop NetworkManager.service
```

It will stop the Network Manager process running in the background, cutting yourself off from the rest of the world, and be alone, finally. If it's enabled, it will be started again the next time your computer will boot.

To have the status of a specific systemd unit, you can do, for example:

```
systemctl status NetworkManager.service
```

Alternatively to `pstree`, you can use the command `ps` to list every p roce s ses running at that precise moment on your system. The options I use the most often is `ps -eF`, which will show you the PID of every process, its parent ID (or PPID), what user owns the process, and so on. As always, you can pipe this output to grep to filter it, or to less to navigate through it more easily.

To list all processes and deamons that systemd manage and their status, you can use the command:

```
systemctl list-unit-files
```

It will automatically use the CLI less by default. You can also filter this list by unit type:

```
systemctl list-unit-files --type service
```

An important step during boot time is to display the login prompt, for you to create a new session of a particular user. After login, a new shell process is started.

With this information, we can complete our puzzle:

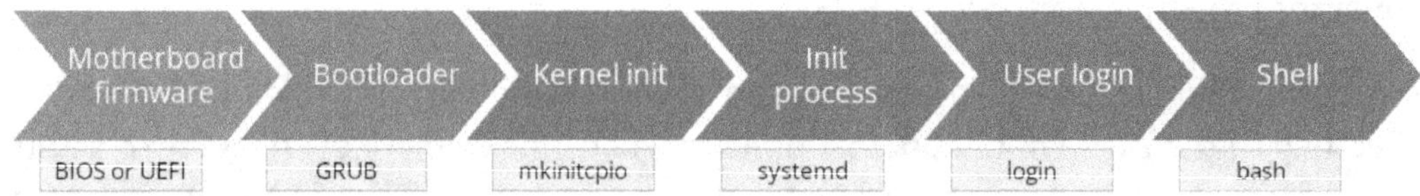

Bash is the default shell for the root user, that's why it's the one started just after login.

Logging the Init Process With journald

You've understood it: systemd is an important process for many Linux distros out there, including Arch Linux. Since it manages so many processes, it would be nice to have some sort of log to see what's happening. Fortunatelly, systemd offers a logging process called journald.

You can interact with this journal using the command `journalctl`. Running it without parameters will display every message logged.

As time pass, you'll have more and more logs. You'll need to filter them most of the time, to get the information you want. Of course, you could pipe the output of `journalctl` to grep or to any other CLIs to filter the output, but systemctl already offer this natively:

- `journalctl -f` - Display only the last entries and print new entries as they are written.
- `journalctl -b` - Display only the logs from the last b oot.
- `journalctl -k` - Only show k ernel messages. This option implies `-b`.
- `journalctl -u <service>` - Display the logs related to the service `<service>`. For example, `journalctl -u NetworkManager`.
- `journalctl --since='yesterday'` - Allow you to filter logs by date range. You can see every possible range you can use with `man 7 systemd.time`.
- `journalctl -p err` - Filter errors by priority.
- `journalctl -o verbose` - Display metadata for each log entry.

The `-o` option stands for o utput and allows you to output journald logs in different format: for example `short`, `json` or even `json-pretty`.

When you filter by priorities, you can use these:

0. "emerg" (0)
1. "alert" (1)
2. "crit" (2)
3. "err" (3)
4. "warning" (4)
5. "notice" (5)
6. "info" (6)
7. "debug" (7)

Processes As Files

You remember when we said that everything on Linux is a file? It won't be a surprise if I tell you that a process is represented as a bunch of files, too. If you execute the command `echo $$` , it will output the process ID of your terminal.

Let's try to run the following command:

```
ls -l "/proc/$$"
```

The output of this command show you the files related to your terminal process. For example, if you do `cat /proc/$$/environ` , you'll see every environment variable set for your terminal process. Environment variables?

Environment Variables

Since we speak about processes, let's quickly see what an environment variable is. It can be defined as a variable attached to a process; this process can use it for different purposes. A child of a process can use the environment variables of its parent, too.

Custom environment variables are usually set when your default shell runs for the first time. Everything running in the shell (becoming child processes of the shell) will be able to access these variables, too. We'll declare many environment variables throughout this book.

To output the environment variables attached to your shell process in a more readable way, you can use the command:

```
printenv
```

You can add the name of an environment variable as argument to only display its value. For example, you can try `printenv SHELL` . It will output the name of the shell the root user use by default. The environment variable SHELL is set by systemd, and therefore every process running on the system can access it.

Creating A New User

Enough explanations, I said! Let's create our first user. Right now, we are the demigod (or demigoddess) root, you remember? It's nice to have so much power, but it's a lot of responsabilities, too. You can do everything you want, including:

- Modifying file you shouldn't modify.
- Crashing your entire system by deleting files you shouldn't delete.
- Let attackers the possibility to control your current user session and, therefore, having all the permissions.

It's not really what we want, do we? We need to protect our system against ourselves, and potential external attackers. If they can take control of root, they'll be the demigods (or almighty demigoddesses), and you'll be their pet. Even if you have nothing to hide, they could use your computer to attack other, more protected systems, and it would be very sad.

The user root has all permissions a user can have, but we don't want the user that we'll create to have that much power.

To manage the permissions on a Linux-based system, we can put our users in different groups. The user will only be allowed to do what the group rules authorize him (or her) to do.

Let's create this user. You need to replace <your_new_user_name> with the best name you can find. Don't take this decision lightly! You're naming your new baby here.

When you're good to go, run this command:

```
useradd -m -g wheel -s /bin/bash <your_new_user_name>
```

What are all these options, you might rightfully wonder?

- -m will create a home directory for the user. You don't want to be homeless, do you?
- -g put the user into the g roup "wheel".
- -s allow you to specify the user's default shell. It's Bash for now, but we'll change it later to use Zsh.

The home directory is a direct child of the root directory: its filepath is `/home` . Every one of its children will be named after the name of each user on your system. Each of these directories will contain all the files and configurations belonging to that user.

For example, if I want to create the user "casimir" (an anthropomorphic orange dinosaur with yellow and red spots), I can run : `useradd -m -g wheel -s /bin/bash casimir` . Its home directory will be `/home/casimir` .

Next, we need to create a password to our user:

```
passwd <your_new_user_name>
```

You can see the users of your system and their groups if you run the command:

```
cat /etc/passwd
```

Now, what should our user be able to do? Everything would be nice, but it's dangerous, as we saw. What about being able to do everything, if we ask each time for a password for the most sensitive commands? This approach has two main benefits:

1. If forces us to think. Instead of only hitting ENTER and regretting it later, we need to enter a password and wonder if what we're doing makes any sense.
2. Even if devilish hackers take control of the user's session, they won't be able to do much without the user's password.

Our user is part of the group "wheel". Every user in this group can use the command `su` (for `su` bstitute). This command creates a new shell process, child of your current shell process. This is called a *subshell*. You'll be incarnating another user in this subshell, by default root. If you want to substitute your current user with one other than root, you can run `su <user_name>` .

For example: try to run:

```
su <your_new_user_name>
```

In my case, I need to do `su casimir` . It will open a subshell, and you'll see that the shell prompt display another user name. You're now the user you've just created! That's totally supernatural and therefore awesome.

This way, we can be our new user most of the time, and run a shell as the root user if we need to perform sensitive operations. That's great, but it's still not really secure: somebody can take control of the subshell. On top of that, it's not really practical to navigate shell processes, and it can get quickly confusing in which shell we're running what command.

To make things more secure and practical, we need to be able to run the command `sudo`, for `su`bstitute `do`. Contrary to `su`, `sudo` won't create a new subshell, but it can substitute our user for a specific command. It will then ask for a password; exactly what we want! Like `su`, if the user name is not given, it will default as the user root.

Now, as your new user, try to run in your shell:

```
sudo echo "I want to use sudo!"
```

After typing your password, you'll receive this message which is, I think, the most helpful, wonderful, and good-willing message you'll ever receive in a Linux-based system. It's a very famous one, too:

```
<your_new_user_name> is not in the sudoers file. This incident will
 ↪  be reported.
```

This incident will be reported! The CIA, the KGB, the GIGN, or your local militia, depending on where you're living, will soon break your door! You'll regret what you just typed and, more generally, to be born. If you have any chair or heavy piece of wood (or even better, metal!), block your door, your windows, and everything else.

If we believe the interpretation of the famous comic "xkcd", it might be even worse than that![1].

To exit this subshell and come back to the parent process (the shell you were before doing these `su` shenenigans), simply type `exit` or, even faster, use the keystroke `CTRL+d`.

We now need to modify a file, for the group "wheel" to be able to use the command `sudo`. Since our new user is part of wheel, he (or she) will have access to the command sudo, too.

To do that, let's be crazy and try Neovim! First, let's install it:

```
pacman -S neovim
```

If you don't want to use it because you hate it, that's fine with me. You can install `nano` or anything else you like. The only condition: if it has a graphical interface, it won't work (yet). We'll see that in the next chapter.

---

[1] https://imgs.xkcd.com/comics/incident.png

The Default Text Editors

The goal is to add the permission for the group "wheel" to use the command `sudo`. To do that, let's run the following command:

```
visudo
```

Bummer. Another error. I'm sorry to push you into errors like that, but it's for you to understand what's happening. We don't have a default text editor set yet, and some commands will need an editor, like `visudo`. To find it, they will look at the value of the environment variable `EDITOR`.

The Return of the Environment Variable

Let's set our first environment variable, using the command `export`. Type in a terminal:

```
export EDITOR=nvim
```

What's `nvim`? It's just the name of the CLI to run Neovim. Note that setting a variable in Bash (or Zsh) doesn't involve any dollar sign `$`. However, you always need to use this sign as prefix when you want to use the value of a variable. For example, try to run these two commands:

```
echo EDITOR
echo "$EDITOR"
```

The first command will output `EDITOR`, the second command will output the value of our variable `EDITOR`, `nvim`. Let's underline some important points:

1. When you use the value of a variable, always surround it with double quotes if you use it as an argument to a command. I'll explain why at the end of this chapter.
2. When you assign a value to a variable, like we did with `EDITOR=nvim`, don't add any space. Many shells, like Bash, are very sensitive to that; they will output an error if you do something like `export EDITOR = nvim`.

Trying visudo Again

Back to our main goal: adding the right to the group "wheel" to run `sudo`. Under the hood, visudo will modify a file; let's back it up first to be sure we won't screw up our system:

```
cp /etc/sudoers ~/sudoers-backup
```

What's the directory `~`? It's an alias for the environment variable `$HOME`; it has the value of the home directory's filepath of the current user. The home directory of the root user is special in the sense that it's not a child directory of the `/home` directory, it's simply the directory `/root`. If you run `ls /root`, you'll see the file you just copied.

Using `~` and `$HOME` will have the same effect. As a result, the following command is equivalent to the one above:

```
cp /etc/sudoers "$HOME/sudoers-backup"
```

Be aware that some CLIs won't expand `~` and your command won't work (or worse: it will do something unexpected). That's why we should always use `$HOME` in shell scripts and in configuration files.

If you modified wrongly (say you deleted half of the file `/etc/sudoers`), you can restore the backup with the following command:

```
cp ~/sudoers-backup /etc/sudoers
```

Let's try `visudo` again. This time, it will correctly open Neovim for you to modify the file!

First Steps In Neovim

Do you remember when you learned to walk? I don't, but I'm sure my first steps were quite clunky. Today, I can walk without consciously thinking about what I'm doing with my legs. It's the same for Neovim: at the beginning you might feel uncomfortable to use all these keystrokes, but after a (little) while it becomes second nature. Neovim's keystrokes will become part of your muscle memory[1].

---

[1] https://en.wikipedia.org/wiki/Muscle_memory

Don't forget to write the different keystrokes on your own cheatsheet as you learn them, as I was advising you in the first chapter of this very book. It will help you tremendously remembering them.

Neovim is very similar to Vim. We'll come back later to explain why Neovim exists and why I'm not using Vim in this book. You can use Vim of course, or you can try to migrate your whole Vim config to Neovim. It's not as daunting as it sounds.

Vim and Neovim are extremely similar: learn one and you'll know how to use the other.

If you already know how Neovim works, find the following line in the open file, un-comment it (delete the character `#`), save and exit. You can now directly jump to that section.

Neovim Modes

Neovim is a modal editor. It's the first big difference between Neovim and the usual text editor or IDE: you need to switch between *modes* to do what you want to do. When I speak about mode in this book, I'll always write them in uppercase for you to spot them more easily.

By default, when you open Neovim, you're in the NORMAL mode. You can move your cursor around using your arrow keys. With the NORMAL mode, you can't write text, but you can edit it. The rationale behind it: developers edit existing content more often than they write new content. That said, Neovim is fantastic to write text, too.

You can come back to NORMAL mode by hitting `ESC` if you're in any other mode.

The second most important mode you can use is the INSERT mode. This mode is the default (and only) mode for most text editors out there: when you type on your keyboard, you write text. You can use different keystrokes in Neovim to switch to INSERT mode, like `i` , `a` , or `A` .

The third most important mode is the COMMAND-LINE mode. It allows you to run commands to perform some precise operations in Neovim. You can go in the COMMAND-LINE mode by hitting `:` . If you try it, you'll end at the lower end of your window. From there, you can type and run Neovim commands.

The most important command in Neovim is `:help` , which gives you access to Neovim's documentation. For example, you can type `:help vim-modes` to learn more about Neovim modes. This help is your best way to learn new tricks in Neovim, and, like the manual `man` in the shell, it contains an insane amount of useful information.

To quit a Neovim window, you can run the command `:q` . Also, if you have only one window, it will quit Neovim.

Editing with Neovim

To authorize the group wheel to run the command sudo, we'll only use the NORMAL mode. First, we need to search for what we want to modify:

1. In normal mode, hit the key `/` . Your cursor will end up at the bottom of your window (like in COMMAND-LINE mode) and you can type your search query.
2. Type `wheel` and press `ENTER` .
3. The first result will be highlighted. You can go to the `n` ext by hitting `n` , or to the previous result with `N` .

While going through the results, you should see at one point these lines:

```
## Uncomment to allow members of group wheel to execute any command
# %wheel ALL=(ALL) ALL
```

We need know to uncomment the second line:

1. Place your cursor on the first character `#` at the beginning of the second line.
2. Hit the key `x` two times. This keystroke in normal mode is meant to delete the character under your cursor.

The result should be the following:

```
## Uncomment to allow members of group wheel to execute any command
%wheel ALL=(ALL) ALL
```

If you deleted too much or if you made a mistake, don't panic! You can undo your change using `u` in NORMAL mode. To redo them, use `CTRL+r` . If you did a bigger mistake and you don't know how to fix it, you can quit without saving with the command `:q!` .

When you're done, you can save your changes with the command `:w` (for write) and quit with `:q` . You can even do both at the same time by running the Neovim command `:wq` . If you made a mistake and you saved your file, you can restore your backup (as we discussed earlier) and try to do the modification again.

When you're done and you're back to the shell, hit `CTRL+l` to c l ean your screen.

Using Sudo

Let's see now if our modification had the impact we wanted:

1. Run the command `su <your_new_user_name>` .
2. A new subshell is created. Run `sudo echo "DO I HAVE POWER?!?"` .
3. Enter your user password.
4. You should see a message which will make you even wiser.
5. Exit the subshell with the command `exit` or by with the keystroke `CTRL+d` .

We're done here! You can now reboot your computer by running:

```
reboot
```

When you're back to the login page, log in with the user you've created in this chapter.

Best Practices For Linux Shells

We said above that we should surround Bash variables with double quote. Why is that? To know more about this, we need to dig a bit deeper in the semantics of different shell syntax.

Strings

First things first: you don't need to quote a string to tell the shell interpreter that it's a string. Try to run the following in a terminal:

```
echo hello
```

The shell interpreter will understand that "hello" is a string. For this precise example, you can surround hello with simple `'` or double `"` quotes to obtain the same result.

Globbing

Many CLIs running in the shell use regular expressions to match patterns of text, but the shell itself doesn't use them. Instead, the shell *expands* or match specific *metacharacters*: this operation is called *globbing*.

Wildcards are often used for globbing. A wildcard is a metacharacter: you can translate the `meta` part of the word by `mean about` . In short, it's a character which has a specific meaning, or *semantics*.

The wildcard is the character `*` , which has different meanings depending on the context. Let's try to use it:

```
ls /usr/share/kbd/keymaps/**/*.map.gz
```

You might already have run this command in the third chapter of the book, to choose a different layout for your keyboard.

The part `*.map.gz` means that we want to display every filename (using `ls`) ending with `.map.gz` . Any character (and any number of characters) can prefix `.map.gz` . Thus, the wildcard has the meaning "0 or more character" in this context.

What about `**/` ? This means "in every sub-directory recursively". Here, we list every file which is in the directory keymaps and all its sub-directories. Be careful however: if you use Bash, it will only parse one level of sub-directories.

If we translate the whole command in plain English, it would be something like this: "Dear shell, please output every file having a filename ending with `.map.gz` , in the directory `/usr/share/kbd/keymaps/` or one of its children, grandchildren, great-grandchildren, and so on. Thanks!".

Strings And Quotes

Now, let's say you want to copy your favorite cat picture in another directory. You don't know the filepath of the source and the destination, but they are stored in two different variables. You could then do that, for example:

```
cp $source $destination
```

There's a problem here: something like the wildcard character could be part of the filename of your cat picture. Let's say that your file is called `*.catpicture` , which is a valid filename on a Linux-based system. When you execute `cp` , the shell will try to expand the wildcard to substitute it with the different files it represents. In short, you might copy every file with filename ending in `.catpicture` , instead of copying your file called `*.catpicture` .

Sometimes you might not be sure of a variable's value; when you parse unknown files from a directory, for example. In that case, you can use double quotes to prevent the globbing to be expanded. For example, if you do something like:

```
cp "$source" "$destination"
```

Even if the variable `$source` or `$destination` contains filepaths with wildcards, they won't be expanded. In short, it treats the wildcard as a normal character, not as a metacharacter.

I would suggest that you always use double quotes around variables when you use them, except if you really want to expand any metacharacter. If you don't do it, you'll have bad surprises. For example, if you use `rm *cat_picture` to delete the file named `*cat_picture` , you might end up deleting every file with filenames that *end* with `cat_picture` .

If you want to be sure that nothing is expanded, not even a variable, you can use single quotes. Try to run the following in your shell:

```
echo '$EDITOR*'
```

It will output `$EDITOR*` .

In a Nutshell

What did we learn in this chapter?

- A process is a program running on your computer. It can create other processes, which will be its children. Each process as a unique process ID (PID).
- The first process (init process) used in many Linux distros is systemd. It will launch basically everything the system needs to run, and stop or start some services depending on what's happening: if a device is plugged to your computer, for example.
- How to create a new user.
- How to edit a file in Neovim. The most important to remember: Neovim has many modes, and each mode allow you to do different things. For example, moving around and editing in NORMAL mode or writing text in INSERT mode.
- A wildcard can be used in a shell to go through child directories recursively with `**` , or match any character with `*` , like in `*.map.gz` .

- When you use a bash variable somewhere, surround it with double quotes.

In the next chapter, we'll see everything we need in order to display graphical user interfaces (GUI) on our new system.

Going Deeper

Links

- Arch Wiki – Sudo[1]
- Arch Wiki – Environment variables[2]
- Arch Wiki – Users and groups[3]
- Arch Wiki – mkinitcpio[4]
- Article announcing systemd[5]

Manual

- `man boot`
- `man useradd`
- `man systemd`
- `man systemd.unit`
- `man systemd.service`
- `man systemd.target`
- `man nvim`
- `man 7 glob`

---

[1] https://wiki.archlinux.org/index.php/Sudo

[2] https://wiki.archlinux.org/index.php/Environment_variables

[3] https://wiki.archlinux.org/index.php/Users_and_groups

[4] https://wiki.archlinux.org/index.php/Mkinitcpio

[5] http://0pointer.de/blog/projects/systemd.html

Graphical Interface

We're now at a crossroad with an existential question: should we reject all graphical interfaces and ban the mouse out of our life forever, or should we use graphical interfaces in *some* cases? Some brave adventurers, after renouncing of any graphical possession except a modest terminal emulator, tried to go the hard way by *only* using the shell.

They never came back to speak about it.

I believe it's possible, but it's difficult. The first problem you'll have is the browser: you have text-based browsers out there for sure, but there is more than text on the Internet. Additionally, if you do some image or video manipulation, good luck trying to do that only with a terminal.

I said it already: the mouse can be useful. It's not the best tool we have, but it's a good one.

Let's stop being philosophical and let's see how to install a graphical interface on top of our beloved shell. Not every system has this layer on top: for example, many servers out there don't offer you any graphical interface at all.

In this chapter, we'll see:

- What's the X Window System.
- A brief introduction of URxvt, the terminal emulator we'll use.
- How to launch X.
- How to install and launch i3 Windows Manager (i3wm).
- How to install new fonts to display characters.

Let's now configure the basics for our graphical interface.

The X Window System

The X What?

In the grand scheme of computing, the X Window System is a dinosaur like many tools we'll use. That's nice, because I like dinosaurs, and I hope you do, too.

The X Window System was created in 1984. It's commonly called "X11" because we use its 11th version since 1987. If something could survive that long, it might be quite stable, and that's great news!

Why hasn't the version of X ever increased? It didn't have to. The X Window System is extremely modular, and the core itself didn't have to change. X11 provides a basic set of tools to create Graphical User Interfaces (GUIs). One of its most surprising features: it can be used over a network.

- An X server can communicate with programs, which are the clients.
- The server accepts request from graphical outputs (commonly windows).
- It sends back user input, like mouse or keyboard input.

The X server only provides a protocol and drawing primitives. It's the task of the different clients, like window managers or desktop environments for example, to do anything they want with it. As a result, it allows great flexibility for the different applications on your computer to have diverse graphical components.

This flexibility shines for the user too: the X server is totally decoupled from the Linux kernel and the shell, so you can choose any window manager or desktop environment you want. Try to do that with Windows and you'll regret it forever. Part of the graphical interface is coupled with part of the Window's kernel. This is simply evil.

This flexibility is one of the greatest benefits you'll get with Linux-based systems, and it's partly why there are so many Linux distros nowadays. The kernel stays the same, but the desktop environment and the applications provided by the distro can vary greatly. It's a good example of a successful separation of concerns.

Installing X

The X Window System is managed by the X.org foundation. That's why we need to install the package `xorg` :

```
sudo pacman -S xorg
```

This is a group of packages: when asked what package you want to install, just press `ENTER` to install everything. Alongside X, many utilities will be installed. We'll be using some of them in the following chapters.

You can also be more selective and just choose what you want from the group of packages if you want to install only what you'll use.

URxvt, Our Terminal Emulator

We'll soon need a terminal emulator. My favorite is URxvt: it's very light, very fast, very everything. The only downsides: it handles fonts weirdly sometimes, and you won't be able to display emojis. I would recommend beginning with it; you can always change it afterward.

To install it, run:

```
sudo pacman -S rxvt-unicode
```

We're not the root user anymore, so we need to use `sudo` each time we want to install a package. If we forget to it, we can repeat the previous command by using `!!` . As a result, `sudo !!` will be expanded to run your previous command using sudo.

This last tip will simplify your life greatly.

Video Terminals and TTYs

Now that we've installed our terminal emulator, it's a good time to explain the importance and often misunderstood concept of TTY.

Historically, TTY is the abbreviation of `t ele ty pe`. It's a physical machine used to send messages long distances, before computers even existed. It looks like a big typewriter.

When computers the size of a room were getting more and more powerful, engineers had the idea to plug teletypes into them to type commands. Why use teletypes? Simply because they were widely available. In the late 70s, physical video terminals (a teletype paired with a screen) also began to be widely used. The goal: displaying the commands typed and getting back an output on a screen.

Nowadays, we don't use teletypes or physical video terminal anymore, but we *emulate* these machines instead. Think of it as the representation of the machine as software, a virtual machine of sort. As a result, a TTY is roughly an emulated terminal with TTY drivers (implemented in the kernel), allowing you - among other things - to run multiple programs at once in the background, and sending input (from a device like a keyboard or a mouse) with a program on the foreground.

You can have many applications running in the background but you can only interact with one application in the foreground with the shell prompt. To change what's running in the background and what's running in the foreground, you can use the commands `fg` or `bg` (for `f` ore `g` round and `b` ack `g` round).

To go through the different TTYs, you can use the range of keystrokes from `CTRL+ALT+F1` to `CTRL+ALT+F6`. The command `tty` can also be used in your shell to see what TTY you're currently using. These TTYs are really useful to debug your system if the one you're using crashed, or because your video drivers display nonsense. They're your friends so don't forget them.

Like everything else in Linux, TTYs are represented using files, and the processes running on our system can directly act on them. These files are in the `/dev` directory.

Right now, the TTY you're using is directly emulated by the kernel. When we use our windows manager i3, we'll use URxvt instead, a graphical terminal emulator which can be run directly by a user. Because of that, URxvt is called a Pseudo Terminal device, or *PTY*. When you start URxvt, a *PTY master* and a *PTY slave* (called *PTS*) will be created, and the shell you have by default for the current user will run as a subprocess (or child process, as we saw) of the PTY slave.

When you use your keyboard with URxvt:

1. The input will be sent to the PTY master and displayed on your screen.
2. When you hit `ENTER`, the TTY drivers will copy the input from the PTY master to the PTY slave (PTS).
3. The shell, child of the PTS process, will interpret your command and send some output back to the PTS if needed.
4. The TTY drivers copy the output from the PTS back to the PTY master.
5. The PTY master displays the output.

It's a very high level overview of the TTY system, which is quite messy when you go into the details. Here's a diagram which can help you understand:

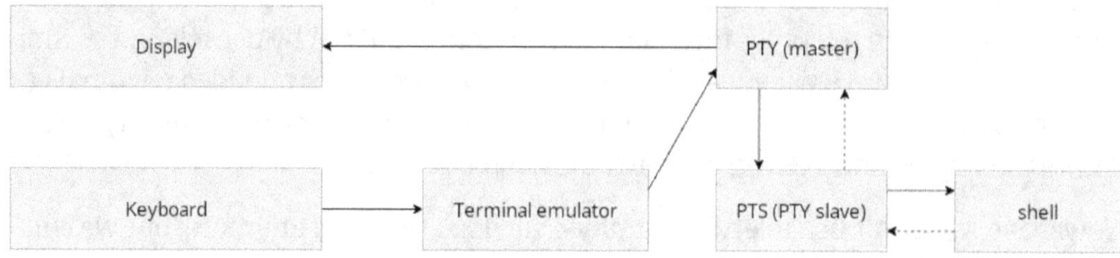

Installing i3 Window Manager

It's about time to install our windows manager i3! You know the drill:

```
sudo pacman -S i3-wm
```

Let's now try to launch it with the command `i3` . Once again, you'll get an error! There is no X server running on our machine yet, so i3 can't use it to display wonderful GUIs.

Launching X

Using `xinit` is the most straightforward way to launch our friend X. Let's install it:

```
sudo pacman -S xorg-xinit
```

A new X server can then be launched with the command `startx` . To launch applications using X (here i3), we can use the configuration file `~/.xinitrc` . Let's use Neovim again to create and setup the file:

```
nvim ~/.xinitrc
```

This command will open Neovim and the file will be automatically created (if it didn't exist already) when you save it.

We are again in the NORMAL mode in Neovim. This time, we need to write into the file, so we'll need to use the INSERT mode. Enter the keystroke:

```
i
```

You should see `--INSERT--` at the bottom of the display to indicate that you're in INSERT mode. The shape of your cursor will also normally change. Let's type now the following:

```
exec i3
```

Press `ESC` to go back to NORMAL mode. If you made a mistake, you can delete the line with the keystroke `dd` . You can also use undo (`u`), and redo too (`CTRL+r`). Then, still in NORMAL mode, write the file and quit with `:wq` .

You can clear the display with `CTRL+l` .

Keyboard Layout for X

If you changed the keyboard layout in the previous installation steps, you need to change it for X too. Simply run this command:

```
localectl --no-convert set-x11-keymap <country_code>
```

Don't forget to replace `<country_code>` with the country code of your keyboard layout. For example, if you want a French layout, use `fr`.

You can also specify some layout variant (like dvorak for example) with this command. You can look at the Arch Wiki[1] to know more about that.

Installing Fonts

Launching i3 now would be a bad idea. Indeed, we didn't install any font to display characters! For now, let's install the font Deja Vu:

```
sudo pacman -S ttf-dejavu
```

We'll install other fonts later.

Launching i3

We'll now launch our new tiling window manager. It's about time! Simply run the command:

```
startx
```

You need to enter this command manually to run i3 each time your reboot your computer. It's a pain, so we'll automate that later.

Welcome to i3!

---

[1] https://wiki.archlinux.org/index.php/Xorg/Keyboard_configuration

Graphic Cards and Video Drivers

Your video drivers can be the cause of some graphical bugs if you don't have the good ones. It really depends on your graphic card, so if you have any problem with your display I would recommend to look at this page in the Arch Wiki[1].

In a Nutshell

What did we learn in this chapter?

- The X Window System, also called X11 or X, is a server providing simple functions for drawing graphical interfaces.
- Video Terminals and TTYs are relics of the past. They were physical machines before being emulated directly by the Linux kernel.
- A PTY is an emulated teletype run by a user (and not by the kernel).

In the next chapter, we'll do our first steps in i3.

Going Deeper

- Arch Wiki - General Recommendations[2]
- Arch Wiki - Xorg[3]
- Arch Wiki - Xorg Keyboard configuration[4]
- Arch Wiki - URxvt[5]
- Arch Wiki - Hardware video acceleration[6]
- Arch Wiki - Intel Graphics[7]
- Arch Wiki - Nvidia[8]
- The TTY demystified[9]

---

[1] https://wiki.archlinux.org/index.php/Hardware_video_acceleration

[2] https://wiki.archlinux.org/index.php/General_recommendations

[3] https://wiki.archlinux.org/index.php/Xorg

[4] https://wiki.archlinux.org/index.php/Xorg/Keyboard_configuration

[5] https://wiki.archlinux.org/index.php/Rxvt-unicode

[6] https://wiki.archlinux.org/index.php/Hardware_video_acceleration

[7] https://wiki.archlinux.org/index.php/Intel_graphics

[8] https://wiki.archlinux.org/index.php/NVIDIA

[9] https://www.linusakesson.net/programming/tty/index.php

Part II - Mouseless Tools

First Steps in i3 Window Manager

You're now inside your new home. It's a bit messy, we need to fix the place up, but soon we'll have a beautiful castle.

In this chapter, we'll see:

- How to change your screen preferences: resolution, orientation, and placement (in case you have more than one screen).
- What are the basic keystrokes you need to know.
- What are i3bar and i3status.
- How to add a launcher to run your favorite applications.

This is a short introduction to i3 to allow us to configure anything we want. We'll dive more into i3 in a subsequent chapter.

Screen Resolution

When you first launch i3, you'll normally see a message asking you if you want to generate some configuration. Accept it. Then, i3 will ask what modifier you want to set: keep the default `WIN` . The next two options are normally preselected so you just need to hit `ENTER` two times.

The modifier in i3 is the most important key: almost every keystroke you'll use will have this modifier as its prefix. The `WIN` key is normally on the left of your keyboard, with a little Windows logo on it, reminding us the crazy monopoly and unfair competition Microsoft has imposed on PC for decades.

At this point you might want to change your screen layout and resolution. Maybe you have two, three, or 42 screens you want to use. We need an application to manage these preferences.

The good news: we already have it! It's called `xrandr` and it comes with the `xorg` package group we installed earlier. That said, I think it's a bit a pain to use in the shell; I prefer using a simple graphical interface on top of it.

Let's first open URxvt with the keystroke `WIN+ENTER` . I know, it's ugly, but we'll fix that soon. Then, let's install ARandR:

```
sudo pacman -S arandr
```

To open the application, let's run it in URxvt:

```
arandr
```

A new window will open, taking half of your screen. From there you can configure your screens' layouts and resolutions.

As an aside, you can see that your terminal is "blocked": you can't really type anything anymore. This is because a terminal allows you to interact with only one program (the program in the foreground, as we saw), here ARandR. It doesn't mean you can only run one program using the shell.

Go back to your terminal and kill ARandR by hitting `CTRL+c` . Now try this command:

```
arandr&
```

The program ARandR will run again, but this time you have the freedom to continue using your terminal. The `&` character indicates that the process will run in the background.

The Basics of i3

It's time to see the basic commands you can use with i3. As with Neovim, I would advise you to create your own cheatsheet as you go, to become the keyboard master you've always wanted to be.

As I was saying above, the keystrokes you can use with i3 very often include the *modifier key*, in our case the `WIN` key. Since the terminal will be the center of our Mouseless Development Environment, it's nice that we can use the easy-to-remember keystroke `WIN+ENTER` to spawn them.

To close the current window in focus, you can use the keystroke `WIN+SHIFT+q` .

Now, try to open two terminals. Automatically, the screen will be divided vertically for the two applications to each take half of the space available. That's the default behavior. You can select the windows with your mouse, but since we're building a Mouseless Development Environment, you can also focus on them using `WIN+LEFT ARROW` of `WIN+RIGHT ARROW` .

Let's try to hit the keys `WIN+e` . The layout changed from vertical to horizontal. You can focus the windows using `WIN+UP ARROW` or `WIN+DOWN ARROW` this time.

Finally, to end your i3 session, you can use `WIN+shift+e` . There will be an ugly bar appearing on top of your screen with a button you need to click on. We'll get rid of that too in the next chapter.

To shut down your computer, you can run the following command in a terminal:

```
shutdown now
```

That's all for the very basics!

i3bar and i3status

I'm sure you saw it with your hawk eyes: you have an error message at the bottom of your screen, `status_command not found`. By default, `i3` comes with a status bar judiciously called `i3bar`, but we need to manually install `i3status` to display something with it:

```
sudo pacman -S i3status
```

To reload i3, you can hit the keystroke `WIN+SHIFT+r`. You now have some information about your system displayed in the status bar! It's still pretty ugly (in my opinion), but, again, no worries. We'll see how to configure that, too.

Installing Your Favorite Browser

It's time to access the Great Internet, again, this time using browser. It will allow you to look at millions of cat pictures, watch videos of ducks rescued and raised by tigers, arguing on Reddit for hours, and downloading this book on your new system (or its companion[1]) in case you want to copy and paste the commands instead of typing all of them.

My heart goes to Firefox but you can install Chromium too (the open source equivalent of Chrome). If you want the original Google Chrome, you'll have to wait a bit: it's on the Arch User Repository (AUR) and we need to see how you can access it.

To install Firefox, run this command:

```
sudo pacman -S firefox
```

If you want to use Chromium, replace `firefox` with `chromium` in the command above. If you want to go mouseless even when you browse the Internet, a chapter in the book is entirely dedicated to this idea.

---

[1] https://github.com/Phantas0s/mouseless-book-companion

When the browser you wanted is installed, one could ask this very profound question: how to launch it? You could do that from the terminal of course (as we did with ARandR), but there is a better solution.

Program Launcher

We'll now install a program called `dmenu` . Its purpose? Creating interactive menus. i3 also uses it as a program launcher. Let's run:

```
sudo pacman -S dmenu
```

Now, you can open the launcher with `WIN+d` . It will appear at the top of the screen; from there, type the name of any application you want to run and validate by hitting `ENTER` .

Copy and Paste

There is a problem in the strategy above: we can't copy and paste in Neovim yet. We need to install the program `xsel` :

```
sudo pacman -S xsel
```

To understand how the clipboard works in Linux-based systems, I encourage you to read the description on xsel's man page.

To paste in `urxvt` , you need to use `CTRL+ALT+v` . I know, it's not `CTRL+v` , but it's close. You can do the same in Neovim (only in INSERT MODE): it's not the idiomatic way we should use, but it's good enough for now.

To copy from URxvt, you can use `CTRL+ALT+c` .

Pasting From a PDF

We'll now begin to configure everything, and I would understand if your fingers are tired at this point. Mine are too by writing this book; but it's my duty, and I accept the suffering! Anyway, you can now download this book to copy and paste the different commands. You don't have a PDF reader on your system yet, but you can normally use your browser to open PDF files, by running something like this in your terminal:

```
firefox <super_cool_book.pdf> &
```

You can also install and use the excellent zathura to read your favorite PDF files. It's a highly configurable PDF viewer using Vim keystrokes. To install it, run:

```
sudo pacman -S zathura-pdf-mupdf
```

Then, you can read the pdf as following:

```
zathura <super_cool_book.pdf> &
```

To copy text from zathura, you need to run a simple command in the application itself:

```
:set selection-clipboard clipboard
```

Like in Neovim, hitting the keystroke `:` will bring you to a command-line at the bottom of the application. From there, you can type the command you want and run it by hitting `ENTER`.

I won't go in detail on how to configure zathura in this book, but as always, zathura's man page can help you. It contains the list of keystrokes you can use, too.

The Book Companion

Unfortunately, copying and pasting commands from a PDF can introduce many formatting issues. In some cases, it might introduce some buggy behaviors if you're not careful. I would definitely advise you to download the book companion. It contains every single line of configuration we'll write throughout the book, giving you a solid reference in case you have a problem.

First, you'll need to download the archive and unzip it. For that, you need to install the application `unzip`:

```
sudo pacman -S unzip
```

Next, let's use the CLI cURL to download the file, and let's unzip it at the same time. Run the following commands in your terminal:

```
curl -L -o ~/companion.zip \
https://github.com/Phantas0s/mouseless-book-
  ↪   companion/archive/master.zip
  ↪   \
&& cd ~ \
&& unzip ./companion.zip \
&& mv ~/mouseless-book-companion-master ~/mouseless_book_companion \
&& cd ~/mouseless_book_companion
```

I won't explain these commands now, we'll speak more about these ideas later in this book.

The book companion will be located in `~/mouseless_book_companion` . You'll find in there all the configuration we'll write, organized by chapter. You can copy and paste from there the commands you want in your own config files.

Troubleshooting

It's possible that you're having an error in your i3 config file, even if you didn't modify it yet! It's often a keystroke declared two (or more) times. If it's the case, you can still use i3 normally except for this specific keystroke. Still, you'll have to live with an annoying error message on top of your screen.

Normally, two buttons will be displayed with the error message. You can click on `show error` to see what's the problem. You can click on `edit config` to fix the config itself. If it's a keystroke declared multiple times, you can search for it and comment out one of these declarations. Then, reload the config with the keystroke `WIN+r` .

In a Nutshell

We'll begin to configure our terminal emulator URxvt in the next chapter. We saw in this chapter:

- How to configure your different screen using Xrandr and ARandR.
- The basic commands to work with i3:
    - `WIN+ENTER` - Create a new client for URxvt.
    - `WIN+SHIFT+q` - Close the focused window
    - `WIN+e` - Change the windows layout.
    - `WIN+SHIFT+r` - Reload i3.

- `WIN+ARROW KEYS` - Move the focus from window to window.

- How to use dmenu with i3 as a program launcher with the keystroke `WIN+d` .
- How to copy and paste in URxvt using `CTRL+ALT+c` and `CTRL+ALT+v` .

Going Deeper

- Arch Wiki - i3[1]
- Arch Wiki - xrandr[2]
- Arch Wiki - zathura[3]

---

[1] https://wiki.archlinux.org/index.php/I3
[2] https://wiki.archlinux.org/index.php/Xrandr
[3] https://wiki.archlinux.org/index.php/Zathura

Configuring URxvt

Let's begin to configure the different tools we'll use. One of the most important is our terminal emulator URxvt. Let's configure it first to make it more pleasing to the eyes. After all, it should motivate you to do some good work, not to switch off your computer as fast as you can, your stomach rotating on itself by such ugliness.

In this chapter, we'll see:

- How to change the colors of our terminal.
- How to configure the basics for URxvt.
- How to use URxvt as a daemon.

You won't recognize your terminal emulator after that!

The Colors of the Terminal

We can configure URxvt using a general purpose configuration file for X. First, let's run in a terminal:

```
mkdir "~/.config/X11"
```

We'll put all the configuration files for X our new directory `X11` . Let's now create the configuration file itself:

```
touch "~/.config/X11/.Xresources"
```

The file `.Xresources` will contain configurations for all applications that are clients of X, like URxvt. Don't forget the dot `.` in the filename! This file is called a "dotfile"; you can see it as a synonym of "configuration file" in the Linux world. Be careful: not every configuration file has a filename beginning with a dot!

Many Linux users put all their configuration files online, in projects they are often called "dotfiles". We'll do that in the subsequent chapters, too. For now, let's go in the directory we just created:

```
cd ~/.config/X11/
```

If you try to run `ls` in your terminal, nothing will be displayed. Why? We created a file in there! It's because all files that begins with a period `.` are hidden in Linux. You need to do `ls -a` (`a`ll) to display them.

Let's now edit the configuration file. Run in the shell:

```
nvim ~/.config/X11/.Xresources
```

Let's add some colors for the foreground, background and the cursor, by writing these lines in the file `~/.config/X11/.Xresources` that we just opened.

```
*.foreground:   #C6C6C6
*.background:   #1C1C1C
*.cursorColor:  #444444
```

The symbols `*.` means that the configuration will be applied to every application using this file. To reload the file `.Xresources` and apply the changes, run the following in another terminal:

```
xrdb -merge ~/.config/X11/.Xresources
```

What does it mean? I'm glad you asked! The option `-merge` will merge the configuration you specified in `.Xresources` with the local settings of the applications using this configuration. To see the whole final settings set, you can run `xrdb -query -all`.

You need to restart URxvt itself to display the changes you've just made.

It would be nice to merge our customized `.Xresources` file at startup. Let's edit again the file `~/.xinitrc`:

```
nvim ~/.xinitrc
```

Now add this line *before* `exec i3`:

```
xrdb -merge ~/.config/X11/.Xresources
```

Why do we need this line before `exec i3`? We want i3 to:

1. Replace the shell process which is started automatically after login with an i3 process.
2. Run i3 continuously in the background.

To do so, we always need the line `exec i3` to be at the end of the file!

Making URxvt Prettier

URxvt is a terminal supporting 256 colors. It might not be enough for you (some terminal support True Color, or 16 million of them), but for me 256 colors is already too much. So many choices!

Let's configure every other color you can configure for a terminal emulator. Many other CLIs will use these colors, too. For example, here are mine you can add to .Xresources :

```
! black 236 238
*.color0: #303030
*.color8: #444444

! red 167
*.color1: #d75f5f
*.color9: #d75f5f

! green 108
*.color2: #87AF87
*.color10: #87AF87

! yellow 221
*.color3: #ffd75f
*.color11: #ffd75f

! blue 110
*.color4: #87afd7
*.color12: #87afd7

! magenta 146
*.color5: #afafd7
*.color13: #afafd7

! cyan 75
*.color6: #afd7ff
*.color14: #afd7ff

! white 239 15
*.color7: #e4e4e4
*.color15: #ffffff
```

You can copy this configuration directly from the book companion[1].

---

[1] https://raw.githubusercontent.com/PhantasOs/mouseless-book-companion/master/part_II/02_urxvt/.Xresources

If you don't like these colors, you make me very sad. That said, you can go on the fantastic website called terminal sexy[1] to help you configure the colors of your terminal easily. You can even import and export your `.Xresources` file back and forth.

The exclamation marks `!` are used for inserting comments. Everything after `!` won't be interpreted. I've added some information using comments for each color.

The first color on the line just after each comment is the darkest version of the color, and the line just below it the lightest version. If an application wants to display light magenta, it will use the `color13` we've configured.

Regarding the comments themselves, the numbers just after the color names are called "Xterm color codes" (xterm is the standard terminal emulator for X). It's a number between 1 and 256 which represents a color. You might need to use this color code for applications which don't support hexadecimal colors (`#ffffff` for example). It's useful to have a consistent color scheme across your system.

You can find all the colors you can use here[2].

Configuring URxvt

Enough colors! If you didn't notice already, the actual font used by URxvt is not really readable in some situations. Let's change that.

Character Fonts

You can display all fonts installed on your system with the command:

```
fc-list
```

You can filter the list using grep as we saw in previous chapters, or you can navigate through it using a pager like less. If you use grep, you can use the option `-i` to filter without case sensitivity. This means that you can use uppercase and lowercase characters without grep making any distinction between them.

Now, let's add the following line in the file `~/.config/X11/.Xresources` :

```
URxvt*font: xft:DejaVuSansMono:size=14:antialias=true
```

---

[1] https://terminal.sexy

[2] http://jonasjacek.github.io/colors

Reload the configuration with `xrdb` as we saw above and restart URxvt. Notice that your font has changed. You can see here that we've written `URxvt*` at the beginning of the line, which means that the following configuration is only applied to URxvt.

If the spaces between the letters are too wide, you can try to add the following line:

```
URxvt*letterSpace: -1
```

Window Default

Let's now improve URxvt's window itself by adding these four lines in our `.Xresources`:

```
URxvt*borderLess: false
URxvt*externalBorder: 0
URxvt*internalBorder: 4

URxvt*scrollBar: false
```

With this configuration we first hide the external border of the window. Then, we set an internal border to create some nice padding. These borders are transparent by default, but you can add a color with the option `URxvt*borderColor`.

We hide the scroll bar, too: it's quite ugly, and we'll see later other ways to scroll up and down.

Let's display more lines in the terminal by adding this line:

```
URxvt*saveLines: 5000
```

It's now possible to scroll through 5000 lines of output in our terminal!

Let's see next how to make our terminal even faster: that's partly why URxvt is such a good choice.

URxvt Daemon

URxvt is a very light terminal emulator. You can even run it as a daemon (program running in the background) as soon as you log in.

We can use instances of the client `urxvtc` to connect to the daemon `urxvtd` (the server). This means that if the daemon crashes, every client process connected to it will crash too. It might look like a major problem, but it's not:

- We'll install tmux later, allowing you to persist tmux sessions even if you close the terminal emulator itself.
- It has never happened to me in years of use.

We should run the daemon `urxvtd` at the beginning of our X session. To do so, let's modify again our file `.xinitrc` :

```
nvim ~/.xinitrc
```

Next, let's add this line at the beginning of the file:

```
urxvtd -o -q -f
```

This line will run URxvt's daemon each time we launch our X server with these options:

- `-q` for `quiet` - By default, `urxvtd` displays a welcome message. Even if it's nice and welcoming, I see it as useless noise.
- `-o` for `opendisplay` - Keep the daemon process running at all time.
- `-f` for `fork` - Bound URxvt to its control socket.

If you log out, it's important to note that the X server is restarted and `urxvtd` killed. As a result, if you modify some configuration for URxvt and it doesn't seem to work, sometimes you only need to log out and log in again to see the change. It has happened to me often when changing the fonts in `.Xresources` , for example.

In a Nutshell

What did we learn in this chapter?

- How to configure the colors for our terminal and every program using `.Xresources` as a configuration file (dotfile).
- How to list all the fonts install on our system with `fc-list` .
- How to change the font for URxvt.
- How to modify slightly URxvt's window.
- What's the URxvt daemon and how it works.

In the next chapter, we'll dive more into the basics of Neovim.

Going Deeper

- Arch Wiki - rxvt-unicode[1]
- Arch Wiki - X resources[2]

---

[1] https://wiki.archlinux.org/index.php/Rxvt-unicode
[2] https://wiki.archlinux.org/index.php/X_resources

The Basics of Neovim

Now that we used a bit more Neovim, it's time to dive deeper into the basics. We'll write quite a bit of configuration in the subsequent chapters, so it will be definitely useful.

I can never say it enough: I encourage you to write the keystrokes we'll see in this chapter on your own cheatsheet. Trust me, you'll learn much more that way.

In this chapter, we'll see:

- The most important modes for Neovim.
- How to forget the arrow keys and use "h", "j", "k", and "l" instead.
- The commands to switch from NORMAL mode to INSERT mode.
- The motions: horizontal, vertical, and scrolling keystrokes.
- The operators and text objects to navigate and edit your text.

There is a lot to cover here. Again, take your time and experiment while reading. If you're already a seasoned Neovim (or Vim) user, feel free to jump to the next chapter.

Neovim Modes

We saw previously three different modes you can use with Neovim. Let's come back to them briefly:

- NORMAL mode - This is the mode by default. You can navigate and edit your text using NORMAL mode.
- INSERT mode - This mode is meant to insert content. It's the default (and only) mode of most editors available out there.
- COMMAND-LINE mode - When switching to this mode, your cursor will automatically jump to the very bottom of your Neovim instance. From there, you can type and execute Neovim ex commands.

You can also search for your open files using the keystroke / , which will bring you to the bottom of the screen. From there, you can search for anything you want. You can then use the keystroke n or N to go to the n ext or the previous result, respectively.

Let's now introduce a fourth mode: VISUAL mode. Its goal? Selecting your content. After selecting it, you can modify, edit, or copy it.

To enter VISUAL mode - you might have guessed it already - you need to type `v` in NORMAL mode. You will see the indicator `--VISUAL--` appearing in the bottom left corner of your Neovim instance, indicating that you're indeed in VISUAL mode.

These four modes are the most important ones you need to know. There are others, but I won't speak about them in this book.

Configuring Neovim

Let's create now the file `init.vim`, the main configuration file for Neovim:

```
mkdir ~/.config/nvim
nvim ~/.config/nvim/init.vim
```

Then, let's add the following:

```
set clipboard+=unnamedplus
```

Here, we set the *option* `clipboard`, allowing us to paste directly from the OS clipboard to Neovim using Neovim paste keystroke. We'll discuss this idea below.

To save and exit the file, you need to go in COMMAND-LINE mode (using the keystroke `:` in NORMAL mode), type `wq` (for `w` rite and `q` uit), and press `ENTER`. In short, you need to use the keystroke `:wq` in NORMAL mode.

Forget the Arrow Keys

That was the hardest part for me, when I learned to use Neovim: not using the arrow keys to move my cursor around. As we saw in a previous chapter, your fingers should be around the row keys as much as possible. First, for your typing skills to improve, and second because the Neovim keystrokes you can use in NORMAL mode are all around the row keys.

Now, try to reach the arrow keys from the row keys. Yes, you need to move your hand! This is definitely not what we want. That's why, instead of using the arrow keys, you should now use the keys `h` , `j` , `k` and `l` to move respectively left, down, up and right.

It's difficult at first to only use these keys: you'll try to go back to the arrow keys more than once, trust me. We'll see below a way to disable the arrow keys for you to commit to this new way of working.

How to remember what action is mapped to what key?

- h moves your cursor to the left, and l moves it to the right. It makes sense: h is on the far left of the sequence hjkl , and l is on the far right.
- j moves your cursor down. With a bit of imagination j looks like an arrow which points down. Another mnemonic you can use: the j key has a little bump at the bottom, which means that the cursor will go down.
- k is the only letter left, so it has to go up. I always imagine a Ninja Turtle jumping, saying "Kowabunga"! It's not even the good spelling (it would be "Cowabunga") but it works for me. You can create ridiculous associations too; it's a good way to remember. The more absurd it is, the better it works.

I see your mind full of doubts. Fear not, dear reader! I've got you covered for this one, with revolutionary AAA games everybody will speak about in twenty years. A snake game I made[1], where you *must* use the keys hjkl to play.

If you dream of a good old Sokoban game where you can use both hjkl and the arrow keys, your dream is now reality[2].

When I first learned Neovim, I disabled the arrow keys to force myself to only use hjkl . I did it as I was learning the good typing techniques we saw at the beginning of the book. If you want to do the same, add the following in the file ~/.config/nvim/init.vim :

```
noremap <Up> <Nop>
noremap <Down> <Nop>
noremap <Left> <Nop>
noremap <Right> <Nop>
```

Again, it might feel weird at the beginning, but don't give up; the rewards are greater than the pain.

Switching To Insert Mode

We saw previously that the keystroke i moved your whole being into the common and reassuring world of INSERT mode. There are other handy keystrokes you can use to make the transition, introducing welcome subtleties:

- i – Switch to i NSERT mode before the current character.
- a – Switch to INSERT mode a fter the current character.

---

[1] https://matthieucneude.com/snake/
[2] https://matthieucneude.com/sokoban/

- `A` – Switch to INSERT mode `A`fter the end of the current line.
- `o` – `o`pen a new line below the current one, and switch to INSERT mode.
- `O` – `O`pen a new line above the current one, and switch to INSERT mode.
- `r` – `r`eplace one character by another one (it doesn't switch to INSERT mode but it's useful anyway).
- `esc` and `CTRL+c` – Bring you back to NORMAL mode if you're in any other mode.

This will normally cover all your secret desires for INSERT mode.

Undo And Redo

What would we do without the essential undo and redo in an editor? Not much, I'm afraid. We would possibly regress to hunting and gathering while living in caves. We've seen these keystrokes earlier in the book, but let's repeat them here for completeness:

- `u` – `u`ndo the last modifications you did.
- `CTRL+r` – `r`edo the last undo.

```
:help search-commands
:help undo-redo
```

Motions

Moving is important: after all, targeting what we want to change is one of the main goal of the NORMAL mode. To do so, we can use *motions*.

Horizontal Motions

Here are the most useful Vim motions:

- `w` – Move to the next `w`ord.
- `b` – Move `b`ackward, to the previous word.
- `0` – Move to the beginning of the current line.
- `^` – Move to the first non blank character on the current line.
- `$` – Move to the end of the current line.

The keys `hjkl` are also considered motions.

You can even add a counter to any motion: if you type the keystroke `6w` for example, you'll move forward to 6 `w` ords; `6j` will move your cursor 6 lines down.

Vertical Motions

You can move vertically by searching for the word you want to move to (using the keystroke `/` as we saw). It's not the most effective in many cases, but it's good enough for the beginning. Other than that, here are other important vertical motions:

- `<number> SHIFT+g` - Move at line `<number>`. For example: `8G`.
- `1 SHIFT+g` or `gg` - Move to the first line of the document.
- `SHIFT+g` - Move to the end of the document.
- `%` - Move your cursor to a matching bracket (if your cursor is on the closing bracket, it will move to the opening one, and vice versa).

Scrolling commands

You have the ability to scroll in Neovim, too:

- `CTRL+u` - Move `u` pward half a screen.
- `CTRL+d` - Move `d` ownward half a screen.

The number of lines scrolled can be adjusted with the `scroll` option. We'll see Neovim's options just below.

```
:help cursor-motions
:help left-right-motions
:help up-down-motions
:help scrolling
```

The Language of Neovim

Some keystrokes in Neovim can be combined to form sentences, describing an action you want to perform in NORMAL mode. I know, it sounds weird, but it's brilliant: it will help you tremendously to remember all these keystrokes.

These "keystrokes-sentences" are so common that you'll associate more easily what you know already (the action you want to perform) with what you need to learn (the keystrokes). Even better: knowing that Neovim has this "keystroke language" will push you to combine keystrokes instinctively to do what you need to do, and, in many cases, it will work!

Operators

Let see some basic keystrokes which *need* to be combined with a motion. These are called *operators*: you can think of them as the *verb* of your actions.

- `d` – `d`elete.
- `c` – `c`hange.
- `y` – `y`ank (or copy).

You can paste what you've copied with the keystrokes `p` and `P`.

Here are some example to combine these operators with motions:

- `d$` – Delete from your cursor to the end of line. You can also use the alias `D`.
- `dgg` – Delete everything from the cursor to the beginning of the file.
- `ggdG` – Move your cursor to the beginning of the file and delete everything till the end. In short, you've deleted the whole content. Congratulations!

`:help operator`

Text Objects

With operators, you can act on *text objects*, which can be considered as the *noun* of your action. Simply put, a text object is a set of characters. For example, in Neovim, a `word`, a `sentence`, a `paragraph` or even a single quote `'` are all text objects.

Here are some keystrokes I use all the time:

- `diw` – `d`elete `i`nside a `w`ord. It will delete the current word under the cursor.
- `ciw` – `c`hange `i`nside the `w`ord. It will delete the current word under the cursor and switch to INSERT mode.
- `ci'` – `c`hange `i`nside the closest single quote on the line. Your cursor doesn't even have to be inside the single quote! It also works for parenthesis.

You can try to *change a word* or *delete a word*, it also works and introduces some sub-tleties. I let you find what could be the keystrokes for these.

That's all! With these keystrokes, you should be able to be much more effective with Neovim. Be creative and try as many keystroke combinations as you like!

```
:help text-objects
```

A Basic Configuration

Let's now write a basic configuration for Neovim to make the experience a bit smoother.

Neovim's Options

Neovim has many options affecting its behavior. You can think of an option as a variable: it can be a boolean (which can be switched on and off), a string, or a number. You can display their values or modifying them using the COMMAND-LINE mode.

If you want to permanently modify some options, assign their new values directly in your file `~/.config/nvim/init.vim`, as we did with the option `clipboard` at the beginning of this chapter.

Here are the basic commands you can use to manage these options:

- `:set no<option>` – Unset the option.
- `:set <option>!` – Toggle the option.
- `:set <option>?` – Return the option's value.
- `:set <option>=<value>` – Set a value `<value>` (string or number).
- `:set <option>+=<value>` – Add the value `<value>` for a number option, append a string `<value>` for a string option.
- `:set <option>-=<value>` – Subtract the value `<value>` for a number option, delete the string `<value>` for a string option.
- `:set <option>&` – Reset the option to its default value.

For example, if you want to display the filetype of the your current file open, you can run:

```
set filetype?
```

Drop the prefix `:` if you want to set these options in `init.vim`.

 `:help options`
`:help option-list`

Swap Files

The swap file is a mechanism forbidding you to modify a file which is already open in another Neovim process. In this world governed by source control (or more precisely Git), I find this functionality quite useless. Let's disable it by adding to the file `~/.config/nvim/init.vim` the following:

```
" no swap file
set noswapfile
```

As you can see, to add a comment in Neovim's configuration, you need to use the character `"` at the beginning of the line.

Undo Tree

The undo and redo system in Neovim is the most powerful one I've seen. It can keep track of *every* undo (or redo) you did per file, and save them to the disk. This means that even when you close Neovim and reopen it, you can still undo or redo your last (hundred) actions on a specific file.

To enable this life-changing functionality, let's add the following in our `init.vim` file:

```
" save undo-trees in files
set undofile
set undodir=$HOME/.config/nvim/undo
set undolevels=10000
set undoreload=10000
```

As you can see in the command, we know save *undo trees* in the directory `$HOME/.config/nvim/undo`. What's an undo-tree? It's a powerful concept we'll discuss later in the book.

General Options

Let's add the following to our init file to display the line numbers:

```
" set line number
set number
```

Now the big question: tabs or spaces for indenting? We all know that 4 spaces are the best.

```
" use 4 spaces instead of tab
" copy indent from current line when starting a new line
set autoindent
set expandtab
set tabstop=4
set softtabstop=4
set shiftwidth=4
```

If you prefer having 2 spaces for JSON files and tabs for Golang files, don't panic. It's possible to overwrite these options depending of the filetype of your open file.

In a Nutshell

What did we learn in this chapter?

- Neovim has many modes. The most used are NORMAL, INSERT, COMMAND-LINE, and VISUAL modes.
- You can use Vim motions to move around. For example: `hjkl` , `gg` , `G` ...
- You can use operators and text-objects to edit your text in NORMAL mode, using Neovim language: `diw` will d elete i nside a w ord, for example.

In the next chapter, we'll see the different package managers we can use in Arch Linux: Pacman and Yay.

Going Deeper

- Arch Wiki - Neovim[1]
- Vimcasts[2]

---

[1] https://wiki.archlinux.org/index.php/Neovim

[2] http://vimcasts.org/

- Learn Vim Progressively[1]
- 7 Habits of Effective Text Editing[2]

---

[1] http://yannesposito.com/Scratch/en/blog/Learn-Vim-Progressively/

[2] http://www.moolenaar.net/habits.html

Pacman and Yay

Now that we have a global understanding of Neovim, let's switch to a totally different but important subject: your future favorite package manager. Pacman is not only a yellow cheese from the 80s trying to eat pills in dark rooms, it's also the official package manager for Arch Linux. It's a very versatile tool, offering you plenty of options to manage your lovely packages.

In this chapter, we'll see:

- What are the different types of arguments you can use with Pacman, and their function.
- What are the official repositories of Arch Linux.
- How to remove packages.
- How to search for packages in the repositories' databases.
- How to clear Pacman's cache.
- What's the Arch User Repository (AUR).
- How to install Yay, a package manager able to pull packages from the AUR.
- How to install tabs for URxvt with Yay.
- How to install Neovim language extensions with Yay.
- Troubleshooting your Pacman problems.

I don't know about you, but each time I use Pacman, I *hear* this well-known yellow cheese trying to escape colorful ghosts. I might be crazy.

Operations and Options

You can perform *operations* with Pacman, and add *options* to control each operation's behavior. For example, to update your whole system you can run `pacman -Syu` :

- `-S` is the operation.
- `-y` is an option.
- `-u` is another option.

These two options `-y` and `-u` have a specific meaning when coupled with the operation `-S` , but can have other meanings (or don't exist at all) when used with other operations.

Official Repositories

As we saw, you can use Pacman to install packages from different repositories. Here are the official ones:

1. Core repository - In this repository, the community accepts only packages with very strict quality requirements.
2. Extra repositories - Includes every package which is not in core.
3. Communities - Packages from trusted users of the Arch Linux User Repository (AUR).
4. Multilib - Allows you to build and run 32-bit applications on 64-bit installations of Arch Linux (which is normally what we install). It's disabled by default.

Most of the time, you'll install packages from one of these repositories. Each repository has a database indicating where you can find the packages.

If you want to install packages from multilib, you need to modify the configuration of Pacman. I speak very briefly about this configuration file at the end of the chapter.

Updating Your System

Let's begin with one of the most important commands: how to upgrade your system. Arch Linux, as we discussed at the beginning of the book, is a rolling distribution. This means that everything can be updated very often: your applications, the drivers, even the Linux kernel itself.

To update everything, you need to use the command `pacman -Syu` :

- `-S` - Operation used to `S` ynchronize packages.
- `-y` - Update the repositories' databases.
- `-u` - Update the packages which are out-of-date on your system.

Sometimes you'll see multiple 404 errors when you try to install a package: this means that you need to update the databases of the different repositories. You might be tempted to run `pacman -Sy` at this point; don't! Installing a new package following this command might break other packages you have.

To keep it simple, always use `pacman -S <package_name>` , or `pacman -Syu` . You can even combine both: `pacman -Syu <package_name>` .

You should update your system every week or two. It's what I've done for years, and it has always worked well. If you didn't update for a month or more, don't panic; keep in mind, however, the more time you leave between updates, the more likely you are to experience package conflicts and problems.

Sometimes, Pacman will ask you questions you have no idea about; 99% of the time, the process to follow is explained on the homepage of the official website for Arch Linux[1].

Removing Packages

You installed this super cool application... but it's not as cool as you thought? The operation `-R` allows you to remove any package you want. You can add the option `-s` (for recur s ive) to remove all the dependencies used by *only* this package.

For example, if you want to remove the package `php` , you can do:

```
sudo pacman -Rs php
```

Note that Pacman won't delete dotfiles created by an application. You need to remove them manually.

Searching Packages

If you want to install an application but you don't know the exact package name, you can:

- Search for it on Google: `<package_name> Arch Linux` works pretty well.
- You can use Pacman with the operation `-S` (for s ynchronize) and the option `-s` (for s earch).

For example, if you want to see every PHP package available, you can run:

```
sudo pacman -Ss php
```

To fetch some information about packages installed on your system, you can use the operation `-Q` . Coupled with the option `-s` (for s earch), you could search for every PHP package you have installed:

```
sudo pacman -Qs php
```

---

[1] https://www.archlinux.org/

If you've installed packages which are not in the databases of the official repositories (for example when you install packages from the Arch User Repository), you can query them with the operation `-Q` and the option `-m` .

Pacman's Cache

When a package is downloaded using the operation `-S` , it goes in the cache directory of Pacman, normally `/var/cache/pacman/pkg/` . Then, the package is installed.

If you want to reinstall a package, Pacman will use the cache and won't download anything. If you reinstall a package you've uninstalled before, Pacman will use the cache, too.

That being said, if you want to empty the cache because you don't have any space on your hard disk left thanks to your addiction to next-gen video games (yes, gaming on Linux is definitely possible), you can clean it with the command:

```
sudo pacman -Scc
```

The two options mean everything will be super `c` lean afterward. You can use one `c` instead of two if you want to delete from cache only the packages which are not installed on your system.

The Arch User Repository (AUR)

The official repositories of Arch Linux contain a very impressive list of packages. But sometimes you won't find what you want in there. A rare gem or a very specific application written in Cobol in the 70s might not be available in the official Arch Linux repositories. In these rare cases, you can try to find what you secretly desire in the Arch User Repository, or AUR.

For example, we would like to add tabs to our terminal emulator URxvt. There is a very good tab management plugin for it, called `urxvt-tabbedex-mina86` .

First, let's try to find it in the official repositories as follows:

```
pacman -Ss rxvt
```

The package we want is definitely not there. If you Google it, you'll find that the package is part of the Arch User Repository (AUR). We've already mentioned it quite often, so let's see how we can install packages from this magical place.

The AUR contains package description files called `PKGBUILD` (for, you know, p ac k a g e build). These can be read by a script called `makepkg` (make p ac k a g e). This script should be run by a regular user and not by the root user (contrary to Pacman). Indeed, you need to keep in mind that these packages should be considered unsafe. Don't allow them to use the great privileges of the root user.

We can go to the official AUR website[1] and search for the package:

```
urxvt-tabbedex-mina86
```

You'll see a list with the package `urxvt-tabbedex-mina86-git` in it. Click on it and you'll see useful information about the package:

- Click on `view PKGBUILD` to see what a `PKGBUILD` file looks like.
- The comments can be useful if you have any problem installing the package.
- It's useful to look at the list of dependencies, too, to know exactly what you're installing on your system.

You know what would be awesome? Having a package manager like Pacman able to access the AUR. Well, that's exactly what we'll install next.

The Package Manager Yay

The package manager Yay is a wrapper around Pacman. If you use Yay for anything concerning the official repositories, Pacman will be used under the hood. For example, `yay -Syu` will fetch the database from the official repositories, update all your official packages and the packages from the AUR.

It also means that every operation and option you can use with Pacman will work with Yay. How great! Yay!

Personally, I like to use Pacman when I use the official repositories, and Yay when I need to install packages from the AUR. It helps me make a clear distinction between the official and safe packages and the possibly unsafe packages from the AUR.

How to install Yay? It's in the AUR! Again, you can search for it on the AUR website. In the list of results, click on the package `yay` . As you can see, there is a "Git Clone URL" on the page.

Now, on a terminal, change your working directory to `/tmp` using the command `cd /tmp` . This directory is for anything temporary. In fact, everything in the whole directory is deleted each time your computer starts.

---

[1] https://aur.archlinux.org

We need Git to clone our package, so let's install it first:

```
sudo pacman -S git
```

Click on `Git Clone URL` on the AUR webpage to copy it. Then, run in a terminal:

```
git clone <git_clone_url>
```

The URL is normally `https://aur.archlinux.org/yay.git`. When you're done cloning, go to the newly created directory: `cd yay`.

If you run `ls`, you'll see there is only the `PKGBUILD` in it. Let's now build the package:

```
makepkg -s
```

The `-s` option (for `s`ync dependencies) will install the dependencies you need, automatically. If it doesn't work and you have some 404 errors, try to update the databases from the official repositories (some dependencies might come from there) with the command `pacman -Syu`.

Normally, Yay will install Golang as a dependency. It's used for compiling the application; you can get rid of it afterward, if you don't want it, with the command `pacman -Rs go`.

When the build is done, there will be more files in your current directory. We can now install the package with:

```
sudo pacman -U yay-<version>.pkg.tar.zst
```

When you're done, you can try to run this command to see if Yay is correctly installed:

```
yay --version
```

You can see where yay is installed with the command `type yay`.

Clearing Yay Cache

You can clear the cache of Yay the same way you clean the cache of Pacman (see above). To do so, you can use this command:

```
yay -Sc --aur
```

If you want to clean both the Pacman and Yay caches, drop the option `--aur` .

Installing Packages With Yay

We wanted to install some tabs for URxvt, remember? Thanks to Yay, we can do it easily with the command:

```
yay -S urxvt-tabbedex-mina86-git
```

Yay will ask you first if you want to see the difference between the `PKGBUILD` you used in the past and this one. Since you never installed `urxvt-tabbedex-mina86-git` , there is no past `PKGBUILD` and, therefore, no difference.

You can still look at the `PKGBUILD` if you want. It's always a good idea to verify that everything looks fine. Then say yes when Yay asks you if you want to install it.

Adding Tabs for URxvt

Now that we've installed a plugin to have some tabs in URxvt, we need to modify URxvt's configuration. Let's edit the file `.Xresources` with the command `nvim ~/.config/X11/.Xresources` .

Then, add these wonderful lines to the file:

```
URxvt*perl-ext-common: default,tabbedex

URxvt.keysym.Control-Shift-N: perl:tabbedex:new_tab
URxvt.keysym.Control-Shift-K: perl:tabbedex:next_tab
URxvt.keysym.Control-Shift-J: perl:tabbedex:prev_tab

URxvt.keysym.Control-Shift-R: perl:tabbedex:rename_tab
URxvt.keysym.Control-Shift-H: perl:tabbedex:move_tab_left
URxvt.keysym.Control-Shift-L: perl:tabbedex:move_tab_right

URxvt*tabbedex.tabbar-fg: 15
URxvt*tabbedex.tabbar-bg: 236
URxvt*tabbedex.tab-fg: 110
URxvt*tabbedex.tab-bg: 236

URxvt*tabbedex.transparent:true
URxvt*tabbedex.new-button: false
```

The first line enables the Perl extension for URxvt we've just installed.

The 6 lines following set the keystrokes to manipulate these tabs. Our prefix key for URxvt's tabs is the keystroke `CTRL+SHIFT` :

- `CTRL+SHIFT+N` – Open a new tab.
- `CTRL+SHIFT+K` – Select next tab.
- `CTRL+SHIFT+J` – Select previous tab.
- `CTRL+SHIFT+R` – Rename tab.
- `CTRL+SHIFT+H` – Move tab to the left.
- `CTRL+SHIFT+L` – Move tab to the right.

The last lines set the colors of the tabs. We use Xterm colors here, as discussed in a previous chapter. If you wonder what `new-button` is, it's just an ugly button we hide.

To try your new tabs, reload the configuration with the command:

```
xrdb -merge $HOME/.config/X11/.Xresources
```

Then, restart URxvt. Also, feel free to uninstall them if you don't like them.

Neovim Language Extensions

Neovim supports plugins written in Python, Ruby, and even Node.js. Now that we have access to the AUR, we can install the *providers* that enable this functionality. Let's install them:

```
yay -S python-neovim python2-neovim ruby-neovim
```

For more information, you can run `:help provider` in Neovim.

Pacman Troubleshooting

If you have any problems while using Pacman, these tips can help you troubleshoot:

1. Have a look at the official website of Arch Linux[1]. You'll find on the homepage the latest news regarding Arch Linux and the problems you can run into while upgrading your system.
2. You can look at Pacman's logs in `/var/log/pacman.log` to understand what happened.
3. If you have 404 errors while installing a package, simply upgrade your system with the command `sudo pacman -Syu`.

I've installed many AUR packages and I've never experienced huge problems with them, but keep in mind that they are potentially insecure and sometimes broken.

Pacman Configuration

If you want to have a look at Pacman's main configuration, you'll find it in `/etc/pacman.conf`. As indicated at the very end of this chapter, there is a manpage dedicated to this configuration if you want to modify it or to simply understand what's in there.

---

[1] https://archlinux.org/

In a Nutshell

What did we learn in this chapter?

- Pacman can receive an operation and multiple options as arguments. The semantics of these options change depending on the operation used.
- You can synchronize packages with the operation `-S` , remove them with `-R` , and query the package databases with `-Q` .
- To update your whole system, you need to run `sudo pacman -Syu` (or `yay -Syu` if you have AUR packages installed).
- Never run the command `sudo pacman -Sy` (without the `u`)!
- The command `pacman -Rs` will safely remove any package you've installed on your system.
- Yay is a wrapper around Pacman. It allows you to manage packages from the Arch User Repository (AUR) seamlessly.
- You have the ability to use tabs in URxvt!

In the next chapter, we'll gather all our dotfiles in one place and make them publicly available online. You'll then be able to synchronize them with any computer you want.

Going Deeper

- Arch Wiki – Pacman[1]
- Arch Wiki – Pacman Troubleshooting[2]
- Arch Wiki – Pacman Tips and Tricks[3]
- Arch Wiki – System Maintenance[4]
- `man 5 pacman.conf`

---

[1] https://wiki.archlinux.org/index.php/Pacman

[2] https://wiki.archlinux.org/index.php/Pacman#Troubleshooting

[3] https://wiki.archlinux.org/index.php/Pacman/Tips_and_tricks

[4] https://wiki.archlinux.org/index.php/System_maintenance

Dotfiles

As we go through the configuration of our entire Mouseless Development Environment, we collect more and more dotfiles in the directory `~/.config`. It would be nice to gather all these dotfiles in a central project to be able to access them easily.

It would also be nice to have a backup of all these configuration files and a way to synchronize them across multiple computers. Modifying our configuration on one system would then replicate the changes everywhere.

Many Linux users have public repositories on GitHub called "dotfiles" (how original!) where they put all their configuration files to share them with the entire community. We'll do exactly the same in this chapter. More specifically, we'll see:

- What are hard and symbolic links.
- The structure we'll adopt for our repository full of dotfiles.
- How to write and run a shell script.
- How to manage file permissions on Linux-based systems.
- How to publish our dotfiles on the Internet using Git and GitHub.
- What is the SSH protocol and how to create SSH tunnels.

We'll manage all our dotfiles in this book manually; if you want to use an external tool for that later, I would recommend GNU Stow[1].

Hard and Symbolic Links

We'll need to use symbolic links in order to create our dotfiles repository. Let's first discuss what they are.

A filesystem doesn't really care about the content of the file itself, but more about its metadata (data describing data), like creation date, file ownership, or permissions. This metadata is stored in a data structure called an *inode* on Linux-based systems.

Hard Links

If you create a hard link to a file, a second file will be created. This second file will point to the same inode as the original file. You can rename or delete one of the files without affecting the other, but if you change the metadata of one file, the other file's metadata will be modified too. Not only the metadata: if you change the content of one file, the other file's content will also be modified.

---

[1] https://www.gnu.org/software/stow/

To know how many hard links a file has, you can use the command `ls -la`. For example, if you run the command `ls -la /etc/pacman.d`, the output will be something like this:

```
drwxr-xr-x 4 root root  4096 Aug 24 22:09 gnupg
-rw-r--r-- 1 root root 20899 Apr  1 05:36 mirrorlist
```

The numbers 4 and 1 in the second column means that the file `gnupg` has 4 hard links and `mirrorlist` has only 1.

Symbolic Links

A symbolic link (or "symlink") is a file pointing to a *target* file. A symlink follows these rules:

- The symlink only contains the path to its target file.
- If you delete the symlink, the target file won't be deleted.
- If you read or write the symlink, the target file will be read or written.
- If you delete the target file, the symlink won't be deleted, but it won't point to anything anymore.

You can see if a file is a symlink by using the command `ls -l`. If the output includes an arrow as shown below, you've just discovered a symlink.

```
program -> /path/to/program
```

This arrow notation means that "program" is a symlink and its *target* file is `/path/to/program`.

The Structure of the Dotfiles Project

If we move all our config files to our dotfiles repository, the different applications using them won't be able to find them anymore. But if we create symlinks to these dotfiles where the different applications look for them, the problem is solved!

Let's first create the directory `dotfiles`, and the two sub-directories `nvim` and `X11`, by running these three commands:

```
mkdir ~/dotfiles
cd ~/dotfiles
mkdir nvim X11
```

Next, let's move the dotfiles we already have into these new directories by running the following:

```
cp -R ~/.config/nvim/init.vim ~/dotfiles/nvim
cp -R ~/.config/X11/.Xresources ~/dotfiles/X11
```

This is where a new journey begins! A journey full of mysteries, pitfalls, rewards, sweat, and blood! We'll write our first Bash script using Neovim! How many exclamation marks do I need to show my enthusiasm?!!

Let's begin with this command:

```
nvim ~/dotfiles/install.sh
```

Our First Bash Script

First things first: each time we write a script, we should always specify what shell should run it. Let's insert this as the first line in our file:

```
#!/bin/bash
```

This weird gibberish is called a *shebang*, which is the contraction of "shell" and "bang". Why "bang"? It's another name for the exclamation mark `!`. When the script is run as an executable, the OS will parse the shebang, find the program `/bin/bash`, and use it to interpret our script.

As an aside, here are the different directories where programs are located in Linux-based systems:

- `/bin` contains global `bin` aries (programs) for every user.
- `/sbin` contains essential binaries for the system to run.
- `/usr/bin` contains binaries which are user-specific.

In Arch Linux, `/bin` and `/sbin` are just symlinks pointing to `/usr/bin`. As a result, we can consider every binary to be in `/usr/bin`. If you want to add binaries manually to your system, you should put them in `/usr/bin` too.

Let's continue writing our install script. To create a symlink, we can use the command:

```
ln -s <target> <symlink>
```

If you don't use the option `-s` , you'll create a hard link. Let's add another line to our install script, creating a symlink for the first of our config files:

```
ln -sf "$HOME/dotfiles/nvim/init.vim" "$HOME/.config/nvim"
```

The option `-f` forces the creation of the link. It removes any existing link or file with the same name before creating a new symlink.

We could create a symlink to the whole directory `$HOME/dotfiles/nvim` , but we don't want to save *everything* in our dotfiles repository. For example, the `undo` directory in `nvim` always changes, and it's not really interesting to synchronize our undo trees with other systems. We want in our dotfiles only the configuration files which are portable and relevant between systems.

Of course, you can disagree and add to your dotfiles everything you want, with one exception: sensitive information, like passwords, for example. Don't forget that your dotfiles will be public, everybody will be able to access them!

What happens if the directory `$HOME/.config/nvim` doesn't exist? The command `ln` will throw an error. Nobody likes errors, so let's create the directory. Let's create the directory "undo", too, by adding these lines in our install script, just before the command creating the symlink:

```
########
# nvim #
########
mkdir -p "$HOME/.config/nvim"
mkdir -p "$HOME/.config/nvim/undo"
```

By default, the command `mkdir` throws an error if you try to create a directory which already exists. To prevent this, we can use the option `-p` ; if the directory already exist, the command does nothing.

Your file `~/dotfiles/install.sh` should now look like this:

```
#!/bin/bash

########
# nvim #
########
mkdir -p "$HOME/.config/nvim"
mkdir -p "$HOME/.config/nvim/undo"
ln -sf "$HOME/dotfiles/nvim/init.vim" "$HOME/.config/nvim/init.vim"
```

We don't have a symlink yet for `.Xresources`. Let's fix that by adding to the script:

```
rm -rf "$HOME/.config/X11"
ln -s "$HOME/dotfiles/X11" "$HOME/.config"
```

We create a symlink targeting the whole directory `X11` this time, because everything in this directory should be shared between systems. Here, we need to remove the directory manually, if it already exists, for the symlink to be created. For symlinks to *files* that already exist, we can use the `-f` option as we saw above, but this doesn't work for directories.

We're now ready to run our first script! The emotional roller-coaster can begin.

Running A Shell Script

There are three different ways to run our script:

1. `./install.sh` - With this command, the OS will run the script as a program. The OS doesn't know what program to use to read the file, so it will use the one specified by the shebang. A new non-interactive subshell will be created where the script will run.
2. `bash install.sh` - This command bypasses the shebang and will run the shell in a Bash subshell.
3. `source ./install.sh` - If you don't want to use a subshell to run the script, this command will run it in your actual shell.

If we create a subshell, all variables declared in the script will populate the environment of the subshell, without creating or overwriting variables in the environment of our current shell. When the script ends, the subshell is terminated.

We haven't created any variables in our script yet, but we'll do so very soon.

Now, let's run it in our terminal:

```
./install.sh
```

Did you get an error? Something like "permission denied"? No worries, it's normal. Let's now go through an essential idea in Linux-based systems: the file and directory permissions. If you already now what to do to bypass this error, feel free to skip the next part.

Changing Directories And Files Permissions

First, let's run in a terminal the following command:

```
ls -l ~/dotfiles
```

If I run it on my system, here's what I get:

```
-rw-r--r--  1 hypnos wheel  562 Oct 19 10:30 install.sh
drwxr-xr-x 15 hypnos wheel 4.0K Oct 19 10:30 nvim/
drwxr-xr-x  2 hypnos wheel 4.0K Oct 19 10:29 X11/
```

Let's have a closer look at this line:

```
-rw-r--r--  1 hypnos wheel  562 Oct 19 10:30 install.sh
```

You can divide the part `-rw-r--r--` into 4 groups:

1. The first `-` is a special flag. For example, if one of the entries were a directory, the `-` would be replaced with `d`, as you can see with the line:

```
drwxr-xr-x 15 hypnos wheel 4.0K Oct 19 10:30 nvim/
```

2. `rw-` represents the *owner* permissions. The owner is the first user name on the line. Here, it's the user `hypnos`.
3. `r--` represents the *group* permissions. The group name is just after the user name. Here, it's the group `wheel`.
4. `r--` represents the permissions for all *other* users.

Each set of permissions for the owner, group, and all other users can be one of these:

- `---` means that no action is authorized.

- `r--` means that the user can only r ead the file.
- `-w-` means that the user can only w rite the file.
- `--x` means that the user can only e x ecute a file.

You can combine them, too. For example, if you have something like `rw-` , the user can read and write the file, but not execute it.

In short, and to go back to our example, the permissions `-rw-r--r--` authorize the user `hypnos` to read and write the file, every user of the group `wheel` to read (but not write) the file, and all other users are authorized to read the file, too.

To run a script or a program, we need to have the permission to execute it. That's why we had the error "Permission denied". To fix it, let's run the following command:

```
chmod u+x ~/dotfiles/install.sh
```

`chmod` is (again!) an abbreviation for ch ange m ode. The mode is the set of permissions for a given file. What does `u+x` mean?

- `u` means u ser (or owner); the user `hypnos` in our example.
- `+` means that we want to add a permission (you can use `-` to delete one).
- `x` means the e x ecute permission.

We could formulate `chmod u+w` as "I want to add the permission 'execute' for the owner".

If you don't want to change the permissions for the owner, but for a group, or for all other users, you can use one of the following instead of `u` :

- `g` - g roup.
- `o` - o ther users.
- `a` - a ll users.

I encourage you to play around with the permissions to really understand how they work. It's an essential mechanism to understand in Linux-based systems.

Keep in mind that it's better to have restrictive permissions for files with sensitive content. Imagine that somebody takes control of your user, who has permission to read and write important files: the hacker will be able to do a lot of damage!

Now that we can execute our script, let's try to run it again. This time, it should work:

```
./install.sh
```

Don't be surprised if there is no output: we didn't add any in our script. If you try to run `ls -l ~/.config` and `ls -l ~/.config/nvim` , you should see the two symlinks created by the script.

Files and Directories Ownership

We just saw how to change the permissions of a file with `chmod` , but what if we want to change the ownership?

To understand this concept, let's create a file by running this command:

```
sudo touch ~/dotfiles/test
```

Next, if you run `ls -l ~/dotfiles` , you should see a new line:

```
-rw-r--r--  1 root    root      0 Oct 19 10:41 test
```

Now, root own the file because you used `sudo` to create it. What if you would like your current user to write into it? You can't: you need to own the file first.

To change the ownership, you can use `chown` (for `ch` ange file `own` er and group) as following:

```
sudo chown <your_user>:<your_group> ~/dotfiles/test
```

For example, if my current user is named `casimir` , and I want the group `wheel` to have permissions on the file too, I need to run `sudo chown casimir:wheel ~/dotfiles/te`

I need to use `sudo` here because only the owner of a file can change its ownership.

If I run again `ls -l ~/dotfiles` , the line should have changed:

```
-rw-r--r--  1 casimir wheel     0 Oct 19 10:41 test
```

Then, you can change the permissions themselves with `chmod` for your user to be able to write to our test file, as we saw just above.

This example illustrate an important points: don't use `sudo` for anything directly related to your current user. Your user should own its files. Said differently, don't use `sudo` with CLIs creating (or modifying) files which are in any home directory.

Even more generally: root should own files only if the files' directory is own by root too. Your home directory is not owned by root (and shouldn't!).

Let's delete the nonsense we've created with the following command:

```
rm ~/dotfiles/test
```

Enough with ownerships and permissions. Let's make our dotfiles available to the world and beyond!

Making Our Dotfiles Public

If we want to be able to download our dotfiles on any system, we need to find a way to synchronize them. We could use a USB key, but nowadays we have a pretty handy tool called the Internet. We'll use the CLI Git to version our dotfiles first (like everybody else), then we'll put our dotfiles on GitHub, a hosting platform.

I won't explain how Git works, it's way outside the scope of this book. If you don't know Git, simply follow my instructions. Let's install it:

```
sudo pacman -S git
```

That's not all. Our new friend Git is curious and wants to know who we are. Run the following commands in your shell and don't forget to replace the placeholders with your email and name:

```
git config --global user.email "<your_mail@example.com>"
git config --global user.name "<your_name>"
```

Now that Git is configured, we need to create an account on GitHub to store our dotfiles. Let's go to the GitHub website[1]. From there, you can create a new account or use an existing one.

The next step: authorizing our new system to be able to modify repositories on this GitHub account. Without this layer of security, everybody could change our dotfiles! We want to be the only masters here.

This is a great occasion to see, at a very high level, how an SSH tunnel works. Again, if you already know all of that, feel free to skip the next part.

---

[1] https://github.com

The SSH Protocol

The protocol *SSH* means `s`ecure `sh`ell. It creates a "tunnel", an encrypted connection between two devices. In other words: a client will connect to a server via SSH. Yes, this client-server model again!

As an aside, if you don't know what a protocol is, it's just a set of rules to transmit data between electronic devices (phones, computers, servers...)

To create this secured connection between the shell of a client and the shell of a server, let's install OpenSSH:

```
sudo pacman -S openssh
```

To guarantee that our connection between the two computers is secure and nobody can intercept the data we send, we need to create an *SSH key*. This key will be used to encrypt our data. Let's run:

```
ssh-keygen
```

Hit `ENTER` each time a question is asked. This command will create three things:

- The directory `~/.ssh`.
- The files `~/.ssh/id_rsa` and `~/.ssh/id_rsa.pub`.

The content of the file `id_rsa.pub` is your `pub`lic key. You can share it with trusted third parties, like GitHub.

The content of the file `id_rsa` is your private key. You need to be careful with this one:

1. NEVER share your private key with anybody.
2. NEVER use the same key on multiple computers.
3. NEVER make copies of the private key.

If you have many different computers, simply generate new keys for each of them as we just did, and add every single public key to your GitHub account.

Adding Your SSH Public Key to GitHub

In our client-server model, GitHub will be our server. It needs to know that our system (the client) is authorized to modify our dotfiles. For that, we add our SSH public key to our GitHub account. On the GitHub website, you can add your SSH public key in "Settings" > "SSH and GPG keys" > "New SSH key". Copy and paste your **public key**, the content of the file `id_rsa.pub` , in there.

To copy the key, simply run `cat ~/.ssh/id_rsa.pub` , select the output from URxvt and copy it with `CTRL+ALT+c` . We'll see mouseless ways to do that in a following chapter.

You also need to create a new repository called "dotfiles" on your GitHub account. It's in this repository that we'll publish all our dotfiles. If you're on the homepage of your GitHub account, you might see a green button `New` . Click on it, and type `dotfiles` for the `Repository name` . Keep the repository public and click on `Create repository` .

We first need to initialize Git in our project, by indicating where the files should be pushed. Go to the root directory of the dotfiles project by running `cd ~/dotfiles` . Then, run the following commands; you need to replace `<your_github_user_name>` by the user name of your GitHub account.

```
git init
git remote add origin
  ↪  git@github.com:<your_github_user_name>/dotfiles.git
```

Now, let's push everything to our GitHub account. Keep in mind that everything in the `dotfiles` directory will be visible to everybody, so you shouldn't have any passwords or sensitive data in there. I repeat myself, I know, but it's important. Let's run the following in the shell:

```
git add *
git commit -m "First commit"
git push origin master
```

When asked if you want to continue connecting, say "yes". If it didn't work, verify that you correctly copied your SSH *public* key (the content of `~/.ssh/id_rsa.pub`) to your GitHub account as described above.

Your dotfiles should now be online! Congratulations! You can see them on the GitHub website, in your new repository "dotfiles".

Don't forget to commit and push your dotfiles each time you modify them. Now, you have a backup of all your configuration files and an easy way to synchronize them between different computers.

In a Nutshell

What did we learn in this chapter?

- A symbolic link is a "dummy" file which points to another file. Modifying the symbolic link modifies its target. Deleting the symbolic link doesn't affect the target file.
- A shebang indicates to the OS what program it should use to read a shell script.
- There are three different ways to run a shell script: by using the program specified in the shebang, by directly using a specific shell, or by running the script in the current shell instead of a subshell.
- You can configure file and directory permissions for three types of users: the owner, the users in a specific group, and everybody else. Each type of user can have the permission to read, write, and execute a file.
- The SSH protocol can create a secure connection (called an SSH tunnel) between two shells on two different devices: a client and a server.
- You can use Git to synchronize and version your projects using hosting platforms, like GitHub or GitLab.

In the next chapter, we'll dive into i3's configuration.

Going Deeper

General Articles

- Arch Wiki – Dotfiles[1]
- Arch Wiki – File Permissions and Attributes[2]
- Arch Wiki – OpenSSH[3]
- Arch Wiki – Git[4]
- Arch Wiki – Command-line Shell[5]
- GNU Stow[6]

---

[1] https://wiki.archlinux.org/index.php/Dotfiles

[2] https://wiki.archlinux.org/index.php/File_permissions_and_attributes

[3] https://wiki.archlinux.org/index.php/OpenSSH

[4] https://wiki.archlinux.org/index.php/Git

[5] https://wiki.archlinux.org/index.php/Command-line_shell

[6] https://www.gnu.org/software/stow

- dotbot[1]
- Unofficial guide to dotfiles on GitHub[2]

Getting Inspired

- Arch Linux users' dotfiles[3]
- Author's dotfiles[4]
- dotshare.it[5]
- For more ideas to improve your dotfiles, a search in GitHub for dotfiles[6] will keep you busy for a while.

---

[1] https://github.com/anishathalye/dotbot

[2] https://dotfiles.github.io

[3] https://wiki.archlinux.org/index.php/Dotfiles#User_repositories

[4] https://github.com/Phantas0s/.dotfiles

[5] http://dotshare.it/

[6] https://github.com/search?q=dotfiles

i3: A Deeper Dive

We saw very quickly in the chapter First Steps In Your Mouseless Development Environment how to use i3. In this chapter, we'll dive deeper into i3 configuration to really understand what we can do with this fantastic windows tilling manager. I hope that at the end of this chapter you'll be able to understand i3's excellent documentation and what to modify in your configuration to answer your own needs.

A tiling window manager is often lighter than a full-blown desktop environment. It provides powerful mouseless functionalities to manage the windows displaying your favorite applications: the terminal, your favorite cat pictures viewer, and whatnot.

Do you think resizing windows manually is an activity providing a lot of value? I don't think so. As we saw already, i3 helps you manage your windows for 99% of your use cases, if you're not in dire needs of floating windows. This percentage has no scientific foundation whatsoever, but it doesn't stop me to believe in it. We have to believe my friends!

In this chapter, we'll see:

- The general organization of i3.
- How to configure i3.
- What are workspaces and how to configure them.
- How to configure a locking screen.
- How to set up a wallpaper.
- How to configure floating windows.
- How to configure the colors and styles of i3's graphical interface.
- How to configure scratchpads.
- What's the i3 bar and how to configure it.
- How to create a menu with dmenu to manage your screens (if you have more than one).
- What do we need to update in our dotfiles project.

We'll cover a lot here: take a solid beverage, a nice snack, and let's go exploring the depth of i3 together.

How To Use i3?

General Organization

Like tmux we'll see in a later chapter, i3 stores its information in a tree data structure. Let's see what each node can represent.

Workspaces

At the top of our tree you'll find the *workspaces*. You can think of them as virtual desktops[1]. A workspace can contain *containers*.

Containers

A container can contain one or multiple *windows*. These windows will be positioned depending on the container's layout. There are three different layouts possible:

- **Split** – Each window shares the container space and are split horizontally (*splith*) or vertically (*splitv*). This is the default layout.
- **Stacked** – The focused window is visible on top and the other ones are stacked below. You can change the window's focus via keystrokes easily. You can see the windows' headers at the top of the container itself.
- **Tabbed** – This layout is similar to the stacked layout, except that the windows' headers are vertically split, not horizontally.

Note that a container can contain other containers too.

To understand this tree of workspaces, container, and windows, here's a possible representation:

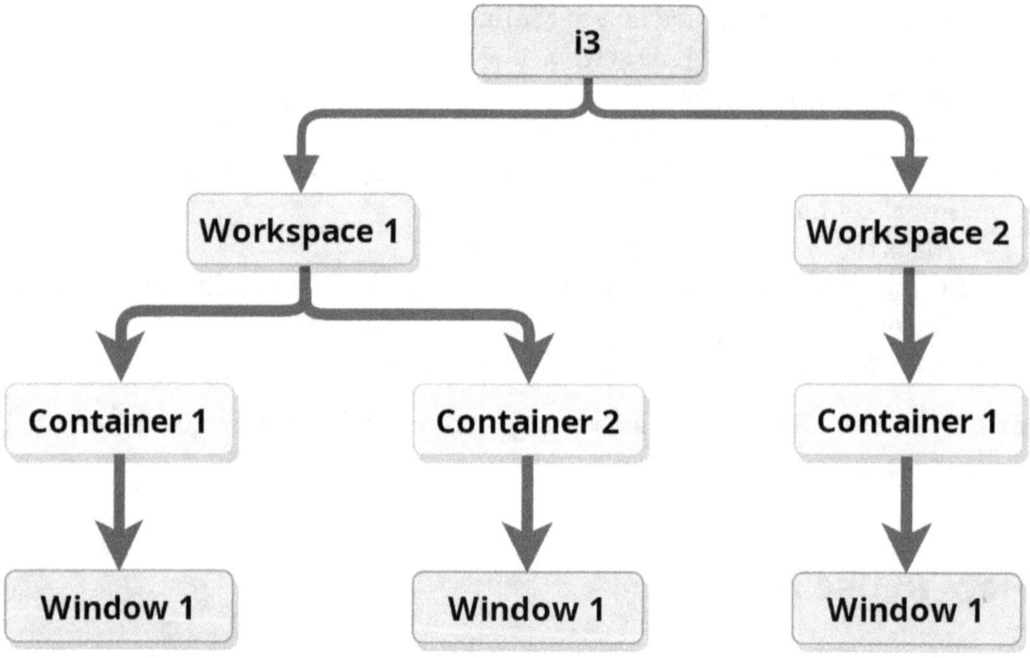

Of course, you can have more workspace, containers, and windows, if you want to. This is just an example to show the hierarchy of the different elements.

---

[1] https://en.wikipedia.org/wiki/Virtual_desktop

The Default Shortcuts

We've seen that i3 uses a special key for (almost) every keystroke. This key is called a *modifier*; by default, it's the `WIN` key (or `CMD` key, if you like Apple keyboards). The variable `$mod` in the configuration is there to set this modifier key. I'll use this variable in this chapter to express the modifier key for the different keystrokes, and you should always use it in your own configuration.

Enough mumbling. Let's practice!

As we saw already, you can move the windows around and see how they are resized automatically. To do so, try to open multiple windows and hit `$mod+SHIFT+ARROW KEY` to see what happens.

We can try to change the layout of the container, too, by using the following keystrokes:

- `$mod+e` – Switch to *split* layout ("splith" or "splitv" depending on your screen).
- `$mod+s` – Switch to *stacked* layout.
- `$mod+w` – Switch to *tabbed* layout.

You can try to create and move windows using each layout to see the differences.

You also need to know the following keystrokes:

- `$mod+SHIFT+c` – Reload i3's configuration. You need to use it each time you modify your configuration file, to apply the changes to the current i3 session.
- `$mod+SHIFT+e` – Logout and quit i3. We will modify that later.

Configuring i3

Configuration Files

Your config file (`~/.config/i3/config`) should already exists. This is not the only configuration file available for i3: different ones can be loaded in a specific order. Here's the complete list; the configuration files on top can overwrite every other configuration files below.

1. `~/.config/i3/config` (or `$XDG_CONFIG_HOME/i3/config` if `$XDG_CONFIG_HOME` is set).
2. `~/.i3/config` .
3. `/etc/xdg/i3/config` (or `$XDG_CONFIG_DIRS/i3/config` if `$XDG_CONFIG_DIRS` is set).
4. `/etc/i3/config` .

The first file overwriting everything else is `~/.config/i3/config`. That's great, because it's the configuration file we'll use. In practice, this means that any option or keystroke set in this file will overwrite the same options or keystrokes set in other files.

Default Configuration

Let's dive a bit more into i3's config. First, let's open the file with Neovim:

```
nvim ~/.config/i3/config
```

One of the first lines of the config will define your modifier key (`$mod`), as I explained above. You can modify it here if you like.

To see every possible value you can use as modifier, you can run in your shell the command `xmodmap`. It will list everything you can use.

As you can see, you can define variables using the keyword `set` followed by the variable name (`$mod` here) and its value (`Mod4`).

Below in the configuration file, you'll see something like this:

```
bindsym $mod+Return exec i3-sensible-terminal
```

The keyword `bindsym` allows you to bind a symbol to a command. Internally, a symbol is mapped to a keycode (a key on your keyboard). To see this mapping, you can run in your terminal `xmodmap -pke | less`.

Here, the symbol `Return` is used. If you prefer using a keycode directly instead of a symbol, you can use the command `bindcode` instead of `bindsym`.

This keystroke will execute (using the command `exec`) `i3-sensible-terminal`, a script[1] trying to find and open an instance of your terminal. Since we use URxvt, we can replace this line with:

```
bindsym $mod+Return exec urxvtc
```

Don't forget to hit `$mod+SHIFT+r` to apply the changes.

Let's continue our exploration. Below you'll find the line:

---

[1] https://build.i3wm.org/docs/i3-sensible-terminal.html

```
bindsym $mod+Shift+q kill
```

It allows you to kill a window. Depending on the application running in that window, some operations might be done before closing. For example, Firefox will save the current session.

Program Launcher

Again, as we saw, there is no start menu where you can find the applications installed on your system. Instead, you can launch your favorite software using a program launcher.

Let's look at the following line:

```
bindsym $mod+d exec --no-startup-id dmenu_run
```

It defines a keystroke to launch dmenu, as we saw in a previous chapter[1].

If you don't like the launcher, you can install and use another one if you want later. As stated in the configuration, rofi is a good alternative.

Moving Windows and Changing Focus

You can focus or move the different windows in your current workspace using `$mod+jkl;` or `$mod+SHIFT+jkl;`. Since we use Neovim, it would make sense to use `hjkl` instead. It's not only Neovim: other CLIs uses `hjkl` too, being consistent will save you some headaches.

Let's modify the binding for focusing windows:

```
# change focus
bindsym $mod+h focus left
bindsym $mod+j focus down
bindsym $mod+k focus up
bindsym $mod+l focus right
```

You'll find below in the file the keystrokes to move focused windows. You can also change them:

1

```
bindsym $mod+Shift+h move left
bindsym $mod+Shift+j move down
bindsym $mod+Shift+k move up
bindsym $mod+Shift+l move right
```

If you reload your config at this point, it's very likely you'll have an error at the top of your screen. We'll fix it next.

Split containers

Sometimes, you'll want to open new windows on the side, or below the windows already open. By default, to open a window horizontally, we need to hit `$mod+h`. But we already use this keystroke; that's why you might see an error if you've reloaded your configuration.

Let reconfigure the splits as follows:

```
# split in horizontal orientation
bindsym $mod+CTRL+h split v

# split in vertical orientation
bindsym $mod+CTRL+v split h
```

Note that changing orientation will create a new container. You can see its delimitation by changing the layout.

Let's now configure the workspaces you've always dreamt of.

Workspaces

Defining Workspaces

You can open and switch to workspaces with the same keystrokes. Here's the default configuration you'll normally find in your current configuration file:

```
# Define names for default *workspaces* for which we configure key
↪   bindings later on.
# We use variables to avoid repeating the names in multiple places.
set $ws1 "1"
set $ws2 "2"
set $ws3 "3"
set $ws4 "4"
set $ws5 "5"
set $ws6 "6"
set $ws7 "7"
set $ws8 "8"
set $ws9 "9"
set $ws10 "10"

# switch to workspace
bindsym $mod+1 workspace number $ws1
bindsym $mod+2 workspace number $ws2
bindsym $mod+3 workspace number $ws3
bindsym $mod+4 workspace number $ws4
bindsym $mod+5 workspace number $ws5
bindsym $mod+6 workspace number $ws6
bindsym $mod+7 workspace number $ws7
bindsym $mod+8 workspace number $ws8
bindsym $mod+9 workspace number $ws9
bindsym $mod+0 workspace number $ws10

# move focused container to workspace
bindsym $mod+Shift+1 move container to workspace number $ws1
bindsym $mod+Shift+2 move container to workspace number $ws2
bindsym $mod+Shift+3 move container to workspace number $ws3
bindsym $mod+Shift+4 move container to workspace number $ws4
bindsym $mod+Shift+5 move container to workspace number $ws5
bindsym $mod+Shift+6 move container to workspace number $ws6
bindsym $mod+Shift+7 move container to workspace number $ws7
bindsym $mod+Shift+8 move container to workspace number $ws8
bindsym $mod+Shift+9 move container to workspace number $ws9
bindsym $mod+Shift+0 move container to workspace number $ws10
```

What does it mean?

1. The first part defines the variables for each workspace. You have 10 of them by default.
2. The second part define keystrokes to switch between each of these workspaces. For example, hitting `$mod+3` will display the third workspace.
3. The third part define keystrokes to move windows to specific workspaces.

For example, `$mod+SHIFT+3` will move the focused windows to the third workspace.

Here's my own config as an example:

```
set $terms "1: terms"
set $web "2: web"
set $db "3: db"
set $file_manager "4: files"
set $mail "5: mails"
set $documents "6: documents"
set $mindmap "7: mindmap"

# switch to workspace
bindsym $mod+1 workspace $terms
bindsym $mod+2 workspace $web
bindsym $mod+3 workspace $db
bindsym $mod+4 workspace $file_manager
bindsym $mod+5 workspace $mail
bindsym $mod+6 workspace $documents
bindsym $mod+7 workspace $mindmap
bindsym $mod+8 workspace 8
bindsym $mod+9 workspace 9

# move focused container to workspace
bindsym $mod+Shift+1 move container to workspace $terms
bindsym $mod+Shift+2 move container to workspace $web
bindsym $mod+Shift+3 move container to workspace $db
bindsym $mod+Shift+4 move container to workspace $file_manager
bindsym $mod+Shift+5 move container to workspace $mail
bindsym $mod+Shift+6 move container to workspace $documents
bindsym $mod+Shift+7 move container to workspace $mindmap
bindsym $mod+Shift+8 move container to workspace 8
bindsym $mod+Shift+9 move container to workspace 9
```

You also have the ability to go back to your last workspace with the same keystroke. For example, if you are on the first workspace and you hit `$mod+2`, you'll switch to the second workspace. Then, if you hit `$mod+2` again, you'll go back to your previous workspace, the first one.

To enable this, you need to add to your configuration:

```
workspace_auto_back_and_forth yes
```

Opening Applications in a Specific Workspace

You can also open a specific application in a specific workspace. Let's say for example that you always want to open Firefox in the workspace 2. You can add in your config:

```
assign [class="firefox" instance="Navigator"] <workspace_variable>
```

In my case, the variable for the workspace 2 is `$web`, so I would need to replace `<workspace_variable>` with `$web`.

You can assign the application to a workspace using its class (its general identifier), its instance (an identifier which is specific to some windows from the application itself), or both. To get the `class` name and the `instance` name of a specific application's window, you need to run the application itself. Then, open a terminal and run the following:

```
xprop | grep WM_CLASS
```

Your mouse cursor will turn into a cross. Click on the window you want the class and instance of. Something similar to the following line will appear in your terminal:

```
WM_CLASS(STRING) = "Navigator", "firefox"
```

The first element is always the instance (`Navigator`), the second always the class (`firefox`). Be careful: the case matters. What's uppercase in these identifiers should stay uppercase in your config.

Resizing Windows

If you continue to go through the configuration, you'll find keystrokes to display a window fullscreen, to reload, or reset i3.

Continuing our descent, we'll find keystrokes to resize windows. Let's modify them, again to match the Neovim key bindings *hjlk*.

```
bindsym h resize shrink width 10 px or 10 ppt
bindsym j resize grow height 10 px or 10 ppt
bindsym k resize shrink height 10 px or 10 ppt
bindsym l resize grow width 10 px or 10 ppt
```

You'll notice that you first need to go in *mode resize* before being able to resize anything. This means that you first need to hit `$mod+r` (you'll see the word "resize" appearing at the bottom of the screen). Then, you can resize your windows using `$mod+hjkl`.

You might have noticed that when you hover your cursor (with your mouse! Blasphemy!) on different windows, it will automatically put them in focus. I hate that, so I always disable it with the following line:

```
focus_follows_mouse no
```

Feel free to add it to your own config. Now, to focus a window with your mouse (don't touch it, you fool!), you need to click on it.

Locking Your Screen

To lock your screen for your coworkers not sending embarrassing messages on Slack on your behalf, you'll need i3lock:

```
sudo pacman -S i3lock
```

Now, you have the power to choose a nice looking lock screen. Here are two solutions you can pick from:

Simple wallpaper

Your lock screen can simply display an image. To do so, add the following to your configuration:

```
set $i3lockwall i3lock -i <path_to_your_png_image.png>
```

Keep in mind that i3lock can only display PNG images using the argument `-i`. Don't use JPEG or any other format.

Display With Blurry Effect

You can also apply an effect on the current display you have when you lock the screen. For that, you need to install imagemagick and scrot:

```
sudo pacman -S imagemagick scrot
```

Then, create a script:

```
mkdir ~/.config/i3/scripts
nvim ~/.config/i3/scripts/lock.sh
```

Add the following lines in your new script:

```
#!/bin/sh

img=/tmp/i3lock.png

scrot -o $img
convert $img -scale 10% -scale 1000% $img

i3lock -u -i $img
```

Finally, add this line to i3's configuration file:

```
set $i3lockwall sh ~/.config/i3/scripts/lock.sh
```

That's it!

The Locking Keystroke

Let's now add a keystroke to lock our system:

```
bindsym $mod+CTRL+Shift+l exec --no-startup-id $i3lockwall
```

To unlock your computer, you have to type your user's password and hit ENTER .

Lock, Shutdown, and Reboot Menu

Let's find and delete the following line:

```
bindsym Mod1+Shift+e exec "i3-nagbar -t warning -m 'You pressed the
  ↪  exit shortcut. Do you really want to exit i3? This will end your
  ↪  X session.' -B 'Yes, exit i3' 'i3-msg exit'"
```

This allowed you to log out of i3. Instead, let's create a menu with `dmenu` to have a nice and discrete way to lock your screen, log out of i3, suspend your computer, hibernate, reboot, shutdown everything, or conquer the world.

Simply add the following to your configuration:

```
# shutdown / restart / suspend...
set $mode_system \
System (l) lock, (e) logout, (s) suspend, \
(h) hibernate, (r) reboot, (Ctrl+s) shutdown

mode "$mode_system" {
    bindsym l exec --no-startup-id $i3lockwall, mode "default"
    bindsym e exec --no-startup-id i3-msg exit, mode "default"
    bindsym s exec --no-startup-id $i3lockwall && systemctl suspend,
     ↳ \
    mode "default"
    bindsym h exec --no-startup-id $i3lockwall && systemctl
     ↳ hibernate, \
    mode "default"
    bindsym r exec --no-startup-id systemctl reboot, mode "default"
    bindsym CTRL+s exec --no-startup-id systemctl poweroff -i, \
    mode "default"

    # to close the menu: Enter or Escape
    bindsym Return mode "default"
    bindsym Escape mode "default"
}

bindsym $mod+BackSpace mode "$mode_system"
```

If you hit `$mod+BackSpace` after reloading your config, you'll see at the bottom of your screen the menu you just defined. You can hit `l`, `e`, `s`, `h`, `r` or `CTRL+s` depending on what you want to do.

To close the menu, you can hit `ENTER` or `ESC`.

Wallpaper

It's nice to have a wallpaper when you open a workspace instead of this dull, black, depressing void. We can use `feh`, a simple application which can display images. Let's install it, and let's create a directory where we'll put our wallpaper:

```
sudo pacman -S feh
mkdir -p ~/.config/i3/feh
```

You can download a nice wallpaper from the Internet and put it in the directory you've just created. Then, add the following line in the config file of i3:

```
exec --no-startup-id feh --no-fehbg --bg-fill \
~/.config/i3/feh/<my_image>
```

You need to replace `<my_image>` with the filename of your wallpaper.

Floating Windows

Some applications are easier to use with floating windows, a more "traditional" window you can move with your mouse. For example, pop-up and task dialog should be floating. To do so, add these two lines in your configuration file:

```
# floating pop up automatically
for_window [window_role="pop-up"] floating enable
for_window [window_role="task_dialog"] floating enable
```

You can specify what application should be open in a floating window automatically, using the `class` and `instance` of that application, as explained above in the workspace section.

For example, it would be a good idea to open ARandR in a floating window. To do so, we can add in the configuration file:

```
for_window [class="Arandr"] floating enable
```

Reload the configuration, try to launch ARandR, and, as expected, it's floating! You can move your floating windows using `CTRL+SHIFT` and the usuals `hjkl`. To resize them, you can use the mode resize we saw above or take your mouse and use `RIGHT CLICK+WIN`.

Colors and Style

You can configure colors and style for i3 directly in the configuration file. Even better: we can re-use the colors we defined in `~/.config/X11/.Xresources` to keep a consistent color scheme throughout our system. To do so, we need to use the `set_from_resource` directive.

For example, `set_from_resource $foreground foreground #C6C6C6` will define a variable `$foreground` which will use the `foreground` color defined in the `.Xresources` file. If `foreground` is not defined, it will fallback to the color `#C6C6C6`.

Here's my own configuration. You can simply copy paste it and change the fallback colors if you want to.

```
# special
set_from_resource $foreground foreground #C6C6C6
set_from_resource $background background #1C1C1C
set_from_resource $cursorColor cursorColor #C6C6C6

# black
set_from_resource $black1 color0 #303030
set_from_resource $black2 color8 #444444
set $trueblack #000000

# red
set_from_resource $red1 color1 #d75f5f
set_from_resource $red2 color9 #d75f5f

# green
set_from_resource $green1 color2 #87AF87
set_from_resource $green2 color10 #87AF87

# yellow
set_from_resource $yellow1 color3 #ffd75f
set_from_resource $yellow2 color11 #ffd75f

# blue
set_from_resource $blue1 color4 #87afd7
set_from_resource $blue2 color12 #87afd7

# magenta
set_from_resource $cyan1 color5 #afafd7
set_from_resource $cyan2 color13 #afafd7

# cyan
set_from_resource $cyan1 color6 #afd7ff
set_from_resource $cyan2 color14 #afd7ff

# white
set_from_resource $white1 color7 #4E4E4E
set_from_resource $white2 color15 #ffffff
```

Instead of using `set_from_resource`, you can define your own variables, such as
`set $black #000000`. We can now use the variables we just declared to change the
colors of i3:

```
##########
# DESIGN #
##########

# hide borders
hide_edge_borders both

# class                  border  backgr. text     indicator child_border
client.focused           #333333 $black2 $white2 #285577
client.focused_inactive #333333 $background $foreground #484e50
client.unfocused         #333333 #222222 #888888 #292d2e   #222222
client.urgent            $red1   $red1   $white2 $red1      $red1
client.placeholder       #000000 #0c0c0c $white2 #000000    #0c0c0c
```

Since we're speaking color and design, let's make URxvt a bit prettier, too. I don't like having borders around it; if you agree, you can add the following to your configuration:

```
for_window [class="URxvt*"] border pixel 1
```

Scratchpad

I like to have a terminal running in the background at all time. It's practical to run scripts or updating the system while admiring cat pictures. I've also configured a scratchpad to look at the precise resource consumption of my application using the application htop.

Let's configure all of that. First, let's install htop:

```
sudo pacman -S htop
```

With i3, you can create scratchpads you can then hide and show with a simple keystroke. Let's add the following lines to the configuration file:

```
# Terminal scratchpad
for_window [instance="urxvt_scratchpad"] move to scratchpad, border
  ↳  none
bindsym $mod+Shift+t [instance="urxvt_scratchpad"] scratchpad show
exec urxvtc -name urxvt_scratchpad

# htop scratchpad
for_window [instance="htop_scratchpad"] move to scratchpad, border
  ↳  none
bindsym $mod+Shift+p [instance="htop_scratchpad"] scratchpad show
exec urxvtc -name htop_scratchpad -e htop
```

This is pretty self-explanatory, so I won't go into the details here. You might need
to log out and log in again for these changes to work. Then, you can try to hit
$mod+SHIFT+t or $mod+SHIFT+p and see what happens.

The i3 Status Bar

It's time to modify the status bar at the bottom! To do so, we need to create a new
configuration file only for i3status:

```
nvim ~/.config/i3/i3status.conf
```

Let's add the following lines:

```
# i3status configuration file.
# See "man i3status" for documentation.

# It is important that this file is edited as UTF-8.

general {
    interval = 1
    colors = true
    color_good="#FFFFFF"
    color_degraded="#ffd75f"
    color_bad="#d75f5f"
}

order += "volume master"
order += "battery 0"
order += "disk /"
order += "cpu_usage"
order += "load"
order += "tztime local"
```

These first lines call the following functions you need to add afterward:

```
tztime local {
        format = " %Y-%m-%d %H:%M:%S "
}

disk "/" {
    format = " %avail "
}

cpu_usage {
    format = " %usage "
}

load {
    format = " %5min 5min "
}

volume master {
    format = " %volume "
    format_muted = " %volume "
    device = "default"
    mixer = "Master"
    mixer_idx = 0
}

battery 0 {
    format = "%status %percentage "
    format_down = " DOWN "
    status_chr = " CHARGING "
    status_bat = " BATTERY "
    status_unk = " UNKNOWN "
    status_full = " FULL "
    path = "/sys/class/power_supply/BAT%d/uevent"
}
```

After that, you need to delete the actual bar block in the file `~/.config/i3/config` and add this one instead:

```
bar {
    status_command i3status --config ~/.config/i3/i3status.conf
    # Disable all tray icons
    tray_output none
    # tray_output primary
    colors {
        background $black2
        statusline $white2
        separator $white2

        #                   border background text
        focused_workspace  $background $background $red1
        active_workspace   $black2 $black1 $white2
        inactive_workspace $black1 $black2 $foreground
        urgent_workspace   $red1 $red1 $white2
        binding_mode       $background $red2 $white2
    }
}
```

I won't explain this configuration in detail, I think it's pretty self-explanatory. We'll improve the status bar even further by adding icons in a later chapter of the book.

Managing Your Screen

To manage different screen setups, you can use dmenu to choose what screen configuration you want. If you want to experiment with that, you need first to open ARandR and configure your screen layout and resolution as you like. Then, click on "Layout" -> "Save as" and save it in `~/.config/X11/monitor.sh`.

You can then add this in i3's configuration file (you know, `~/.config/i3/config`):

```
set $mode_display Config monitor resolution - Default config (d)

mode "$mode_display" {
    bindsym d exec --no-startup-id sh
    ↪  "$HOME/.config/X11/monitor.sh", mode "default"


    # back to normal: Enter or Escape
    bindsym Return mode "default"
    bindsym Escape mode "default"
}


bindsym $mod+x mode "$mode_display"
```

Using the keystroke `$mod+x` will display a menu for you to choose your screen setup. There is only one in this example, but you can create as many as you want.

Updating Our Dotfiles

Congratulation! You've successfully configured i3 Windows Manager. This configuration is not part of our dotfiles yet, so let's fix that.

First, let's move the i3 directory:

```
mv ~/.config/i3 ~/dotfiles
```

The command `mv` stands for m o v e: it first copies files or directories, and, if it was successful, it deletes the source. You can also use it to rename a file; for example: `mv <name> <new_name>`.

It's time to edit `~/dotfiles/install.sh`. Simply add the following:

```
######
# i3 #
######


rm -rf "$HOME/.config/i3"
ln -s "$HOME/dotfiles/i3" "$HOME/.config"
```

We first delete the directory in case it exists, then we create a symlink targeting the whole `i3` directory.

To test the changes, let's run:

```
cd ~/dotfiles && ./install.sh
```

If everything worked fine, push your changes to GitHub:

```
git add *
git commit -m "Add i3 config"
```

In a Nutshell

What did we learn in this chapter?

- You can think of i3 as a tree: at the top you have the workspaces, containing containers, containing themselves windows, where applications display their graphical interfaces.
- You can configure keystrokes to move containers in a workspace, move containers from a workspace to another, resizing windows, and so on.
- We can use i3lock to lock our screen, dmenu to create helpful menu (even a program launcher), and i3status to have a nice status bar at the bottom of the screen.
- We can create floating windows for any application we want.

In the next chapter, we'll switch shells, from Bash to the Z-shell (Zsh).

Going Deeper

- Arch Wiki – i3[1]
- Official documentation[2]

---

[1] https://wiki.archlinux.org/index.php/I3

[2] https://i3wm.org/docs/

The Z-Shell (Zsh)

We'll now switch shells. We were using Bash; the future is Zsh. Why is that, you might ask? Why do you have to say goodbye to a shell that did so much for you?

- The level of flexibility and customization of Zsh is crazy.
- You have access to a powerful auto-completion engine for your favorite CLIs.
- The Vi mode is golden for every Vim lover.
- There is an important and active community around Zsh.
- Bash scripts are (mostly) compatible with Zsh.

One of the goals of this book is to try different tools to see if you like using them. Feel free to go back to Bash if you don't find Zsh appealing. Bash can mostly do what Zsh does, except for the auto-completion. Some prefer mastering Bash first, but I don't think it's a requirement.

In this chapter we'll see:

- How to configure the basics of Zsh.
- How to use Zsh's Vi mode to be able to modify commands using Neovim keystrokes.
- How to edit commands directly in Neovim with one keystroke.
- How to install very useful Zsh plugins.
- How to automatically start i3 without the need to enter `startx` each time we boot our system.

You can test your Zsh configuration while you're writing it by simply running `zsh` in your shell. It will create a subshell you can exit with the command `exit` or by using the keystroke `CTRL+d`.

Again, we'll cover quite a lot in this chapter: prepare yourself, stretch a bit, do some yoga, meditate, eat a banana, then let's go.

Framework Or No Framework?

You'll see many articles on the Internet advising you to install a Zsh framework with a crazy number of plugins, options, and aliases all fully configured. The most famous ones are Oh My Zsh[1] and prezto[2].

I tried this approach for years and I think the drawbacks outweigh the benefits:

---

[1] https://ohmyz.sh/

[2] https://github.com/sorin-ionescu/prezto

- It's difficult to know what's included in these frameworks. When I read their documentation, I can't possibly remember everything they set. Therefore, I barely use 10% of their functionalities.
- Zsh already has a lot of functionality and many options by default. It's even more daunting to have a framework on top.
- A framework is a big external dependency which brings more complexity. If there is a conflict with our own configuration or a bug, it can take a long time to figure out what's happening.
- A framework imposes rules and ways of doing things we don't necessarily want or even need.

Don't get me wrong: these frameworks are incredible. They can be useful to get some inspiration for your own configuration, too. But I wouldn't couple them to my own configuration.

Zsh Config Files

First and as always, let's install our new shell:

```
sudo pacman -S zsh
```

To configure Zsh for your user's session, you can use the following files:

- `$ZDOTDIR/.zshenv`
- `$ZDOTDIR/.zprofile`
- `$ZDOTDIR/.zshrc`
- `$ZDOTDIR/.zlogin`
- `$ZDOTDIR/.zlogout`

In case you wonder what the environment variable `$ZDOTDIR` stands for, we'll come back to it soon.

Zsh reads these configuration files in the following order:

1. `.zshenv` - Should only contain user's environment variables.
2. `.zprofile` - Can be used to execute commands just after logging in.
3. `.zshrc` - Should be used to configure the shell itself and for running commands.
4. `.zlogin` - Same purpose as `.zprofile`, except that it's read just after the file `.zshrc`.
5. `.zlogout` - Can be used to execute commands when a shell exits.

We'll only use the files `.zshrc` and `.zshenv` in our own configuration. Let's create them directly in our dotfiles repository this time:

```
mkdir ~/dotfiles/zsh
touch ~/dotfiles/zsh/.zshrc
touch ~/dotfiles/zsh/.zshenv
```

Next, let's directly modify our installation file for our dotfiles by running the command `nvim ~/dotfiles/install.sh` in a terminal.

Add the following lines to the file:

```
mkdir -p "$HOME/.config/zsh"
ln -sf "$HOME/dotfiles/zsh/.zshenv" "$HOME"
ln -sf "$HOME/dotfiles/zsh/.zshrc" "$HOME/.config/zsh"
```

Run your script and verify that your symlinks are properly created, then push your modifications to your GitHub repository:

```
git add *
git commit -m "Add Zsh config"
```

Basic Zsh Configuration

Environment Variables

Now we'll configure our first environment variables for the XDG Base Directory. A couple of variables set special locations for our user's data, like dotfiles or cached data. Only your current users will have access to these directories.

Normally, the different applications you install on your system will use the values of these variables to locate the user's dotfiles and other user-specific files. This is also where new files would be added if needed. Unfortunately, some applications will install their dotfiles in other locations, like your `$HOME` directory.

Let's modify `.zshenv` with the command `nvim ~/dotfiles/zsh/.zshenv`. Then, let's add the following lines:

```
# For dotfiles
export XDG_CONFIG_HOME="$HOME/.config"

# For specific data
export XDG_DATA_HOME="$XDG_CONFIG_HOME/local/share"

# For cached files
export XDG_CACHE_HOME="$XDG_CONFIG_HOME/cache"
```

Many CLIs use the `$EDITOR` or `$VISUAL` environment variables to launch your favorite editor if they need to. Let's set them:

```
export EDITOR="nvim"
export VISUAL="nvim"
```

Next, let's set the variable `$ZDOTDIR`. It determines where the config files for Zsh should be located. Let's add to `.zshenv` the following:

```
export ZDOTDIR="$XDG_CONFIG_HOME/zsh"

# History filepath
export HISTFILE="$ZDOTDIR/.zhistory"
# Maximum events for internal history
export HISTSIZE=10000
# Maximum events in history file
export SAVEHIST=10000
```

This last piece of configuration is related to Zsh's command history:

- Your history will be stored in the file `$ZDOTDIR/.zhistory`.
- Your history will have 10000 entries maximum.

An important note: don't add your history file `.zhistory` to any repository on GitHub! Everything you're running in your shell will end up in there, which can include passwords and other sensitive information about your favorite cat. Beware!

We can also add the variable `$DOTFILES` in `.zshenv`, with the following:

```
export DOTFILES="$HOME/dotfiles"
```

We'll use this environment variable soon.

Aliases

Aliases, in Linux-based systems, allow you to call a command with a string of characters of your choosing. For example, let's imagine that I've an alias `gp` for `git push`. When I want to run `git push`, I only need to type the shorter `gp` instead. The shell will then expand the alias, which means that instead of running `gp`, it will run `git push`.

Let's first create an alias file:

```
touch ~/dotfiles/zsh/aliases
```

We need now to source our new alias file. Let's add the following line in our `zshrc`:

```
source "$XDG_CONFIG_HOME/zsh/aliases"
```

We saw already different ways to execute shell scripts in a previous chapter. Sourcing a shell script will run it in the current shell.

Let's now modify `~/.dotfiles/install.sh` to add this line:

```
ln -sf "$HOME/dotfiles/zsh/aliases" "$HOME/.config/zsh/aliases"
```

As always, run the script `install.sh` to verify that everything works as expected.

That's great and all, but we haven't set any aliases yet. We could add the following to the file "$HOME/dotfiles/zsh/aliases", for example:

```
alias ll='ls -lah'
alias ga='git add'
alias gc='git commit'
alias gp='git push'
```

You'll be soon able to add, commit, and push files with Git by running `ga`, `gc`, and `gp` respectively.

Life is not easy however, and everything has drawbacks. Here are some thoughts to keep in mind:

1. Don't try to create aliases for everything, or you'll get lost in your forest of aliases. Create aliases only when you really need them. Good candidates are commands you're annoyed to type every single time.
2. Don't copy and paste random aliases from the Internet. You'll never remember them if you just add them blindly to your dotfiles.

3. If you help somebody on his or her computer, or if you end up on a server, you'll get very frustrated if you've aliased too many commands and you don't remember the original commands. Your aliases are (often) only on your computer.

Another detail: the aliases are not expanded when the shell is not interactive. In other words, your aliases won't work in your shell scripts. That's a good thing for portability.

When you're done configuring your first aliases, we can move forward to configure some Zsh options.

Options

Zsh provide many options you can set with `setopt` or unset with `unsetopt` in the file `~/dotfiles/zsh/.zshrc`. For example:

```
setopt AUTO_PARAM_SLASH
unsetopt CASE_GLOB
```

I won't detail every possible option here. Your can read the detailed Zsh documentation[1] to hour heart's content.

Zsh Completion System

Compared to other shells, Zsh's completion system is one of its bigger strengths. To initialize completion for the current Zsh session, you'll need to call the function `compinit`. More precisely, you'll need to add this to the file `~/dotfiles/zsh/.zshrc`:

```
autoload -U compinit; compinit
```

What does it mean?

The `autoload` command loads a file containing shell commands. To find this file, Zsh will look in the directories of the *Zsh file search path*, defined in the variable `$fpath`. From there, it will try to find a file named `compinit`.

When the file `compinit` is found, its contents will be loaded as a *function*. The function name will be the name of the file. You can then call this function like any other shell function.

---

[1] http://zsh.sourceforge.net/Doc/Release/Options.html

Why use autoload, and not source the file by doing `source /path/of/compinit`, as
we did before?

- It avoids name conflicts if you have an executable with the same name.
- It doesn't expand aliases thanks to the `-U` option.
- It will load the function only when it's needed (lazy-loading), which nicely
  speeds up Zsh startup!

Now, let's add the following to our file `.zshrc`:

```
# Autocomplete hidden files
_comp_options+=(globdots)
source ~/dotfiles/zsh/external/completion.zsh
```

By default, auto-completion doesn't work for dotfiles. We change that with the first
line. The second line is the source file `completion.zsh`.

First, let's create a directory:

```
mkdir ~/dotfiles/zsh/external
```

You might have noticed that you don't have the file `completion.zsh`. You can find
it in the book companion[1].

Copy its content into the new file `~/dotfiles/zsh/external/completion.zsh`.

What's the purpose of this file, you might rightfully ask? It's from the Zsh framework
prezto[2] and it improves the auto-completion system. I basically pruned everything
I didn't want. The original file is here[3].

If you look at the file's content, you'll see many instances of the command `zstyle`.
It can be used to define and lookup styles for Zsh[4]. You can play around with it to
understand what it does, if you feel like it of course.

Next, let's add the following command to the file `~/dotfiles/install.sh`:

```
rm -rf "$HOME/.config/zsh/external"
ln -sf "$HOME/dotfiles/zsh/external" "$HOME/.config/zsh"
```

---

[1] https://raw.githubusercontent.com/PhantasOs/mouseless-book-companion/master/part_II/08_zsh
/dotfiles/zsh/external/completion.zsh

[2] https://github.com/sorin-ionescu/prezto

[3] https://raw.githubusercontent.com/sorin-ionescu/prezto/master/modules/completion/init.zsh

[4] http://zsh.sourceforge.net/Doc/Release/Zsh-Modules.html#The-zsh_002fzutil-Module

We'll put in the directory `~/dotfiles/zsh/external` everything we didn't write with our soft and gracious hands. To be able to autoload everything in this `external` directory, we need to add this line in our file `~/dotfiles/zsh/.zshrc`:

```
fpath=($ZDOTDIR/external $fpath)
```

We've already seen the `$fpath` variable. Here we prepend `$ZDOTDIR/external` to the variable's value, which means that Zsh will first search in this directory for any function we want to autoload.

We don't autoload anything from this `external` directory at the moment, but that will change soon.

You can now run `~/dotfiles/install.sh`. Then, let's run `zsh` to try the auto-completion:

- If you type `cp` followed by a space (`cp `) and hit the tab key, you'll see that Zsh will auto-complete the command.
- If you type `cp -` and hit the tab key, Zsh will display the possible arguments for the command.

Lovely, isn't it?

Pimp My Zsh Prompt

The time of the dull, lifeless, and depressing Zsh prompt has ended! We'll now configure a better one, before our eyes start crying blood. Let's define our needs first:

- The prompt needs to be on one line. It's simpler and it avoids display bugs. Been there, done that.
- The prompt needs to display some information related to Git when necessary (branch, stash, and so on).

If these needs are not yours, that's fine. You'll be able to modify the prompt as much as you want. You can even make it completely different, I won't stop you. Do everything your heart dictates. You're free, like a little bird.

First, let's create a new file:

```
nvim ~/dotfiles/zsh/external/prompt_purification_setup
```

Then, let's copy the content of our new prompt[1] into this new file.

---

[1] https://raw.githubusercontent.com/PhantasOs/mouseless-book-companion/master/part_II/08_zsh/dotfiles/zsh/external/prompt_purification_setup

Finally, let's add the following lines into our `.zshrc` :

```
autoload -Uz prompt_purification_setup; prompt_purification_setup
```

I won't explain the code of the prompt here, we'll see bash scripting in more detail in the next chapters. Still, I'd like to point out two things:

- Two variables are set in this script: `$PROMPT` and `$RPROMPT` . The first one formats the left prompt, the second displays Git information on the right.
- You can add some formatting styles using, for example, `%F{blue}%f` to change the color, or `%Bmy-cool-prompt%b` to make everything bold.

This prompt doesn't need any external dependencies. You can modify it as much as you want. The icons for the right prompt (Git information) won't work for now, but we'll take care of that later.

Zsh Directory Stack

You can push and pop directories on a directory stack[1] with Zsh. By manipulating this stack, you can set up a history of directories visited and jump back to these directories easily.

First, let's set some options in our file `~/dotfiles/zsh/.zshrc` :

```
# Push the current directory visited on to the stack.
setopt AUTO_PUSHD
# Do not store duplicate directories in the stack.
setopt PUSHD_IGNORE_DUPS
# Do not print the directory stack after using pushd or popd.
setopt PUSHD_SILENT
```

From there, we can create a very handy alias in our file `~/dotfiles/zsh/aliases` :

```
alias d='dirs -v'
for index ({1..9}) alias "$index"="cd +${index}"; unset index
```

What does it mean?

- Thanks to the options we've set, every directory we visit will populate the stack.
- When you use the alias `d` in a terminal, it will output the directories on the stack prefixed with a number from 1 to 9.

---

[1] http://zsh.sourceforge.net/Intro/intro_6.html

- The line `for index ({1..9}) alias "$index"="cd +${index}"; unset index` will create aliases from 1 to 9. They will allow you to jump directly into a specific directory present in the stack.

For example, if you run the command `1` in Zsh, you'll jump to the directory prefixed with `1` in your stack list. You can also increase `index ({1..9})` to `index ({1..100})` for example, if you want to be able to jump back to 100 different directories!

Zsh, Your New Best Friend

It's time to set Zsh as the default shell of our user. Are you now psychologically ready to switch from Bash to Zsh? Great! Let's run this command:

```
chsh -s $(which zsh)
```

When you're done, restart your computer for the file `~/dotfiles/zsh/.zshenv` to be sourced (all the commands of the file will be read and executed). Normally, Zsh should run directly after logging in with your user.

Zsh With Vim Flavors

We will now enable some very nice functionalities to be able to edit our commands "Neovim style".

Enabling the Vi Mode

Zsh has a Vi mode you can enable by adding the following into your file `.zshrc`:

```
bindkey -v
export KEYTIMEOUT=1
```

You can now switch between INSERT and NORMAL mode with `ESC` directly in Zsh. The second line `export KEYTIMEOUT=1` makes the switch between the two modes quicker.

Changing Cursor

A visual indicator to show the current mode (NORMAL or INSERT) would be nice. In Neovim, the cursor is a beam | when we're in INSERT mode, and a block when we're in NORMAL mode. Let's do the same for Zsh.

First, we need to create a new file: `nvim "$DOTFILES/zsh/external/cursor_mode"`. Then, copy and paste the content of this file[1] in it.

Next, we need to autoload this script as a new function. Add the following to your `.zshrc`:

```
autoload -Uz cursor_mode && cursor_mode
```

To apply the change, simply source your `.zshrc` as follows:

```
source "$DOTFILES/zsh/.zshrc"
```

You can now speak about the beam and block with passion and verve to all your friends.

Vim Mapping For Completion

To give Zsh even more of a Vim taste, we can set up the keys `hjkl` to navigate the auto-completion menu.

First, add the following to your `zshrc`:

```
zmodload zsh/complist
bindkey -M menuselect 'h' vi-backward-char
bindkey -M menuselect 'k' vi-up-line-or-history
bindkey -M menuselect 'l' vi-forward-char
bindkey -M menuselect 'j' vi-down-line-or-history
```

This configuration should be added before autoloading `compinit`.

Here we load the Zsh module `complist`. Modules have functionalities which are not part of Zsh core, but they can be loaded on demand. This module gives you access to `menuselect`, to customize the way you can move your cursor around while auto-completing.

---

[1] https://raw.githubusercontent.com/PhantasOs/mouseless-book-companion/master/part_II/08_zsh/dotfiles/zsh/external/cursor_mode

The command `bindkey -M` binds a key to the command `menuselect`.

Editing Commands In Neovim

You can also configure Zsh to use Neovim (or any editor running in a terminal) to directly edit what you type at the command-line prompt. To do so, add the following in your `.zshrc`:

```
autoload -Uz edit-command-line
zle -N edit-command-line
bindkey -M vicmd v edit-command-line
```

We autoload `edit-command-line`, a function from zshcontrib[1], a melting pot of contributions from Zsh users. This function lets you edit the command using the default text editor we've set in the environment variable `$EDITOR`. Great! That's what we wanted.

We've seen `bindkey -M` at the beginning of this chapter. If you add `vicmd` to it, the keystroke will only work when you're in NORMAL mode (called COMMAND mode in the documentation). In short, you can hit `v` in NORMAL mode to launch your editor to edit your command. When you're done editing it, save and quit with `:wq`, as you would do with a file.

Zsh Plugins

The term "plugin", as I use it, is nothing official. People often speak about Zsh plugins as external pieces of configuration you can add to your own. There are many of these plugins available, and many of them are part of Zsh frameworks.

Zsh Additional Completion

There are many auto-completion files for different CLIs which are not included in the basic installation of Zsh. Let's fix that with this command:

```
sudo pacman -S zsh-completions
```

Zsh now supports even more CLIs to auto-complete their arguments.

---

[1] https://linux.die.net/man/1/zshcontrib

Zsh Syntax Highlighting

What about having syntax highlighting directly in the shell? Let's install the following plugin by running in your shell:

```
sudo pacman -S zsh-syntax-highlighting
```

Then, let's source it in our file `~/dotfiles/zsh/.zshrc` :

```
source /usr/share/zsh/plugins/zsh-syntax-highlighting/zsh-syntax-
    ↪ highlighting.zsh
```

You should source this plugin at the very bottom of your zshrc. Everything loaded before will then be able to use syntax highlighting if needed.

Jumping To A Parent Directory

Do you like to type `cd ../../..` to go back to the great-grand-parent of the current directory? Me neither.

It's where bd[1] can help you. Imagine that you're in the directory `~/a/b/c/d` . You can jump directly to `a` with the command `bd a` . The auto-completion for Zsh is even included. Awesomeness!

As always, let's first create a file: `nvim "$DOTFILES/zsh/external/bd.zsh"` . Then, let's copy and paste the content of the file bd.zsh[2] into your new file.

Finally, let's source it in our `.zshrc` :

```
source ~/dotfiles/zsh/external/bd.zsh
```

Alternatively, you can source it in another file (say `~/dotfiles/zsh/external/bd`), and then autoload this file in your `.zshrc` .

---

[1] https://github.com/Tarrasch/zsh-bd

[2] https://raw.githubusercontent.com/Phantas0s/mouseless-book-companion/master/part_II/08_zsh/dotfiles/zsh/external/bd.zsh

Custom Scripts

Using a shell allows you to automate many parts of your workflow with shell scripts. That's a major benefit we should take advantage of! While you're working, ask yourself what tasks you repeat again and again to automate them as much as you can. This is the real power of the shell, and it will make your whole workflow even more efficient!

Let's create a new file:

```
nvim $DOTFILES/zsh/scripts.sh
```

Let's add the following to the file:

```
#!/bin/zsh

compress() {
    tar cvzf $1.tar.gz $1
}
```

We can then source our functions in our file `$DOTFILES/zsh/.zshrc` by adding this line:

```
source $DOTFILES/zsh/scripts.sh
```

That's it! Now you can use the command `compress` to compress a directory. Joy and happiness!

You can also look at the scripts I have in my dotfiles[1] for inspiration. I even documented them[2]. It's not perfect, but it works.

The Fuzzy Finder fzf

If there is one program which can significantly improve your shell experience, it's fzf. It's a fast and powerful tool to basically search for anything you want: an entry in your Zsh history, in your filesystem, or in your Git commits. The sky's the limit!

As always, let's first install it:

```
sudo pacman -S fzf
```

---

[1] https://github.com/Phantas0s/.dotfiles/blob/master/zsh/scripts.zsh

[2] https://github.com/Phantas0s/.dotfiles/blob/master/zsh/README.md

Then, add the following to your `.zshrc` :

```
if [ $(command -v "fzf") ]; then
    source /usr/share/fzf/completion.zsh
    source /usr/share/fzf/key-bindings.zsh
fi
```

These four lines simply verify that the command "fzf" exists, and if it does, it sources fzf completion for Zsh and creates some key bindings you can use in the shell. What are these key bindings?

- `CTRL+t` – Search for a file in the current directory and sub-directories.
- `CTRL+r` – Search for an entry in the command history.
- `ALT+c` – Allow you to select a sub-directory and make it your working directory.

Additionally, you can fuzzy search for a process you want to kill by typing `kill` in your terminal followed by `TAB` . How awesome is that?

By default, fzf uses the CLI `find` under the hood, but we can do better. First, let's install a faster alternative to grep called `ripgrep` :

```
sudo pacman -S ripgrep
```

You can now use the command `rg` in your terminal instead of `grep` (if you want to). We're now ready to modify the behavior of fzf by adding the following in the file `$DOTFILES/zsh/zshenv` :

```
export FZF_DEFAULT_COMMAND="rg --files --hidden --glob '!.git'"
export FZF_CTRL_T_COMMAND="$FZF_DEFAULT_COMMAND"
```

Now you have more control over what fzf is doing. Here, we ask fzf to use ripgrep by default when we're searching for files. Then, we add some options to ripgrep:

- `--files` – Search for files.
- `--hidden` – Search for hidden files, too.
- `--glob '!.git'` – Exclude any file or directory called `.git` .

You can also use `fzf` in Neovim with the plugin fzf.vim. We'll come back to fzf and fzf.vim later in this book.

Automatically Starting i3

Thanks to `.zshrc` being sourced just after login, we can start i3 automatically without the need to type `startx` each time. By doing so, we're able to specify a path in the filesystem for the file `.xinitrc`, too. So let's move it to where it should belong:

```
mv ~/.xinitrc ~/dotfiles/X11/.xinitrc
```

Then, run the install script of our dotfiles:

```
cd "$DOTFILES" && ./install.sh
```

Now, we can configure i3's startup. Add the following in your `.zshrc`:

```
if [ "$(tty)" = "/dev/tty1" ];
then
    pgrep i3 || exec startx "$XDG_CONFIG_HOME/X11/.xinitrc"
fi
```

Let's look at this in more detail:

- The CLI pgrep (for `p`rocess `grep`) allow you to fetch a specific process.
- `||` is a logical OR. If the process "i3" does exist, "true" is returned and nothing else is executed.
- The command `exec startx "$XDG_CONFIG_HOME/X11/.xinitrc"` will be executed if the process i3 doesn't exist.
- The command `exec` *replaces* the shell process (running after logging in) with the `startx` process, which is then replaced by `i3` thanks to our `.xinitrc` file and its last line `exec i3`. That's why, when you log out, you can't come back to the shell process anymore, because it has been replaced by i3. Instead, you come back to the login prompt.
- The `$()` notation runs a command and return its output. If it wasn't there, the string of characters "tty" would be compared to the string `/dev/tty1`, which is never true.
- We saw the `tty` command in a previous chapter. We verify here that we are in the first tty and, in that case, we launch i3. Why? Because we don't want to launch i3 in every tty!

You can now restart your computer and see if everything works. Don't forget to push the changes you've made to GitHub. By the way, when you're committing your changes, you can run `git commit` instead of `git commit -m "my changes"`.

Neovim will open automatically (thanks to the environment variable `$EDITOR` we've set) for you to add your commit message.

In a Nutshell

What did we learn in this chapter?

- Using a framework with Zsh is a risky move. Having many dependencies coupled to something as important as the shell might not be the best idea.
- Zsh read a bunch of config files in order to load environment variables and some configuration. The most important ones are `.zshenv` (for your environment variables) and `.zshrc`.
- The XDG directories are a set of environment variables containing directory paths. They are used by most applications to store user specific files, like dotfiles or caching.
- Aliases allow you to define shorter commands. You should use them when you're annoyed by repeatedly typing long commands you use often.
- There are many options you can set or unset to customize Zsh.
- The Zsh completion system can auto-complete many CLIs' arguments. Try it with Pacman for example. How nice is that?
- You can use a directory stack to be able to jump back easily to a previous directory you've visited.
- We can edit commands in Zsh with the Vi mode, or even edit them using Neovim directly.
- There are many plugins (external scripts) available for Zsh. You can find many of them on GitHub.

In the next chapter, we'll improve our Mouseless Development Environment by installing and configuring useful applications.

Going Deeper

- Arch wiki – XDG Base Directory[1]

Zsh Documentation

- Options[2]

---

[1] https://wiki.archlinux.org/index.php/XDG_Base_Directory

[2] http://zsh.sourceforge.net/Doc/Release/Options.html

- Prompt[1]
- Modules[2]
- Keymaps (Vi modes)[3]
- Directory stack[4]

Author's dotfiles

- Scripts[5]
- Scripts "documentation"[6]

---

[1] http://zsh.sourceforge.net/Doc/Release/Prompt-Expansion.html

[2] http://zsh.sourceforge.net/Doc/Release/Zsh-Modules.html

[3] http://zsh.sourceforge.net/Doc/Release/Zsh-Line-Editor.html#Keymaps

[4] http://zsh.sourceforge.net/Intro/intro_6.html

[5] https://github.com/Phantas0s/.dotfiles/blob/master/zsh/scripts.zsh

[6] https://github.com/Phantas0s/.dotfiles/blob/master/zsh/README.md

Improving Your Mouseless Development Environment

Now that we have most of our tools installed and configured, let's see how we can improve our new system even further. Here's the program:

- We'll first improve the install script for our dotfiles.
- We'll see how we can install new fonts.
- We'll install Dunst to have nice desktop notifications.
- We'll see how to mount and unmount new plugged devices automatically.
- We'll see some ways to replace the caps lock key with a `CTRL` or `ESC` key.

With these small modifications, we'll make our system even more enjoyable to use.

Improving the Dotfiles Install Script

We'll now refactor the install script for our dotfiles, using the environment variables we've created in the file `~/dotfiles/zsh/.zshenv` in the last chapter. More precisely, we'll substitute every filepath in the file `~/dotfiles/zsh/install.sh` with equivalent environment variables.

The CLI `sed` is very good at performing operations on plain text, like replacing text using following precise patterns, for example. This command takes an input and returns the modified content as output. For example, you can try to run in your terminal:

```
echo "I like you" | sed "s/like/appreciate/"
```

You'll get `I appreciate you` as output: you've just substituted `like` with `appreciate`. By default, remember that `sed` only replace the first occurrence of the match. Try to run:

```
echo "I like you and you like me" | sed "s/like/appreciate/"
```

You could expect to have `I really appreciate you and you appreciate me` as output, but you only get `I appreciate you and you like me`. What if you want to replace every single "like"? You need to add the flag "g" (for `g`lobal) to your substitution:

```
echo "I like you and you like me" | sed "s/like/appreciate/g"
```

In a more general way, we can use the substitution provided by sed like this:

```
sed s/<search>/<replacement>/<flag(s)> <input>
```

It will use your input and replace `<search>` with `<replacement>`, then it will output the result.

We are using the character `/` as the separator between the search, the replacement, and the flags, but you can use another one if you want to. The following example does exactly the same thing:

```
echo "I like you and you like me" | sed "s#like#appreciate#g"
```

How can sed helps us to refactor our dotfiles? First, let's change our working directory with the command `cd $DOTFILES`. Then, let's run the following in Zsh:

```
sed "s#\$HOME/dotfiles#\$DOTFILES#g" "install.sh"
```

It will output the whole file with the occurrence of `$HOME/dotfiles` replaced with `$DOTFILES`. Before going further, let's clarify some key points here:

1. `sed` accept regular expressions as search patterns. This means that some characters (called meta-character) can select precise patterns of text, because these meta-characters have a specific meaning (or *semantics*).
2. The character `$` is part of this set of meta-characters, but we don't want to use its special meaning. We want to search for the character itself. To do that, we need to *escape* it by adding `\` as a prefix.
3. If you want to search for the character you use as separator between `<search>` and `<replacement>`, you need to escape it, too. The more you'll escape characters with `\`, the less your regular expression will be readable. That's why we changed the usual separator `/` to `#` in our substitution.

By running the above command, we didn't actually modify anything; we've just output the whole contents of the file and replaced the string `$HOME/dotfiles` with `$DOTFILES`. The file itself didn't change.

You can write the changes you make directly into the file using the option `-i`. That being said, I would like to show you a different way to do the same thing, using Neovim this time. Let's edit the file:

```
nvim $DOTFILES/install.sh
```

Then, let's type the following command:

```
:%s#$HOME/dotfiles#$DOTFILES#g
```

We don't need to escape the characters `$` here because Neovim's regular expression engine works a bit differently, and `$` is not considered a meta-character by default. The new symbol `%` is a range, to specify that we want to apply our command to the whole file.

Let's run another command to replace `$HOME/.config` with `$XDG_CONFIG_HOME` :

```
:%s#$HOME/.config#$XDG_CONFIG_HOME#g
```

Now, if one day we want to use another directory to store our configuration files, we just need to set a new value for the variables `$DOTFILES` and `$XDG_CONFIG_HOME` respectively, in the file `$DOTFILES/zsh/.zshenv` .

Adding And Configuring Fonts

Installing Fonts

Let's switch to a totally different topic: what about having nice icons to please our marvelous eyes? These icons can be included in font files, so let's see how to install them first.

To display icons in URxvt, we need mono fonts (fonts with the same fixed size for every character), and another font to display icons in i3. If we use the same fonts for both, the icons displayed by i3 will be too small.

If there's a place where we can find font files with icons included, it's definitely in Ryan L. McIntyre's GitHub repository, aka ryanoasis.

Let's use for now, the font Inconsolata for the whole system: you can find the fonts for URxvt and i3 in the book companion[1]. You can change it later, of course: the repository of ryanoasis[2] is full of tasty fonts waiting to be downloaded and installed. You can also directly use his tool if you want to become a true nerd font.

---

[1] https://github.com/Phantas0s/mouseless-book-companion/tree/master/part_II/09_improving_sys
tem/dotfiles/fonts

[2] https://github.com/ryanoasis/nerd-fonts

Again, let's create a new directory:

```
mkdir "$DOTFILES/fonts"
```

Next, let's move the fonts downloaded using `mv` . You probably downloaded the fonts to the directory `~/Downloads` ; check the setting of your browser if it's not there. Then, run this command in a shell:

```
mv ~/Downloads/<my_font_file> ~/Downloads/<my_other_font_file>
  ↪  ~/dotfiles/fonts
```

You can now add the following to the file `$DOTFILES/install.sh` :

```
##########
# Fonts #
##########

mkdir -p "$XDG_DATA_HOME"
cp -rf "$DOTFILES/fonts" "$XDG_DATA_HOME"
```

We don't create a symbolic link here since we'll never modify these fonts manually, so we just copy them. The option `-r` copies a directory r ecursively, and the option `-f` f orces overwriting the directory if it already exists.

As always, run your install script to see if everything is working as expected.

Next, we need to refresh the font cache:

```
fc-cache -f
```

This cache is populated with some information about your fonts. This information is useful for the different applications on your system to find the fonts they need. The option `-f` f orces the regeneration, even if the fonts are apparently up to date.

To see all the fonts available on the system, you need to run this command in a shell:

```
fc-list
```

Don't hesitate to pipe the output to the pager `less` to navigate the list more easily. You can also use grep to see if the cache files for our new fonts have been correctly generated:

```
fc-list | grep -i "nerd"
```

We filter for "nerd" here simply because it's part of the name of the font. The option `-i` means case i nsensitive: grep will match "nerd" uppercase or lowercase.

Changing URxvt's Fonts

We need to modify the file `$DOTFILES/X11/.Xresources` for URxvt to use our new fonts. You can modify the value of the key `URxvt*font` as follows:

```
URxvt*font: xft:Inconsolata Nerd Font
    ↪  Mono:style=Medium:size=14:pixelsize=16:antialias=true
```

I've got the name `Inconsolata Nerd Font Mono` thanks to the command `fc-list` we used above. Since we've changed our file `.Xresources`, we need to run the following command to apply the changes:

```
xrdb -merge $HOME/.config/X11/.Xresources
```

That's not all: you might also need to log out from your i3 session and login again to see our new wonderful fonts. If there's too much space displayed between the characters of your font in URxvt, you can add the following option to the file `.Xresources`:

```
URxvt*letterSpace: -1
```

Changing i3's Fonts

Next step: configuring i3 with the second font we've downloaded. Let's open the file `$DOTFILES/i3/config` with Neovim and let's search for the string of characters `font pango`. Then, we can modify the line found as following:

```
font pango:Inconsolata NF 12
```

Reload i3 with the keystroke `$mod+SHIFT+c` (if it doesn't work, reset i3 with `$mod+SHIFT+r`). Remember: `$mod` is normally the `WIN` key or any key you've configured in i3's configuration.

With all of that done, it's time to add nice icons to our i3 status bar. I like the icons from font-awesome, but you can also use material icons or others.

You can directly copy paste the icons you want to use in the i3bar to the file `$DOTFILES/i3/i3status.conf`. For example, you can add a calendar icon in the string defining the clock as follows:

```
format = " <my_icon> %Y-%m-%d %H:%M:%S"
```

You can replace `<my_icon>` with the icon itself. You can copy and paste from a cheat-sheet like this one[1].

Desktop Notifications With Dunst

Our dotfiles use nice environment variables for important filepaths. We have nice icons all over the place. What else can we do to make our system even better? What about desktop notifications?

I personally hate notifications (it breaks my focus when I need it the most), but I admit that they can be useful for some cases, like reminding me of an important meeting, for example.

I like to use the application dunst to manage desktop notifications. Let's install it:

```
sudo pacman -S dunst libnotify
```

To test our new notification system, let's first run dunst in the background.

```
dunst&
```

If you wonder what's this `&`, it allows us to run programs in the background. We've seen it when we configured the layout of our screen(s).

Next, let's try to run the following command:

```
notify-send "hello" -u low
```

The option `-u` lets you specify the `u`rgency level of the notification: `low`, `normal` or `critical`.

---

[1] https://fontawesome.com/cheatsheet?from=io

As you can see, the notifications are quite simple by default (some would say "ugly", and I'm part of them), so let's improve that. The default configuration of Dunst for the whole system is in `/usr/share/dunst/dunstrc` . It's often better to configure the applications we use only for a specific user, not for the whole system.

I won't describe Dunst's configuration in detail. It's not an essential component for our Mouseless Development Environment, and the default configuration has many comments which can help you to configure it as you wish.

For now, let's download the configuration I'm using from the book's companion[1]. Then, create a new directory:

```
mdkir "$DOTFILES/dunst"
```

Next, move the file you've downloaded:

```
mv ~/Downloads/<file> "$DOTFILES/dunst/dunstrc"
```

We also need to start dunst when we boot our system. Let's add the line in `$DOTFILES/i3/config` :

```
exec --no-startup-id dunst
```

As always when we add new dotfiles, we need to install them via our script `$DOTFILES/install.sh` . Let's add these lines:

```
mkdir -p "$XDG_CONFIG_HOME/dunst"
ln -sf "$DOTFILES/dunst/dunstrc" "$XDG_CONFIG_HOME/dunst/dunstrc"
```

That's it! We now have a desktop notifier. Long live the desktop notifier!

Automatically Mounting Devices

As we saw in a previous chapter, you need to manually mount any block device you plug in your system to a directory in order to access it. A block device can be a USB key or an external hard disk, for example. You can do it using both commands `mount <your_block_device>` and `umount <directory>` , but you also can automate the process.

---

[1] https://raw.githubusercontent.com/PhantasOs/mouseless-book-companion/master/part_II/09_imp
roving_system/dotfiles/dunst/dunstrc

To do so, we'll now install `udiskie` to automatically mount block devices when they're plugged:

```
sudo pacman -S udiskie
```

The block devices will be mounted `/run/media/<your_user_name>` by default.

To unplug your devices safely, you need to unmount them. You can use `udiskie` to do so, too:

```
udiskie-umount <device>
```

Since we use Zsh, we can auto-complete the `<device>` we want to unplug. We can also use the option `-a` (for a ll) to unmount everything we've plugged manually.

To have more information about what's mounted, you can run in a terminal:

```
udiskie-info -a
```

To automatically run udiskie when you're booting your system, you can add the following line in your file `$DOTFILES/X11/.xinitrc`.

```
udiskie &
```

Don't forget: the line `exec i3` needs to be at the end of the file `$DOTFILES/X11/.xinitrc`.

Visual Configuration

When developers create desktop applications for Linux-based systems, they mainly use two toolkits (libraries) for the graphical user interface (GUI): GTK[1] or QT[2]. It's usually easy to differentiate an application using one or the other; both libraries give a specific look and feel to their GUI.

As a user, you can configure the appearance of GTK+ GUI. If you want to do so, let's install the very lightweight LxAppearance:

```
sudo pacman -S lxappearance
```

---

[1] https://wiki.archlinux.org/index.php/GTK

[2] https://wiki.archlinux.org/index.php/Qt

I know, applications with GUIs are evil because you need the mouse to use them, most of the time. But for some applications, we have little choices. Your browser is a good example, even if we'll see different ways to make your internet experience kind-of-mouseless.

You can then install any GTK theme you want[1] and switch to it using LxAppearance. Some of them are available directly from the Arch Linux official repositories, others can be found on the AUR. Most of them need to be installed manually.

Personally, I like the GTK theme shades of gray[2].

Remapping Your Caps Lock

Do you use often the `Caps Lock` key? I never use it. If I want some majestic uppercases, I use the `SHIFT` key.

Let's remap it to something more useful!

The only downside remapping the `Caps Lock` key: you'll hit this same key very often when you try to help your colleagues on their computers, and you'll be confused to see uppercase letters suddenly appearing. As a result, many keyboards almost ended up out the window.

A New Escape Key

I've said, in a previous chapter, that it wasn't very nice to use your arrow keys because they were too far away from the row keys of your keyboard. When you look at your `ESC` key, it's far away too, isn't it?

That's why I've realized, a long time ago, while watching dinosaurs by my window, that I could remap the `Caps Lock` key to the `ESC` key.

You know what? We have everything already installed to make it work. Try to run the following in your terminal:

```
setxkbmap -option caps:escape
```

The tool setxkbmap allows you to change the layout of your keyboard. Let's add the line just above to the file `~/dotfiles/X11/.xinitrc` to always have this `Caps Lock` key mapped to the `ESC` key.

---

[1] https://www.gnome-look.org

[2] https://aur.archlinux.org/packages/gtk-theme-shades-of-gray/

Two Keys in One

We can do even better: remapping the `Caps Lock` key to behave both like the `ESC` key and the `CTRL` key! Sounds confusing? Do you think you can handle it? Do you think you need it? There is only one way to know: just try it!

I was also doubtful about this idea, now I can't live without it.

We'll first remap the `Caps Lock` key with the `CTRL` key. Run the following in your shell:

```
setxkbmap -option 'caps:ctrl_modifier'
```

Then, we need to use a new tool which allows us to send a key's event when the physical keyboard's key is released. Let's install it:

```
sudo pacman -S xcape
```

Then, we can run xcape in the background. Run in your shell the following:

```
xcape -e 'Caps_Lock=Escape'&
```

Now, when you press the key `Caps Lock` with another key, it will act as the left `CTRL` key. When you press `Caps Lock` by itself, it's like pressing the `ESC` key.

In short, you have two very useful keys on the same physical key. Is it a problem? Not really, since you never use `CTRL` *and* `ESC` at the same time. Additionally, you always use `CTRL` with another key.

To always have this mapping when you boot your system, you can add the following in the file `~/dotfiles/X11/.xinitrc`:

```
setxkbmap -option 'caps:ctrl_modifier';xcape -e 'Caps_Lock=Escape'&
```

The Problem of the External Keyboard

There is another downside when you remap one of your key: if you plug in an external keyboard while your system is running, your remapping won't be applied automatically.

The best solutions I've found is to re-apply the mapping manually with a keystroke of your choosing. To do so, add the following to the i3's config file `$DOTFILES/i3/config`:

```
bindsym $mod+z exec "setxkbmap -option 'caps:ctrl_modifier';xcape
↪   -e 'Caps_Lock=Escape' &"
```

Here, I've configured the keystroke `$mod+z` to apply the remapping of my `Caps Lock` key; feel free to use any keystroke you want.

Git diff

Finally, let's install `diff-so-fancy`, a script to make our `git diff` more readable:

```
sudo pacman -S diff-so-fancy
```

Then, modify Git's configuration by running the following line:

```
git config --global core.pager "diff-so-fancy | less --tabs=4 -RFX"
```

If you try to run `git diff` in the `$DOTFILES` directory for example, you'll see the magic!

While we're speaking about Git, you might notice that we didn't add our Git config file `~/.gitconfig` in our dotfiles repository, simply because there is an email address in there.

If you don't care that everybody can see this email address, you can add `~/.gitconfig` to your repository if you want to. I would even advise you to move `~/.gitconfig` to `~/.config/git/config` to keep as many dotfiles as you can in the `$XDG_CONFIG_HOME` directory.

In a Nutshell

What did we learn in this chapter?

- If you have the same filepath all over your shell scripts, you can create variables (or environment variables) to be able to modify them easily if you need to.
- When you install a new font on your system, you first need to generate the cache with `fc-cache`.
- To list the fonts installed on your system, use `fc-list`.
- Dunst and libnotify allow you to have desktop notification.
- You can automatically mount devices when they're plugged, thanks to udiskie.

- Remapping the `Caps Lock` key to the `ESC` key is a nice useful trick, especially if you use Vim or Neovim.
- If you want to feel the power, don't be afraid: try to remap the `CAPS LOCK` key to the `ESC` key *and* the left `CTRL` key.

In the next chapter, we'll come back to Neovim to prepare ourselves to write more complex bash scripts.

Going Deeper

- Arch Wiki – Environment Variables[1]
- Arch Wiki – Fonts[2]
- Arch Wiki – USB storage devices[3]
- Arch Wiki – Dunst[4]
- Arch Wiki – GTK[5]
- Arch Wiki – QT[6]
- Arch Wiki – Xorg/Keyboard configuration[7]
- diff-so-fancy[8]

---

[1] https://wiki.archlinux.org/index.php/Environment_variables

[2] https://wiki.archlinux.org/index.php/Fonts

[3] https://wiki.archlinux.org/index.php/USB_storage_devices

[4] https://wiki.archlinux.org/index.php/Dunst

[5] https://wiki.archlinux.org/index.php/GTK

[6] https://wiki.archlinux.org/index.php/Qt

[7] https://wiki.archlinux.org/index.php/Xorg/Keyboard_configuration

[8] https://github.com/so-fancy/diff-so-fancy

Neovim: A Deeper Dive

To be comfortable writing our installer for our new system, we'll now dive even more into the wonderful world of Neovim. Specifically, we'll see in this chapter:

- Different places in Vim where we can modify and organize open files.
- Useful motions to jump quickly from one place to another in your codebase.
- How to create new keystrokes.
- Powerful functionalities to repeat some of your keystrokes easily.
- Ways of manipulating the command history.
- Plugins which offers different ways to manage some ideas we've already seen.

You'll see at the end of each section the help commands related to what we've discussed. You can read these help sections directly in Neovim when you're ready to dive even deeper.

Neovim Spatial Organization

If you've used an IDE before, you're certainly used to managing your files with tabs. Neovim uses other ways to represent and organize open files. Indeed, there are four layers of abstraction you can use for that: the *buffers*, the *windows*, the *tabs*, and the *argument list*.

Buffers

A *buffer* directly matches to an open file in memory. To make a comparison with a standard IDE, a buffer would be the *content* of a tab. The big difference is that when you close a tab in an IDE, you also close the open file in it. Not in Neovim; if you close a window containing a buffer, the buffer is still there but it's *hidden*.

In fact, a buffer can have three different states:

- *active* - The buffer is displayed in a window.
- *hidden* - The buffer is not displayed, but it exists and the file is still open.
- *inactive* - The buffer is not displayed and *empty*. It's not linked to any file.

The content of a file in a hidden buffer is not directly visible in Neovim. But how do we know that this buffer is still open if we can't see the content of the file displayed?

To see all opened buffers, we can look at the *buffer list*. You can use the commands `:buffers` or `:ls` to display it. Each line contains:

1. The buffer unique ID.
2. Indicators displaying different information (for example `a` for active, `h` for hidden, or   for inactive).
3. The name of the buffer, if any. It can be the filepath of the file linked to the buffer.
4. The line number where the cursor is.

For example: `27 %a   "layouts/shortcodes/notice.html" line 18` means that the buffer ID 27 is in state `a` (active), its name is `layouts/shortcodes/notice.html` and the cursor in this specific buffer is on line 18. You can also see that the current buffer is displayed with the flag `%` just before its state.

You might have noticed that the path of the file is relative, but relative to what? To Neovim's current directory. You can display its path with the command `:pwd` , and you can change it using `:cd <new_path>` .

To navigate through the buffer list, you can use these commands:

- `:buffer <ID_or_name>` - Move to the buffer using its ID or its name.
- `:bnext` or `:bn` - Move to the next buffer.
- `:bprevious` or `:bp` - Move to the previous buffer.
- `:bfirst` or `:bf` - Move to the first buffer.
- `:blast` or `:bl` - Move to the last buffer.
- `CTRL+^` - Switch to the alternative buffer. It's marked in your buffer list with the symbol `#` .
- `<ID>CTRL+^` - Switch to a specific buffer with ID `<ID>` . For example, `75CTRL-^` switch to the buffer with ID 75.

You can also apply a command to all buffers using `:bufdo <command>` .

Not all buffers are displayed in the buffer list. To display unlisted buffers, you can use the command `:buffers!` or `:ls!` . You'll see any unlisted buffers with an indicator `u` just after its ID.

Now, let's ask this existential question: how can we create buffers?

- If you create a window, a buffer will be created automatically.
- `:badd <filename>` - Add `<filename>` to the buffer list.

If we can create buffers, we should be able to delete them:

- `:bdelete <ID_or_name>` - Delete a buffer by ID or name. To delete more than one buffer, you can specify more than one ID or name separated with spaces.
- `:1,10bdelete` - Delete buffers from ID 1 to 10 included.
- `:%bdelete` - Delete all buffers.

Do you want an error message? Follow these steps:

1. Modify a buffer.
2. Forget to save it and hide it.
3. Try to quit Neovim

Neovim will complain that you're hidden buffer is not saved. To get around that, I would recommend setting the option hidden in your Neovim configuration file (`$DOTFILES/nvim/init.vim`) as follows:

```
set hidden
```

You can try it directly in your current session by running the command `:set hidden!` to toggle the option on and off. You can play around with it and see what you prefer.

To see the value of any option, you can use a question mark. For example: `:set hidden?` or `:set filetype?` .

To be honest with you, the way I'm explaining this whole `hidden` concept is not totally accurate; I'll let you dig into Neovim's help if you want to know more.

Finally, to see if a buffer was modified you can use the keystroke `CTRL+G` .

```
:help buffers
:help :buffers
:help current-directory
:help hidden
```

Windows

A window in Neovim is a space (or a place) you can use to display the content of a buffer. Don't forget: when you close the window, the buffer is still in the buffer list.

To create windows, you can use the command `:new` or one of these keystrokes:

- `CTRL+W s` - Split the current window horizontally.
- `CTRL+W v` - Split the current window vertically.
- `CTRL+W n` - Split the current windows horizontally and edit a new file.
- `CTRL+W ^` - Split the current window with the *alternate file* (the buffer marked with a # in your buffer list).
- `<buffer_ID>CTRL+W ^` - Split windows with the buffer of ID `<ID>` . For example, `75 CTRL-W ^` will open a window with a buffer of ID 75.

To move your cursor from one window to another, you can use:

- `CTRL+W <Down>` or `CTRL-W j` .

- `CTRL+W <Up>` or `CTRL-W k`.
- `CTRL+W <Left>` or `CTRL-W h`.
- `CTRL+W <right>` or `CTRL-W l`.

You want to move the windows? Here we go:

- `CTRL+W r` - Rotate the windows.
- `CTRL+W x` - Exchange the focused window with the next window.

Who wants windows without being able to resize them? Here are the keystrokes you've always dreamt of:

- `CTRL+W -` - Decrease window's height.
- `CTRL+W +` - Increase window's height.
- `CTRL+W <` - Decrease window's width.
- `CTRL+W >` - Increase window's width.
- `CTRL+W =` - Resize windows to the same size for them to fit on the screen

I think it's pretty tedious to move the cursor from window to window and to move the windows themselves using these vanilla keystrokes. We'll see later a plugin which can help us make everything a tad easier.

If you want to quit windows, you can use the commands:

- `:q` - To `q` uit the current window. People lied to you! `:q` doesn't quit Neovim, but a window. Although, if there is only one window open, Neovim will close.
- `:q!` - To `q` uit the current window, even if there is only one window open with an unsaved buffer `!`.
- `:qa` - To `q` uit all the current windows. Add `!` if you don't want to save your changes in unsaved buffers.

```
:help windows
:help opening-window
:help window-move-cursor
:help window-moving
:help window-resize
```

Tabs

We saw that a buffer is a document (often an open file), and a window is the container for an active buffer. We can see tabs as a container for a bunch of windows. As a result, Neovim's tabs are different from the usual tabs you can find in many IDEs!

Here are the commands to create and delete tabs:

- `:tabnew` or `:tabe` – Open a new tab.
- `:tabclose` or `:tabc` – Close the current tab.
- `:tabonly` or `:tabo` – Close every other tab except the current one.

To move from tab to tab, you can use these keystrokes:

- `gt` – g o to the next t ab.
- `gT` – g o to the previous tab.

You can also add a count before the last two keystrokes. For example, `1gT` goes to the first tab. Yep, tabs are indexed from 1, not from 0.

`:help tab-page`

Argument List (arglist)

The argument list (also called arglist) is the fourth and last abstraction allowing you to organize your open files. It's useful to see it as a *stable subset* of the buffer list, as Drew Neil points out in one of his vimcast[1]. As a result, it follows these two rules:

1. Every file in the arglist will be in the buffer list.
2. Some files in the buffer list might not be in the arglist.

The files you want to open when you run Neovim (`vim file1 file2 file3` for example) will be automatically added to the arglist and, as we just saw, to the buffer list.

The arglist can be useful to isolate some files from the buffer list to do some operations on them. Here are some commands you can use to manipulate the arglist:

- `:args` – Display the arglist.
- `:argadd` – Add file to the arglist.
- `:argdo` – Execute a command on every file in the arglist.

To edit the files in the arglist, you can use these commands:

- `:next` – Move to the next file in the arglist.
- `:prev` – Move to the previous file in the arglist.
- `:first` – Move to the first file in the arglist.

---

[1] http://vimcasts.org/episodes/meet-the-arglist/

I never use the arglist, but many users do. The buffer list can be modified by other actions unrelated to buffers, like opening new windows. The arglist stays the same, except if you explicitly modify it. That's why it's more stable.

```
:help arglist
```

Mapping Keystrokes

We've seen a great deal of vanilla keystrokes and commands. It would be nice to be able to create our own! For that, you can use mapping commands for every Neovim mode:

- `:nmap` – Create a new mapping for NORMAL mode.
- `:imap` – Create a new mapping for INSERT mode.
- `:xmap` – Create a new mapping for VISUAL mode.

It might sound confusing to have different mappings for different modes, but it's actually easy to remember, thanks to our muscle memory[1].

Let's try an example together by mapping `w` to `dd`. By default, `dd` deletes a line, and `w` is a motion to move your cursor from word to word.

1. Run the command `:nmap w dd`
2. Try to hit the keystroke `dd`. It will delete a line.
3. Try to hit `w`. It deletes a line too.

However, `w` can't be used anymore to move from word to word. Let's try to fix that by running: `:nmap w v`.

Try to hit `v` now. It deletes a line too! You just did a recursive mapping: `v` maps to `w` which maps to `dd`. It would be nice to:

1. Map `w` to `dd`
2. Map `v` to the motion made by `w` *before* its mapping with `dd`.

To do that, you can use the following mapping commands:

- `:nnoremap` – Create mapping for NORMAL mode (non recursive).
- `:inoremap` – Create mapping for INSERT mode (non recursive).
- `:vnoremap` – Create mapping for VISUAL mode (non recursive).

---

[1] https://en.wikipedia.org/wiki/Muscle_memory

To do the silly mapping we wanted to do before, restart Neovim to have the default mapping, then execute these commands:

```
:nnoremap w dd
:nnoremap v w
```

This time, `w` deletes a line and `v` moves from word to word.

If you didn't get this concept of recursive mapping, no worries: just use the non-recursive `noremap` commands when you need to map a keystroke.

You can also use special characters in your mapping. For example:

- `<space>` for `SPACE`.
- `<c-w>` for `CTRL+W`.
- `<cr>` for `c`arriage `r`eturn (`ENTER`).

To see the complete list, run the command `:help key-notation` in Neovim.

Now that you have *The Power*, try to avoid changing the default Neovim's keystrokes as much as you can. Don't map `w` to `dd`, for example: it was just an example to show you how it works. It's more practical for you to use the default keystrokes as much as you can, because you can use them on any instance of Vim or Neovim, even in a docker container or on a remote server.

If you want to create new mappings, you should use a special key called the *leader key*. It's a way to create namespaces for keystrokes: first you use your leader key, then you use your keystroke. Thanks to the leader key, your new keystroke will never conflict with the default Neovim keystrokes.

You need to set the variable mapleader to use the key you want as leader key. Here's an example:

```
:let mapleader = "\<space>"
```

The mapping commands we saw above are often written in Neovim's configuration file to set them automatically when you open Neovim. For example, you can write the following in the file `$DOTFILES/nvim/init.vim`:

```
nnoremap <space> <nop>
let mapleader = "\<space>"

nnoremap <leader>bn :bn<cr> ;buffer next
nnoremap <leader>tn gt ;new tab
```

First, we remap `<space>` to `<nop>`. By default, SPACE in normal mode moves your cursor to the left; but we don't want to keep this mapping. When you map a key to `<nop>`, the key doesn't do anything anymore.

Then, we define our leader key and other keystrokes. The keystrokes SPACE bn will move to the next buffer, and SPACE tn will move to the next tab. Notice that when you want to map a keystroke to a command, you need to add `<cr>` (for c arriage r return) at the end, exactly like you would type ENTER to execute the command.

You're now a space leader! How awesome!

```
:help mapping
:help leader
:help key-notation
```

Jump! Jump! Jump!

There are special motions in Neovim called jump-motions. These motions move your cursor several lines away, like the keystroke gg we saw already in a previous chapter.

Jump List

Each time we use a jump motion, the position of the cursor before the jump is saved in the *jump list*. You can move through it with the following keystrokes:

- CTRL+o - Go to the previous cursor positions.
- CTRL+i - Go to the next cursor positions.

You can move from line to line and even from buffer to buffer with these holy commands. I use them all the time, and I'm pretty sure you will too.

Change List

I find the change list really useful. Each time you insert something (using INSERT mode), the position of your cursor is saved in the change list. You can navigate through it using these keystrokes:

- g; - Jump to the next change.
- g, - Jump to the previous change.

Discovering them was like seeing the light for the first time. At least.

Method Jump

Being able to jump from method to method, if you're programming with some OOP languages, is a nice feature to have. You can do that with the following keystrokes:

- `[m` – Move to the start of a method.
- `]m` – Move to the end of a method.

The methods should have similar syntax to Java's methods for these keystrokes to work.

```
:help jump-motions
:help jumplist
:help changelist
```


Repeating Keystrokes

You know what's great? Automation. You know what's great with Vim? Keystroke automation. That's a very powerful feature, so get ready!

Single Repeat

When I heard about the sacred single repeat, my life in Neovim changed (again). Here's how you can feel like a powerful superhuman:

- `.` – Repeat the last change.
- `@:` – Repeat the last command executed.

The keystroke `.` is now my best friend. It's simple and diabolically effective.

```
help single-repeat
```

Complex Repeat: The Macro

1. `q<letter>` - Begin recording keystrokes in a register. You can think of a register as a place in memory.
2. Every keystrokes you'll do onward will be saved.
3. `q` - Stop the recording.
4. `@<letter>` - Redo the keystrokes you've recorded.

For example, let's say that you need to repeat keystrokes on multiple lines:

1. Hit `qq` .
2. Do what you have to do. For example: `^cawhello<Esc>` .
3. Hit `q` again.
4. To repeat your series of keystrokes, hit `@q` .

Here, I use the `<letter>` `q` as an example; but you can actually use any lowercase letter you want. If you need to repeat your keystrokes again after the first repeat, you can even use `@@` which repeats your previous `@` command.

```
:help complex-repeat
```

The Command Window

You can access the command history directly in Neovim:

- `q:` - Open the command history.
- `q/` and `q?` - Open the search history.
- `CTRL+f` - Open the command history while in COMMAND-LINE mode.

From there, you can modify any commands you want and execute it with `ENTER` . Very handy when you need to repeat command lines with slight differences.

```
:help cmdline-window
```

Revisiting the Undo Tree

We saw before how to undo and redo a command; Vim allows you to also save all these undos in a file for each file you modify. As a result, even if you close Neovim and come back to edit your file again, you'll have access to your last changes by "undoing" or "redoing" them.

We've already configured that in a previous chapter, but that's not all: you might think that Vim will only save a *list* of undos, but it actually saves an *undo-tree*. It changes everything!

Let's take an example: when you do three changes, then undo two of them, and do one (or more) changes afterward, a new branch will be created. You can picture it like this:

```
@ -> last change after two undos
|
| o -> third change
| |
| o -> second change
|/
o -> first change
|
o
```

The second and third change have been undone, @ represent where you are now. You can revert to any of these change (first, second or third), which means in general that you can revert to *any last changes* you've made.

It's a bit difficult to navigate in this tree with vanilla Vim, but we'll see in the next section a very useful plugin to improve that. You'll then be able to search for the entire undo tree for a piece of content you want to find back!

```
:help undo-redo
:help undo-persistence
:help undo-tree
```

Plugins

Everything we saw till now can be managed differently using a couple of plugins. Here are the ones which make my life easier regarding everything we saw before.

Let's be clear here: plugins can modify many things in Neovim. I would suggest you use plugins which work well with the idiomatic ways to use Neovim, and to use the default keystrokes. Otherwise, each time you use Vim without your config files (like on a remote server or a docker container), you'll be totally lost.

Plugin Manager

First of all, we need a plugin manager. It's a plugin helping you to manage your plugins (that's so meta). There are many available out there; I've settled for `vim-plug`. To install it:

1. Go to the plugin's GitHub page[1]. You'll have to type a command to fetch the plugin, something like this:

```
sh -c 'curl -fLo "${XDG_DATA_HOME:-
↪  $HOME/.local/share}"/nvim/site/autoload/plug.vim --create-dirs
↪  \
       https://raw.githubusercontent.com/junegunn/vim-
↪  plug/master/plug.vim'
```

Now, add the following at *the beginning* of `~/.config/init.vim`:

```
call plug#begin("$XDG_CONFIG_HOME/nvim/plugged")
call plug#end()
```

You now have a new superpower: you can extend Neovim's native functionalities with plugins. Let's take a concrete example: we'll write a CSV file later in this book when we write shell scripts to install the Mouseless Development Environment you're building right now. The plugin `csv.vim` can help you to display CSVs in a more readable way, so let's install it:

You need to put between the two lines we've added to your file `init.vim` the following:

```
Plug 'chrisbra/csv.vim'
```

The final result in should look like this:

```
call plug#begin("$XDG_CONFIG_HOME/nvim/plugged")
    Plug 'chrisbra/csv.vim'
call plug#end()
```

Before installing the plugin, you need tor reload `init.vim`. Run the following command in COMMAND-LINE mode:

```
:source $MYVIMRC
```

---

[1] https://github.com/junegunn/vim-plug

Then, run the command:

```
:PlugInstall
```

You now have a new plugin. Congratulation!

Where does the string `chrisbra/csv.vim` come from? It's only the last part of the GitHub repository's URL: `https://github.com/chrisbra/csv.vim`. If the plugin is hosted on GitHub, you can always take the part of the URL with the user name and the repository's name, and add it to your `init.vim` file as we did.

You can also install plugins from sources other than GitHub; you'll find all this information on the GitHub page of vim-plug itself.

You can configure the plugins you've installed directly in `init.vim` too. For example, we can configure our new plugin for handling `csv`, as follows:

```
augroup filetype_csv
    autocmd!

    autocmd BufRead,BufWritePost *.csv :%ArrangeColumn!
    autocmd BufWritePre *.csv :%UnArrangeColumn
augroup END
```

Here's what these lines do:

- Format in a more readable way each cell of your CSV when you read or write your buffer.
- Doesn't save this formatting when you write your file.

I won't go into lengthy explanations about each command here. You don't need to know them to use Neovim. Remember: Neovim's help is your best resource if you want to know more.

Closing Buffers Without Closing Windows

By default, when you use `:bdelete` to close a buffer, the window will also be closed. If you want to keep your window layout, you can use the plugin moll/vim-bbye[1].

It's a very small plugin which gives you a new command, `:Bdelete` (with an uppercase `B`), allowing you to close a buffer without closing a window. You can try to create a new keystroke for this command to easily close any buffer.

---

[1] https://github.com/moll/vim-bbye

Managing Windows Easily

I'm not a big fan of the vanilla way to resize windows. The plugin simeji/winresizer[1] gives you a new mode to resize them. To enter this mode, you need to use the keystroke `CTRL+e` .

If you don't like the keystroke, you can add this line to your vimrc to change it:

```
let g:winresizer_start_key = "<leader>w"
```

Now, you can use this new resize mode with the keystrole `LEADER w` . It's just an example, use the keystroke which works for you.

When you're in this new resize mode, you'll see some help at the bottom of Vim. You can use `hjkl` to resize the window, `e` to change modes from `resize` mode to `focus` mode to `move` mode. The last one allows you to swap windows.

Navigating Through The Buffer List

We saw fzf already in a previous chapter. I use the plugin fzf.vim intensively too. It allows you to fuzzy search in the buffer list, the command history, or even files in your current path (set up with the option `path`).

That's only a tiny subset of what fzf.vim can do for you. I invite you to go on the GitHub repository[2] for your mind to be blown away.

Manipulating the Undo Tree

As promised, here's a very useful plugin to go back to any change you want: simnalamburt/vim-mundo[3]. The command `:MundoToggle` will show you the undo-tree of your current buffer in a new buffer.

From there, you can select any undo you want to go back to. I invite you to play a bit with this plugin to really understand how the undo-tree works in Neovim. It can be real life savior!

---

[1] https://github.com/simeji/winresizer

[2] https://github.com/junegunn/fzf.vim

[3] https://github.com/simnalamburt/vim-mundo

Automatically Installing the Plugin Manager

What about automatically installing our plugin manager when we install our dotfiles on a new system?

Let's add the following commands in the file `$DOTFILES/install.sh` .

```
# install neovim plugin manager
[ ! -f "$DOTFILES/nvim/autoload/plug.vim" ] \
    && curl -fLo "$DOTFILES/nvim/autoload/plug.vim" --create-dirs \
    https://raw.githubusercontent.com/junegunn/vim-
    ↪ plug/master/plug.vim

mkdir -p "$XDG_CONFIG_HOME/nvim/autoload"
ln -sf $DOTFILES/nvim/autoload/plug.vim"
    ↪ "$XDG_CONFIG_HOME/nvim/autoload/plug.vim"


# Install (or update) all the plugins
nvim --noplugin +PlugUpdate +qa
```

The expression `[ ! -f "$DOTFILES/nvim/autoload/plug.vim" ]` is a conditional. I'll explain later in more detail how to use them. Here, the `-f` flag verifes if the given file exists. The bang "!" is the negation operator: the expression will be true if it's false, and false if it's true.

In short, `curl -fLo "$DOTFILES/nvim/autoload/plug.vim" --create-dirs` will be executed if the file `$DOTFILES/nvim/autoload/plug.vim` doesn't exist.

The slashes `\` are only there to write on multiple lines a command which *should* be on one line. For example, `echo hello` can be written as:

```
echo \
hello
```

In a Nutshell

What did we learn in this article?

- Neovim has many abstractions to represent open documents (often files). A buffer is a file, a window can contain a buffer, and a tab can contain multiple windows.

- If you want to create a new keystroke, you should use a non-recursive mapping command depending on the mode you want your keystroke to be available in.
- It's possible to jump from one place to another in a file and even in multiple files. The jump list and the change list are very useful to quickly navigate through a codebase.
- You can repeat previous keystrokes with the period `.` or by recording them.
- You can save many undos per file and come back to them even after closing and re-opening the file.
- Plugins can extend the functionality of Neovim and simplify your life. Beware: don't install everything and anything, or you'll get lost in an ocean of plugins.

In the next chapter, we'll see how to configure another useful tool to improve our experience in the shell: tmux, the terminal multiplexer.

Going Deeper

- Vim for advanced users[1] - Your obedient servant
- Youtube channel - ThePrimeagen[2] - Theprimeagen
- Vimcast - Working with buffers[3] - Drew Neil
- Vimcast - Meet the arglist[4] - Drew Neil

---

[1] https://thevaluable.dev/vim-advanced/

[2] https://www.youtube.com/channel/UC8ENHE5xdFSwx71u3fDH5Xw

[3] http://vimcasts.org/episodes/working-with-buffers/

[4] http://vimcasts.org/episodes/meet-the-arglist/

The Terminal Multiplexer tmux

It's time to configure the last major tool we'll use for our Mouseless Development Environment: tmux. It will offer you many new powerful functionalities. More precisely, we'll explore in this chapter:

- What's tmux, and what it can bring to your workflow.
- How to configure tmux, step by step.
- What are the best tmux plugins you can use.
- How to automate the creation of tmux sessions.

I already mentioned numerous times that creating a personal cheatsheet is a very good way to learn and have a solid reference for all your keystrokes. I'm sorry to repeat myself; it's for your own good.

What's tmux?

How could we possibly know what tmux is without installing it on our system? Let's do that with our favorite Pacman command:

```
sudo pacman -S tmux
```

As the title of this chapter whispers, tmux is a t erminal mu ltiple x er. You can create multiple tmux *sessions* which can be attached to a terminal emulator. If you already know GNU-screen (another terminal multiplexer), tmux is somehow similar (but better, of course!).

To understand this concept of terminal multiplexer, we'll try to create a tmux *session*. But first, open a terminal and run `tty` : it will output the current tty you're using.

Then, simply run `tmux` in your terminal. You've just opened your first tmux session! Wonderful. If you run `tty` again, you'll see that tmux created a new one. If you have no idea what I'm speaking about with ttys, we previously discussed it in a previous chapter.

You can list every tmux session currently running with the command:

```
tmux list-sessions
```

You normally have only one session named `0` .

Now, let's run this in the terminal:

```
while :; do echo 'This will never end, except if you hit CTRL+C';
 ↪ sleep 1; done
```

We've just created an infinite loop; don't stop it yet! Now, close the terminal with `$mod+SHIFT+q` . Did the loop stopped? Not at all! It continues to run *in the background*. Even if you closed your terminal, the tmux session itself is still alive.

You don't believe me? You're right; you need to experiment by yourself. Let's do the following:

1. Open a new terminal and type `tmux list-sessions` .
2. Reattach the session by running `tmux attach-session -t <session name>` .

Your infinite loop is back, and as you can see, that it was still running in the background. Let's really kill it this time by pressing `CTRL+c` .

Why use Tmux?

I know there are developers using only i3, arguing that you can already spawn as many terminal emulators as you want. That's true, and you can go down this road too, but I would argue that tmux offers more than just a couple of terminals.

Background Operations

As we saw above, you can detach a tmux session from a client (the terminal) and you can attach it back. Yes, we're back with our good old server–client paradigm.

Since your tmux session is independent of your terminal, you don't need to worry anymore if you close it or even if it crashes. You can always reattach your session afterward in a new terminal. This means that you can run any process in the background, even if you have no terminal open. For example, let's imagine that you need to run a slow script on your remote server. You could:

1. Connect to your remote server via SSH.
2. Launch tmux on the remote server.
3. Run a script which takes hours.
4. Close the SSH connection. The script will still run on the remote server, thanks to tmux!
5. Switch off your own computer and go home.

For this scenario to work, you'll need tmux installed on your server.

More Terminals! Everywhere!

Tmux allows you to create multiple ttys on a single screen. This is the functionality I use the most. You can configure it easily and precisely, according to your specific needs. It works very well with Neovim too, as we'll see later.

Saving tmux Sessions

It's possible to save tmux sessions in a file and reopen them later, even after switching off your computer.

Remote Pair Programming

A tmux session can be attached to many clients (terminals), even via SSH. Which means that you can do pair programming with another developer using tmux and Neovim by sharing the same tmux session!

How to use tmux?

General Organization

Let's see in more details how to use tmux. Here's an example of what kind of hierarchy you can have:

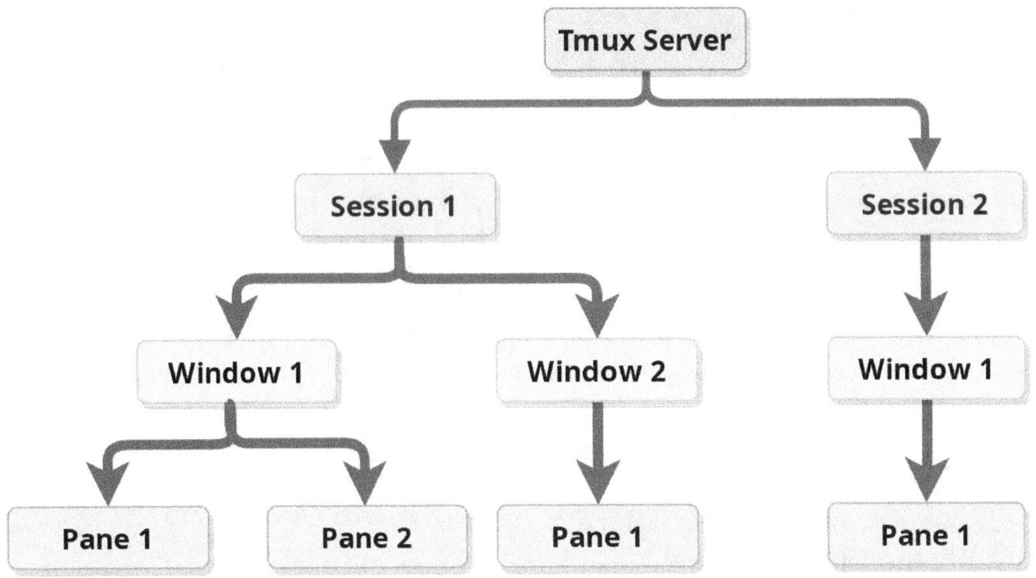

When you launch tmux, it will create a *tmux-server*, a tmux session, a *window*, and a *pane*.

tmux Server

The tmux server manages every single tmux session. If you kill it, you also kill every session. You can try it by yourself with the command `tmux kill-server`.

Sessions

We mentioned this concept before. You can detach sessions from a client (often a terminal) and attach them back.

Windows

In tmux, a window represents the entire terminal. You can have multiple windows open in one session. Each of them are represented by a tab in the status bar at the bottom of the terminal.

Panes

You can split your windows in panes to have multiple ttys in one window. These panes are independent by default, but you can synchronize them if you want to.

tmux Workflow

tmux Keystrokes

Like i3 or Neovim, tmux needs a way to separate its own shortcuts with the CLIs's shortcuts running in the different panes. If you run Neovim in tmux, the keystrokes you use in the first should be different from the ones you use in the second, or they will conflict with each other.

That's why most of the keystrokes in tmux need to be done *after* entering a prefix key. As we saw already in the previous chapter, it's a bit like having a namespace for your keystrokes.

The tmux's prefix key is `CTRL+b` by default. Let's try it:

1. Go back to a tmux session and press `CTRL+b`.
2. Hit the double quote key `"`.

Congratulation! You just opened a new pane. You can close it by simply typing `exit` (or hitting `CTRL-d`). If you think that this prefix key is awkward and difficult to remember, no worries: we'll change it later.

Command Prompt

You can execute special tmux commands via a command prompt:

1. Hit the prefix key `ctrl+b`
2. Hit `:`
3. Look at the bottom of the terminal: welcome to the command prompt! Now, type `split-window` and press `ENTER` . You've just created another pane.

Managing tmux Sessions

Here are the most useful tmux commands to manage your sessions:

- `tmux list-sessions` - List the tmux sessions open.
- `tmux attach-session -t <session_name>` - Attach the session named "" to a client (often a terminal).
- `tmux new-session -s <session_name>` - Create a new session named "".
- `tmux kill-session -t <session_name>` - Kill the session named "".
- `tmux kill-server` - Kill the tmux server and, as a result, every session.

I would advise you to create aliases into your file `$DOTFILES/zsh/aliases` to shorten these commands a bit. For example, instead of typing `tmux attach-session -t` , you could create an alias `tmuxa` . If you use a tool to automate the creation of your sessions, like tmuxp, you will barely use these commands anyway. More on that later!

Configuring tmux

Let's now configure tmux. We need to create a new configuration file with this command:

```
mkdir $DOTFILES/tmux && touch $DOTFILES/tmux/tmux.conf
```

As usual, let's add a symlink in `$DOTFILES/install.sh` :

```
########
# tmux #
########

mkdir -p "$XDG_CONFIG_HOME/tmux"
ln -sf "$DOTFILES/tmux/tmux.conf" "$XDG_CONFIG_HOME/tmux/tmux.conf"
```

You know what to do next: run the script and verify that everything worked as expected.

The Essentials of tmux

Changing the Default Prefix Key

The default prefix key CTRL+b is not very easy to type or to remember. I prefer using CTRL+SPACE ; it works nicely with Neovim's leader key, SPACE .

Let's add the following in our file $DOTFILES/tmux/tmux.conf :

```
unbind C-b
set -g prefix C-Space
set -g default-terminal "rxvt-256color";
```

The flag -g stands for g lobal: this means that this prefix key will be set for every session, window, and pane in tmux. You could set the option only for a specific window, for example directly in the command prompt using set -w prefix C-Space . It can be useful if you want to try multiple prefix keys on the fly.

Only add set -g default-terminal "rxvt-256color"; if you use URxvt as terminal emulator.

Reloading tmux Config File

Each time you change your config file, you need to reload it in tmux to apply the changes. Let's set a keystroke to reload it easily:

```
unbind r
bind r source-file $XDG_CONFIG_HOME/tmux/tmux.conf \; display
 ↪ "Reloaded tmux conf"
```

Here, we have two commands combined into one, on the second line:

1. We bind the key `r` to reload the config file.
2. We display a message when we hit `PREFIX+r` .

I'll use the notation `PREFIX` in this chapter when referring to the tmux prefix key.

Next, let's kill every possible tmux session with the command `tmux kill-server` . Then, run `tmux` again and, if you hit `PREFIX r` , you'll normally see the message `Reloaded tmux conf` appearing quickly at the bottom of your tmux session.

Now, to apply any change you make in tmux's configuration file, you'll need to reload it with this keystroke. Some changes might not be applied even if you do; in that case, you have no other choice than killing the tmux server with `tmux kill-server` and running `tmux` again.

Mouse Mode

If you want to use your mouse at the beginning because you're afraid to only use your keyboard, you can definitely do so. Enabling the mouse allows you to use it for:

- Selecting panes.
- Selecting windows (via the status line).
- Resizing panes.
- Scrolling windows.
- Copying text.

To enable all of that, add to the configuration file:

```
set -g mouse on
```

Additionally, you can display a menu when you use the right button of your mouse. This option doesn't forbid you to only use the keyboard, that's why I like to keep it on.

Splitting Windows in Panes

One of the most common operation you'll do in tmux is splitting a window into multiple panes. Let's add some useful keystrokes in our config to do exactly that:

```
# v and h are not binded by default, but we never know in the next
  ↳ versions...
unbind v
unbind h

unbind % # Split vertically
unbind '"' # Split horizontally
bind v split-window -h -c "#{pane_current_path}"
bind h split-window -v -c "#{pane_current_path}"
```

You might think that something is reversed here, between my keystroke v (for vertical) and the tmux flag -h (for horizontal). Well, it's complicated[1].

The flag -c executes a shell command, and #{pane_current_path} sets the same working directory for the pane you were in and the new one.

You could also change Neovim's configuration to be able to split your windows horizontally in Neovim with the keystroke CTRL+w h instead of CTRL+w s to keep some consistency. If you want to do so, just add the following in $DOTFILES/nvim/init.vim :

```
nnoremap <c-w>h <c-w>s
```

Resizing Panes

You can resize the panes with the keystroke PREFIX ALT+ARROW KEY .

Navigating Panes

To navigate from pane to pane, you can use the keystroke PREFIX ARROW KEY by default. Since I'm doing that very often, I don't use the tmux prefix key for these bindings.

Let's ditch the arrow keys in favor of our good old friends hjkl , to stay consistent with i3 and Neovim keystrokes:

---

[1] https://github.com/tmux/tmux/issues/213

```
bind -n C-h select-pane -L
bind -n C-j select-pane -D
bind -n C-k select-pane -U
bind -n C-1 select-pane -R
```

The flag `-n` disable the prefix key for these bindings.

We'll see later that we can even use these keystrokes to jump seamlessly between Neovim windows and tmux panes.

That's great, but we've got a problem now: we can't use `CTRL+1` to clean our shell anymore. We need to configure another keystroke for this task.

To do so, add the following to your file `$DOTFILES/zsh/.zshrc` :

```
bindkey -r '^l'
bindkey -r '^g'
bindkey -s '^g' clear-screen
```

These lines will unbind the keystroke `CTRL+1` and rebind the keystroke `CTRL+g` to clear the shell. It takes a bit of practice to get used to it, but nothing bad.

Increasing The Maximum Output Lines

One of the functionalities I love in tmux is being able to have thousands of output lines. Let's add the following to `$XDG_CONFIG_HOME/tmux/tmux.conf` :

```
set -g history-limit 10000
```

You can then do some search on the output of past commands directly in tmux. It's very easy if you use the search plugins I'll discuss below.

Managing Windows

Let's now modify the vanilla keystrokes to create a new window and to rename an existing one. Let's add the following in our configuration file:

```
unbind n  #DEFAULT KEY: Move to next window
unbind w  #DEFAULT KEY: change current window interactively

bind n command-prompt "rename-window '%%'"
bind w new-window -c "#{pane_current_path}"
```

After reloading the file you'll be able to use `PREFIX w` to create a new window and `PREFIX n` to rename the current window.

If you look at the bottom of your tmux session, you'll see a status bar and one (or multiple) tab(s) on the left. Each tab represents one window. You can select the windows open with the keystroke `PREFIX <number>`, with `<number>` being the window's number you want to display.

You can see that a little star in the window's tab indicates what window is currently displayed in your terminal. If you think that it's not visible enough, I totally agree. We'll improve the status bar later.

You can also see that the windows' numbers begin with 0. It's more practical, however, to set it to 1 instead. To stay consistent, let's do the same with the pane numbers by adding in the config:

```
set -g base-index 1
set-window-option -g pane-base-index 1
```

You might think it's annoying to hit the keystroke `PREFIX <number>` to change windows, and I agree with you. Let's add keystrokes to go through each of the open windows more easily. Just add the following to the tmux's config file:

```
bind -n M-j previous-window
bind -n M-k next-window
```

With these keystrokes, we can go through our windows with `ALT+k` and `ALT+j`. Again, these keystrokes don't use the prefix key, so be careful not to bind them in any other CLI.

Copy Mode

Like Neovim, tmux has modes:

- The default mode.
- The copy mode.

The default mode is equivalent to the INSERT mode in Neovim. Speaking about Neovim, we can set the Vi mode in our configuration file as follows:

```
set-window-option -g mode-keys vi
```

Now, let's try the copy mode! Hit `PREFIX+[` . To go back to the default mode, you need to hit `q` .

You can see that you're in copy mode thanks to the two numbers on the top right corner of your pane. The number on the left indicate the total number of lines which are below the visible output, and the one on the right how many lines are above.

From there, you can use the vanilla Neovim keystrokes to navigate your current terminal output. For example:

- `Ctrl-u` – Scroll up.
- `Ctrl-d` – Scroll down.
- `/` – Search.

Unsurprisingly, you can use copy mode to copy some content from your terminal. If you tried to copy terminal outputs already from tmux with your mouse, you might have been confused: it doesn't really work. Indeed, tmux by default doesn't copy anything in your system clipboard, but it uses one of its *paste buffer*. But, for convenience, I like to use the system clipboard directly when I copy something from the terminal.

Let's now configure exactly that by adding the following in our tmux configuration file:

```
unbind -T copy-mode-vi Space; #Default for begin-selection
unbind -T copy-mode-vi Enter; #Default for copy-selection

bind -T copy-mode-vi v send-keys -X begin-selection
bind -T copy-mode-vi y send-keys -X copy-pipe-and-cancel "xsel
  ↪  --clipboard"
```

To stay consistent with Neovim's keystrokes, we did the following:

1. Changing the keystroke to select text from the default SPACE to v (for v isual).
2. Changing the keystroke to copy the selected text from the default ENTER to y (for y ank).

Then, we pipe the action to `xsel` , to copy the selection to the system clipboard.

Be aware that you can past what's in the tmux `paste buffer` , by using `PREFIX+]` , if you don't want to use the system clipboard directly.

And voila! Now, copy and pasting in tmux will normally work like a charm. You can also copy using the mouse: select what you want and hit y without releasing the left button. If you release it, the selection will disappear before you had the chance to copy it.

Symbiosis Between tmux and Neovim

There are some additional configurations you need to make for tmux to work seamlessly with Neovim. First, if you use Neovim in tmux, you might experience a cursor problem: it doesn't change from rectangle to pipe when you go from Normal Mode to Insert Mode.

Adding this line in $DOTFILES/tmux/tmux.conf will help:

```
set -g -a terminal-overrides ',*:Ss=\E[%p1%d q:Se=\E[2 q'
```

It would also be nice to navigate between Neovim's windows and tmux's panes with the same keystroke. To do so, let's add the following in our tmux.conf file:

```
# Smart pane switching with awareness of Vim splits.
# See: https://github.com/christoomey/vim-tmux-navigator

is_vim="ps -o state= -o comm= -t '#{pane_tty}' \
    | grep -iqE '^[^TXZ ]+ +(\\S+\\/)?g?(view|n?vim?x?)(diff)?$'"
bind -n C-h if-shell "$is_vim" "send-keys C-h"  "select-pane -L"
bind -n C-j if-shell "$is_vim" "send-keys C-j"  "select-pane -D"
bind -n C-k if-shell "$is_vim" "send-keys C-k"  "select-pane -U"
bind -n C-l if-shell "$is_vim" "send-keys C-l"  "select-pane -R"
bind -n C-\\ if-shell "$is_vim" "send-keys C-\\" "select-pane -l"
```

You'll also need to install the Neovim plugin christoomey/vim-tmux-navigator for everything to work as expected.

Design

It's time to improve the colors and look of tmux. I won't copy all the configuration for the design here, but you'll find it in the mouseless book companion[1].

When you're done, restart the tmux server with the command:

---

[1] https://raw.githubusercontent.com/Phantas0s/mouseless-book-companion/master/part_II/11_tmux/dotfiles/tmux/tmux.conf

216

```
tmux kill-server && tmux
```

Now, you can enjoy the beauty. If you don't like it (I would definitely understand that), you can change the colors easily; they match the colors you've defined already in `$DOTFILES/X11/.Xresources` .

Plugins

Even if we made tmux pretty and more consistent with the other tools, we can improve it even more by adding some useful plugins.

The tmux Plugins Manager

To manage our tmux plugins, we need the tmux plugin manager. Let's first clone the project with Git:

```
git clone https://github.com/tmux-plugins/tpm \
$XDG_CONFIG_HOME/tmux/plugins/tpm
```

Then, let's add the following line in our tmux config:

```
set -g @plugin 'tmux-plugins/tpm'
```

With this line, we install the plugin `tpm` , for t mux p lugin m anager. Finally, let's add the following line **at the very end** of the config file:

```
run -b "$XDG_CONFIG_HOME/tmux/plugins/tpm/tpm"
```

As always, reload your tmux config with `PREFIX r` . Each time you add a new plugin to your configuration, You need to hit `PREFIX SHIFT+I` . Let's do exactly that.

A message will appear, saying that you can continue with `ENTER` , but you really need to hit `q` .

It's time now to modify our install script `$DOTFILES/install.sh` to automatically download the tmux plugin manager if it's not already on the system:

```
[ ! -d "$XDG_CONFIG_HOME/tmux/plugins/tpm" ] \
&& git clone https://github.com/tmux-plugins/tpm \
"$XDG_CONFIG_HOME/tmux/plugins/tpm"
```

Next step: installing some nice tmux plugins to make it even better!

A Better Search With CopyCat

As we saw, tmux copy mode allows you to search in the output of the current pane. But if you want advanced search capabilities, you can try tmux copycat[1]. Here's the superpower you'll gain:

- You won't need to be in copy mode to search for something.
- You'll be able to search using regex patterns or plain strings.
- You'll have new keystrokes to automatically select filepaths, Git status output, urls, and IP addresses, from any output. You can then copy them easily.
- The search result will be automatically selected. You can yank it (copy it) directly with the `y` keystroke we configured above.

Like in Neovim, you can use `n` and `N` to jump to the next or previous result, respectively. To install copycat, copy this line to your `tmux.conf` file:

```
set -g @plugin 'tmux-plugins/tmux-copycat'
```

You then need to reload your tmux config and hit `PREFIX SHIFT+I` to install copycat.

To use it, you need to kill the tmux server with the command `tmux kill-server` (all your sessions will be lost!) and relaunch `tmux`.

Then, simply hit `PREFIX /` to search in your shell output. You'll see at the bottom of your session that copycap is indeed working.

Fuzzy Search And Copy with fzf and Extrakto

Extrakto allows you to search for some content in your pane using `fzf`. Let's add the following in our configuration file:

```
set -g @plugin 'laktak/extrakto'
```

---

[1] https://github.com/tmux-plugins/tmux-copycat

Again, reload your tmux configuration and hit `PREFIX SHIFT+I` to install the new plugin. To use extrakto, kill the tmux server and relaunch it.

You can now fuzzy search for the output of your terminal using `PREFIX TAB`. Select what you want and press `ENTER` to copy the search in your system clipboard.

Creating tmux Sessions Automatically

The power of tmux doesn't stop here. The CLI tmuxp allows you to automate the creation of tmux sessions via YAML (or JSON) config files. You can automate almost everything, from the number of windows and panes you want to the commands to run in each pane.

```
sudo pacman -S tmuxp
```

To try it, we first need to create a configuration describing what we want in our tmux session. Let's run the following command first:

```
mkdir "$XDG_CONFIG_HOME/tmuxp"
nvim "$XDG_CONFIG_HOME/tmuxp/dotfiles.yml"
```

Then, let's add these lines in the file `$XDG_CONFIG_HOME/tmuxp/dotfiles.yml` :

```
session_name: dotfiles
start_directory: $HOME/dotfiles

windows:
  - window_name: nvim dotfiles
    layout: tiled
    panes:
      - nvim +FZF
  - window_name: terms
    layout: tiled
    panes:
      -
      - ls -lah
      -
```

This configuration sets up a session with 2 windows. The first contains one pane, the second three. Neovim will run in the first window called `nvim dotfiles`. In the second window called `terms`, three panes will be set, and the command `ls -lah` will run in one of them.

This is just an example: you can configure your tmux sessions in a more granular way if you want.

You could add the file we've just created directly in your dotfiles project, create a symlink as we did many times before (in the file `$DOTFILES/install.sh`), and sync everything with Git. But keep in mind that it will become public. It's fine if you don't have any passwords or sensitive data in there; otherwise, don't do it!

To try your tmuxp configuration, execute the following command in a terminal without tmux:

```
tmuxp load dotfiles
```

It should create a tmux session called "dotfiles", two windows and the different panes we described above.

i3 Scratchpad Running tmux

I don't know if you remember, but we added the following lines in our i3 config file `$DOTFILES/i3/config` when we configured our tiling window manager:

```
# Terminal scratchpad
for_window [instance="urxvt_scratchpad"] move to scratchpad, border
  ↵   none
bindsym $mod+Shift+t [instance="urxvt_scratchpad"] scratchpad show
exec urxvtc -name urxvt_scratchpad
```

With this configuration you can toggle a magical terminal with the keystroke `$mod+SHIFT+t`. It would be even better if we could automatically have tmux running in this terminal! We can make this wish comes true: replace the lines above with the following ones in the file `$DOTFILES/i3/config`:

```
# Terminal scratchpad with tmux and two windows: 1.Terminal |
  ↵   2.Neovim temp file
for_window [instance="urxvt_scratchpad"] move to scratchpad, border
  ↵   none
bindsym $mod+Shift+t [instance="urxvt_scratchpad"] scratchpad show
exec urxvtc -name urxvt_scratchpad \
-e tmux new-session -d -s scratchpad \; \
new-window -n vim 'nvim +e /tmp/nvim-tmp.md' \; \
attach-session -d -t scratchpad
```

Let's explain this gibberish:

- `tmux new-session -d -s scratchpad` – Create a new tmux session.

    - `-d` – Doesn't attach the session to the current terminal.
    - `-s scratchpad` – The tmux session is named `scratchpad`.

- `new-window -n nvim 'nvim +e /tmp/nvim-tmp.md'` – Create a new tmux window.

    - `-n nvim` – The window is called `nvim`.
    - `nvim +e /tmp/nvim-tmp.md` – Create the file `/tmp/nvim-tmp.md` (if it doesn't exist yet) and edit it with Neovim. Practical to have a quick access to Neovim at all times!

- `attach-session -d -t scratchpad` – Create a new client in the current terminal and attach a tmux session to it.

    - `-d` – Detach the session to other possible attached clients.
    - `-t scratchpad` – Attach the session named `scratchpad`.

The semi-colon `;` is used to execute multiple tmux commands on one line; here `new-session`, `new-window` and `attach-session`. Since `;` has another meaning for the shell interpreter, we need to escape it with a backslash `\`.

I could have used a tmuxp layout here, but it was to show you that it's possible to automate your tmux sessions without using any other external tool. It's quite cumbersome but it works.

As always, feel free to experiment with that by adding or modifying some options depending on what you want.

Choosing Your tmux Session With fzf

Now, let's imagine that you love creating tmuxp layout files. You're creating more and more of them, and soon there are so many you forgot how you named them. If you don't have their names, you can't use them.

To solve this problem, I've written a script which allows you to choose what you want to do: running a new tmux session, not running tmux at all, or using a specific layout file with tmuxp.

You can add the following in the file `$DOTFILES/zsh/scripts.sh`:

```
ftmuxp() {
    if [[ -n $TMUX ]]; then
        return
    fi

    # get the IDs
    ID="$(ls $XDG_CONFIG_HOME/tmuxp | sed -e 's/\.yml$//')"
    if [[ -z "$ID" ]]; then
        tmux new-session
    fi

    create_new_session="Create New Session"

    ID="${create_new_session}\n$ID"
    ID="$(echo $ID | fzf | cut -d: -f1)"

    if [[ "$ID" = "${create_new_session}" ]]; then
        tmux new-session
    elif [[ -n "$ID" ]]; then
        # Rename the current urxvt tab to session name
        printf '\033]777;tabbedx;set_tab_name;%s\007' "$ID"
        tmuxp load "$ID"
    fi
}
```

I won't go into the details here. You'll normally be able to understand this script after finishing part III of the book.

Now, source the file in your shell (or open a new one) and try to run `ftmuxp` *outside* a tmux session. You can create a new tmux session with the option `Create New Session`. If you don't want any tmux session, simply hit `ESC`.

Note that the line `printf '\033]777;tabbedx;set_tab_name;%s\007' "$ID"` is only useful if you use tabs for URxvt, something you might have installed in a previous chapter. It automatically renames the tab according to the name of the tmuxp's layout you've chosen.

If you want to run this function each time you open a new terminal, simply add the following to your file `$DOTFILES/zsh/.zshrc`, after the command which sources your scripts:

```
ftmuxp
```

Magic!

In a nutshell

What did we learn in this chapter?

- A tmux server manages all your tmux sessions. These sessions include windows and panes.
- You can configure tmux depending on your own workflow, needs and personality.
- Almost every tmux keystroke includes the prefix key. It's easier to remember and doesn't conflict with other keystrokes from other CLIs.
- You can enhance tmux even further with useful plugins.

The next chapter quickly describes what Neovim plugins I use to have a fantastic experience in the editor.

Going Deeper

- Arch Wiki - tmux[1]
- tmux repository[2]
- tmux plugins repository[3]

---

[1] https://wiki.archlinux.org/index.php/Tmux

[2] https://github.com/tmux/tmux

[3] https://github.com/tmux-plugins

Neovim Plugins

A choice is now given to you, mouseless adventurer: you can dive into this chapter and begin to enter the wonderful world of plugins for Neovim, or you can skip it and continue to part III to build an installer for your new system.

In this chapter, I'll briefly describe the plugins for Neovim I'm using. I encourage you to look at my dotfiles on Github[1], and more precisely:

- The file init.vim[2] to find the plugins I'm using and the options I've set.
- The different config files I have for each plugin I use[3]. If you're interested in some of my configuration, copy it directly in your file `$DOTFILES/nvim/init.vim`.

In the companion of this book[4], you'll find a basic Neovim configuration with a couple of plugins configured, including coc.nvim and Neomake. It's a good start if you want to make an IDE out of Neovim, and it will help you debug your bash scripts when you'll be ready for the part III of this book.

I would recommend you to make sure that you understand what you're copying from any external dotfiles you'll find. Also, make sure that you really need it. Otherwise, you'll have a hard time understanding what your system can do for you, and modifying your dotfiles later will be more challenging than it should be.

That's why I spend time explaining the pieces of configuration we've added to our system throughout the book.

The Language Server Protocol

A developer expects many functionalities in a modern editor (or IDE), like auto-completion with documentation, go to definition, or automatic refactoring. To implement these functionalities, many editors out there use the Language Service Protocol, or LSP. We're coming back to the client server paradigm we've encountered numerous times in this book:

1. A client (the editor) communicate with a language server you need to install beforehand.

---

[1] https://github.com/Phantas0s/.dotfiles

[2] https://github.com/Phantas0s/.dotfiles/blob/master/nvim/init.vim

[3] https://github.com/Phantas0s/.dotfiles/tree/master/nvim/pluggedconf

[4] https://raw.githubusercontent.com/Phantas0s/mouseless-book-companion/master/part_II/12_neovim_plugins/dotfiles/nvim/init.vim

2. The server gives back to the editor everything it needs for nice IDE-like functionalities to work.

The Plugin coc.nvim

Neovim's core team is developing a native solution[1] to communicate with language servers at the time I'm writing these lines. But this functionality is not yet officially released, so I prefer relying on the plugin coc.nvim[2] to communicate to these language servers for now.

This plugin will be our client. What else do we need to do?

1. Install `nodejs` and `yarn` for coc.nvim to work. Both are available in the Arch Linux official repositories.
2. Install a language server itself, often specific to a programming language. You'll find many of them on the Github page of coc.nvim[3]. Since we're using Arch Linux, they'll very often be available in the official repositories or in the AUR.
3. Configure coc.nvim for it to know what language server you want to use for what language, and how. Again, I provided an example in the companion of this book[4].

If everything is correctly configured, you'll have access to many new functionalities depending on what the language server provides. Neovim will feel like a real IDE!

Extensions to coc.nvim

You can also install extensions to coc.nvim to communicate with precise language servers without the need to configure them manually in our JSON file `coc-settings.json`. For example, you can add the following in your file `$DOTFILES/nvim/init.vim`:

```
let g:coc_global_extensions = [
    \ 'coc-snippets',
    \]
```

---

[1] https://neovim.io/doc/user/lsp.html

[2] https://github.com/neoclide/coc.nvim

[3] https://github.com/neoclide/coc.nvim

[4] https://github.com/Phantas0s/mouseless-book-companion/blob/master/part_II/12_neovim_plugins/dotfiles/nvim/coc-settings.json

The next time you'll launch Neovim, this piece of configuration will automatically download the plugin `coc-snippet` . Coupled with the plugin honza/vim-snippet[1], it will allow you to auto-complete code snippets for many languages.

- coc.nvim[2]

tmux completion

You can install the plugin `tmux-complete.vim` to auto-complete anything in Neovim from your tmux session (commands, output, filepaths, and whatnot). It works out of the box if you've configured coc.nvim already.

- tmux-complete.vim[3]

Fuzzy Finder in Neovim With fzf

We've already installed fzf in a previous chapter. You can also install fzf.vim, a plugin allowing you to use it in Neovim.

Here are some commands I use very often:

- `:Files` - Search recursively for a file in your working directory.
- `:History` - Search the history of open files.
- `:Buffers` - Search through your open buffers.

You can even combine ripgrep with fzf to parse your files and find any pattern you want in your working directory and all its sub-directories.

- fzf.vim[4]

Navigating files

As we just saw, the plugin fzf.vim allows you to navigate easily through your files. But if you want to see your filesystem in a tree, you can use the built-in `netrw` . You can launch it with `:Explore` , `:Lexplore` , or `Hexplore` .

---

[1] https://github.com/honza/vim-snippets

[2] https://github.com/neoclide/coc.nvim

[3] https://github.com/wellle/tmux-complete.vim

[4] https://github.com/junegunn/fzf.vim

If you don't like it, you can use the plugin NERDTree instead. There are many other alternatives: coc-explorer, chadtree, nvim-tree.lua, or fern.vim. The choice is yours!

- nerdtree[1]
- coc-explorer[2] (coc.nvim plugin)
- chadtree[3]
- nvim-tree.lua[4]
- fern.vim[5]

Linter

How would our coding lives be without a good linter? Full of failures and disappointments, I'm afraid. You could alternatively use coc.nvim, but I prefer the Neomake plugin.

You remember the paradigm client server? Well, Neomake acts as a client to different linters that you need to install manually, a bit like coc.nvim act as a client to many language servers that you need to install manually.

Many Vim and Neovim users use Ale instead of Neomake. Again, it's a question of preference.

Neomake is not just a linter; in fact, it's a plugin which allows you to run programs asynchronously.

- Neomake[6]
- Ale[7]

Surrounding

It's often useful to be able to surround some text with special characters. For example, if you want to surround a couple of words with parenthesis, you can do it easily with the plugin vim-sandwich.

---

[1] https://github.com/scrooloose/nerdtree

[2] https://github.com/weirongxu/coc-explorer

[3] https://github.com/ms-jpq/chadtree

[4] https://github.com/kyazdani42/nvim-tree.lua

[5] https://github.com/lambdalisue/fern.vim

[6] https://github.com/neomake/neomake

[7] https://github.com/dense-analysis/ale

Everybody else uses vim-surround but I think vim-sandwich has better defaults.

- vim-sandwich[1]
- vim-surround[2]

Navigating in Open Buffers

Many plugins out there will allow you to modify the way that you can move your cursor in an open buffer. We saw already that Neovim offers many keystrokes to do that natively, so I don't feel the need to add any plugin on top. There is one exception: when using `f`, `F`, `t` or `T` in NORMAL mode, vim-snipe allows you to choose exactly where you want to land.

There is another plugin working similarly, but way more powerful: vim-easymotion. My brain doesn't like it, but I know that many people are happy with it.

If you're a fan of vim-easymotion, you'll be delighted to learn that there exists a similar plugin for tmux[3] that allows you to do rougly the same... but in tmux!

- vim-snipe[4]
- vim-easymotion[5]

Text Objects

What about adding new text objects? This is exactly what targets.vim does. For example, you'll be able to change text between commas with the keystroke `ci,` in NORMAL mode. Handy!

- targets.vim[6]

---

[1] https://github.com/machakann/vim-sandwich

[2] https://github.com/tpope/vim-surround

[3] https://github.com/schasse/tmux-jump

[4] https://github.com/yangmillstheory/vim-snipe

[5] https://github.com/easymotion/vim-easymotion

[6] https://github.com/wellle/targets.vim

Register History

The nvim-miniyank plugin will create a yank history that you can go through with whatever keystroke you want. I find it very useful. There are many alternatives to this one too.

- nvim-miniyank[1]
- Yoink.vim[2]
- vim-easyclip[3]

Snippets

Having a set of snippets for the most common programming languages will save you some precious time. The plugin vim-snippets will add them to Neovim. You can then use coc.nvim and its extension coc.snippets to auto-complete them.

If you don't want to use coc.nvim for your snippets, you can instead use the UltiSnips plugin.

- vim-snippets[4]
- UltiSnips[5]

Search And Replace

What about searching and replacing some text recursively in your working directory? That's what quickfix-reflector allows you to do.

You can also use coc.nvim for that, with the command `:CocSearch`. It will open a buffer with all the search results. You can modify them and save the buffer to apply the modifications to the different files.

Another good alternative: a plugin called ferret.

- Quickfix Reflector[6]
- ferret[7]

---

[1] https://github.com/bfredl/nvim-miniyank

[2] https://github.com/svermeulen/vim-yoink

[3] https://github.com/svermeulen/vim-easyclip

[4] https://github.com/honza/vim-snippets

[5] https://github.com/sirver/UltiSnips

[6] https://github.com/stefandtw/quickfix-reflector.vim

[7] https://github.com/wincent/ferret

Status Bar

Do you like the status bar of Neovim? If you don't, you can replace it with plugins like lightline or vim-airline. You can also find countless tutorials on the Awesome Internet to build your own.

- lightline[1]
- vim-airline[2]

Color Scheme

I like to have more or less the same colors for basically everything I'm running on my system. That's why I've decided to write, step by step, my own color scheme for Neovim.

I would understand if you don't want to do that; it's not easy and it takes time. Instead, you can just pick one you like and simply install it. I put a few popular ones below, but there are many others if you take the time to search a bit.

- gruvbox[3]
- vim-colors-solarized[4]
- iceberg.vim[5]

Manual Pages In Neovim

What about opening your `man` pages in Neovim? This plugin is one of my personal favorites. It's so nice to have all of your Neovim keystrokes while consulting the manual!

To make it work, you'll need the plugin vim-superman. With it, you can open a man page with the following command:

```
nvim -c "SuperMan <the_man_page>"
```

---

[1] https://github.com/itchyny/lightline.vim

[2] https://github.com/vim-airline/vim-airline

[3] https://github.com/morhetz/gruvbox

[4] https://github.com/altercation/vim-colors-solarized

[5] https://cocopon.github.io/iceberg.vim/

For example, if I want to read the man page of the command `cp` , I can run `nvim -c "SuperMan cp"` .

To make it easier to use, you can add to `$DOTFILES/zsh/scripts.sh` the following:

```
vman() {
    nvim -c "SuperMan $*"

    if [ "$?" != "0" ]; then
        echo "No manual entry for $*"
    fi
}
```

Don't forget to source the file in your current shell to apply the changes, by running in your shell:

```
source $DOTFILES/zsh/scripts.sh
```

Opening a new shell will have the same effect.

You can then use the command `vman <section> <the_man_page>` to open any man page you want with Neovim! Like with `man` , the argument `<section>` is not mandatory.

- vim-superman[1]

The Undo-tree

We already saw the vim-mundo plugin in a previous chapter, but I also add it here for completeness. Did I mention that this plugin is awesome?

- vim-mundo[2]

Tmux

These three plugins are a must-have to make your experience with Neovim inside tmux even smoother.

---

[1] https://github.com/jez/vim-superman

[2] https://github.com/simnalamburt/vim-mundo

- vim-tmux[1]
- vim-tmux-focus-events[2]
- vim-tmux-navigator[3]

Startup

With the plugin vim-startify, you can personalize the content of the first window open in Neovim. I love it mostly because a cow will greet you with a nice quote, always related to programming. Who doesn't want a greeting cow?

- vim-startify[4]

Git

What about having some nice plugins to display information from Git? The plugin vim-fugitive will allow you to do exactly that. There are many plugins out there which extend its functionalities, too.

- vim-fugitive[5]
- gv.vim[6]
- git-messenger.vim[7]
- vim-gitgutter[8]

Syntax Highlighting

Neovim already has some functionalities built-in to enable syntax highlighting for many programming languages. Some plugins extend it for specific niches, like the config file for i3 or even systemd's config files.

- i3-vim-syntax[9]

---

[1] https://github.com/tmux-plugins/vim-tmux

[2] https://github.com/tmux-plugins/vim-tmux-focus-events

[3] https://github.com/christoomey/vim-tmux-navigator

[4] https://github.com/mhinz/vim-startify

[5] https://github.com/tpope/vim-fugitive

[6] https://github.com/junegunn/gv.vim

[7] https://github.com/rhysd/git-messenger.vim

[8] https://github.com/airblade/vim-gitgutter

[9] https://github.com/PotatoesMaster/i3-vim-syntax

- vim-systemd-syntax[1]
- vim-tmux-syntax[2]

Misc

Here's an assortment of miscellaneous plugins that you might find useful:

- vim-abolish[3] - Add... many things.
- vim-commentary[4] - Comment your code with a single keystroke. Supports many common programming languages out of the box.
- vim-highlightedyank[5] - Highlight briefly anything you yank.
- suda.vim[6] - Allow you to write a file if you forgot to use sudo when you opened it.
- vim-css-color[7] - Display the *approximate* color for any given hexadecimal notation.
- vim-matchup[8] - Extend the possibilities given by the keystroke % in NORMAL mode.
- auto-pairs[9] - Automatically close a bracket when you open it.
- vim-repeat[10] - Increase the power of the single repeat (the dot . in NORMAL mode).
- splitjoin.vim[11] - Allow you to split arrays or lists of arguments on multiple lines, or condense them on a single line. All of that can be done with one keystroke, and it supports many programming languages out of the box.

In a Nutshell

What did we learn in this chapter?

---

[1] https://github.com/wgwoods/vim-systemd-syntax

[2] https://github.com/whatyouhide/vim-tmux-syntax

[3] https://github.com/tpope/vim-abolish

[4] https://github.com/tpope/vim-commentary

[5] https://github.com/machakann/vim-highlightedyank

[6] https://github.com/lambdalisue/suda.vim

[7] https://github.com/ap/vim-css-color

[8] https://github.com/andymass/vim-matchup

[9] https://github.com/jiangmiao/auto-pairs

[10] https://github.com/tpope/vim-repeat

[11] https://github.com/AndrewRadev/splitjoin.vim

- You can add many plugins in Neovim. But they come at a cost: they might slow down Neovim's startup.
- Try to spend some time with vanilla Neovim before adding 3048309842 plug-ins.

In the next chapter, we'll explore solutions to go on The Great Internet while trying to use the keyboard as much as we can.

Going Deeper

- Vim Search, Find and Replace: a Detailed Guide[1]
- Vim for PHP: The Complete Guide for a Powerful PHP IDE[2]

---

[1] https://thevaluable.dev/vim-search-find-replace/
[2] https://thevaluable.dev/vim-php-ide/

Mouseless Browsers

We're now finding ourselves in slippery territory: browsing the web without using the mouse. Unfortunately, I haven't found any way to go through *every possible website* only using the keyboard. The solutions out there work most of the time, but if you're on a page relying heavily on JavaScript, for example, it might cause some problems.

In this chapter, we'll look at:

- Lynx, a text-based browser you can run in your shell.
- The fantastic Qutebrowser, a browser allowing you to browse with vim-like keystrokes.
- A list of plugins adding nice vim-like keystrokes for Firefox and Chrome (or Chromium).

Let's improve our virtual life by using more of the keyboard, less of the mouse!

Lynx

You thought that Internet Explorer was the oldest browser still actively developed and maintained? You were wrong. Lynx is the owner of the title. It's a text-based browser you can run in your shell. I use it mainly for websites where I don't necessarily need to look at images or videos, like Wikipedia for example.

I'm sure by now you have an idea how to install it.

You can use it as follows:

```
lynx <URL>
```

For example, if I want to go to Wikipedia, I can run `lynx https://en.wikipedia.org` in my terminal. If you run that in a shell, Lynx will ask you (in the status bar at the bottom) if you want to accept cookies: you can hit `SHIFT+a` for a lways. You can also use the argument `-accept_all_cookies` when launching Lynx if you're annoyed by this question.

Lynx can ask you more questions in the status bar when a choice needs to be made. This status bar will also display the different requests in progress and their responses. Below it, you've got some help you can disable in the options.

You can also scroll with the keys `jk` and use `h` to go to the previous page if you add the argument `-vikeys` when launching Lynx.

You can even add the following into your file `$DOTFILES/zsh/scripts.sh` if you wish:

```
wikipedia() {
    lynx -vikeys -accept_all_cookies
      ↳   "https://en.wikipedia.org/wiki?search=$@"
}

duckduckgo() {
    lynx -vikeys -accept_all_cookies
      ↳   "https://lite.duckduckgo.com/lite/?q='$@'"
}
```

You can then use the command `wikipedia <anything_you_like>` to directly search on Wikipedia, or `duckduckgo <search>` to search for anything you want.

Let's quickly review the basic keystrokes you can use in order to browse easily:

Help

- `?` – Display Lynx help.
- `K` – Display a list of keystrokes.

Navigation

- `jk` – Go up and down the page's links (only with the argument `-vikeys`).
- `h` – Go back to the previous page (only with the argument `-vikeys`).
- `1` or `ENTER` - Follow the link you're on.
- `space` or `+` – Scroll down to the next page.
- `-` – Scroll up to the previous page.
- `g` – Allows you to g o to another URL.
- `CTRL+g` – Abort the connection to a page.

You can also use `TAB` and `CTRL+TAB` instead of `j` and `k` to go through every link and form element of the page. This is useful if you're on an input text field, for example.

History

- `backspace` – Jump to your history.

Page Data

- `=` – Display information about the page, including its URL.
- `\` – Toggle between source code and rendered view.

Bookmarks

- `a` – Save a bookmark.
- `d` – Save a bookmark as `d` ocument.

Downloading

- `d` – Download the current link.

Options

- `o` – Configure Lynx.

Quitting Lynx

- `q` – Quit lynx. You'll need to hit `y` (or `q` again) to confirm.
- `Q` or `CTRL+D` – Quit lynx without confirmation.

Qutebrowser

Qutebrowser is a very nice browser that you can use with your keyboard. Again, I'm sure you'll find the way to install it.

Like many other plugins we'll see below, you can hit `f` in qutebrowser to go into "hint mode". From there, each interactive element (links, buttons, input fields, and whatnot) gets a combination of one or more letters displayed on top, in a wonderful yellow. From there, if you type one of these combinations, you'll interact with the corresponding element, exactly like if you clicked on it.

To escape this "hint mode", simply hit `ESC`.

It's one of those things you need to try to really understand how it works. You can also use `SHIFT+f` to open a new tab after choosing what you want to "click" on.

Here are some useful keystrokes you can use in Qutebrowser:

Basics

- o – Open URL and fuzzy find the history. You can navigate through the history with `TAB` and `CTRL+TAB` .
- go – Edit the current URL.
- gO – Same as go but in a new tab.
- yy – Copy the current URL into the clipboard.
- pp – Open a URL from the clipboard.
- Pp – Open a URL from the clipboard in a new tab.

Navigation

- k – Scroll up.
- j – Scroll down.
- CTRL+f – Page up (f orward).
- CTRL+b – Page down (b ackward).
- CTRL+u – Half page u p.
- CTRL+d – Half page d own.
- shift+g – Scroll to the very bottom of the page.
- gg – Scroll to the very top of the page.

Tabs

- CTRL+t – Open a new tab.
- K – Display the previous tab.
- J – Display the next tab.
- ALT+NUMBER or NUMBER SHIFT+t – Display a specific tab depending on NUM-BER.
- d – Close tab.

Modes

Like in Neovim, qutebrowser has different modes:

- v – Go to visual mode (to yank something from the page). Then, to select some text, hit v (or SHIFT+v).
- y – Yank (copy) the selected text.
- i – Go to insert mode when you need to fill some fields (input text fields or textareas, for example).

Browser Plugins

You can also install a plugin to Firefox or Chromium to add some vim-like keystrokes for a mouseless browser experience. These plugins work similarly to Qutebrowser: one key (often `f`) will allow you to switch to "hint mode". From there, you can type a combination of letters displayed on the screen to interact with anything you want.

There is a drawback to this approach, however: there is no "keystroke namespaces", so every keystrokes which are already used by your browser *and* your plugin will conflict.

In my experience, Qutebrowser works better in general than these plugins. That being said, I often need to access developer tools and Qutebrowser doesn't have any, so I often need to fall back to Firefox.

I won't describe every single plugin here. Using the usual Vim (or Neovim) keystrokes will often do the action you were expecting.

Firefox

- Vimium[1]
- Vim Vixen[2]
- Tridactyl[3]
- Saka Key[4]
- Surfingkeys[5]

Chrome

- Vimium[6]
- cVim[7]
- Saka Key[8]
- Surfingkeys[9]

---

[1] https://github.com/philc/vimium

[2] https://github.com/ueokande/vim-vixen

[3] https://github.com/tridactyl/tridactyl

[4] https://github.com/lusakasa/saka-key

[5] https://github.com/brookhong/Surfingkeys

[6] https://github.com/philc/vimium

[7] https://github.com/1995eaton/chromium-vim

[8] https://github.com/lusakasa/saka-key

[9] https://github.com/brookhong/Surfingkeys

In a Nutshell

What did we learn in this chapter?

- The solutions discussed in this chapter will allow you to browse most websites only using the keyboard, but not all.
- Lynx is a good solution if you want to browse websites in your comfy shell and if you don't care about images, videos, and other rich content.
- Qutebrowser is the best solution if you want to browse with Vim-like keystrokes.
- You can add existing plugins to Firefox or Chrome to be as mouseless as possible.

In part III we'll embark in another journey: creating bash scripts to install the whole Mouseless Development Environment on any computer you want in one command line.

Going Deeper

- Web Browsers – Arch wiki[1]
- Official Lynx website[2]
- Lynx user guide[3]
- Arch Wiki – Qutebrowser[4]
- Official Qutebrowser website[5]
- Qutebrowser cheatsheet[6]

---

[1] https://wiki.archlinux.org/index.php/List_of_applications/Internet#Web_browsers

[2] https://lynx.invisible-island.net

[3] http://condor.cc.ku.edu/~grobe/docs/Lynx_users_guide.html

[4] https://wiki.archlinux.org/index.php/Qutebrowser

[5] https://qutebrowser.org

[6] https://qutebrowser.org/img/cheatsheet-big.png

Part III - Building Your System Installer

The Installer

It's time for being proud of yourself.

You went from an empty hard disk to a nicely configured system you can modify for your own needs. You built, layer by layer, a Mouseless Development Environment. Congratulations! Go pour your favorite drink and take the time to appreciate how great you are.

But it's not over. Let's continue this adventure by creating a set of scripts to install your whole system (Arch Linux and all your software) in one command. I used these scripts successfully on a dozen PCs, and even on a Macbook Pro, without any problems.

But they're not perfect; they're not meant to be extremely flexible either. That said, they're good enough for our purpose. These last chapters will also be a good occasion to talk about the basics of shell scripting.

If you use tmux and Neovim to write these scripts, try to use the new functionalities we saw in the last chapters as much as you can. Practicing is the best way to memorize your new keystrokes and to find new ways to use your tools.

In this chapter, we'll see:

- How to use the CLI dialog.
- What the different output streams we can manipulate for a given process are.
- How to create variables and arrays in Bash scripts.
- How to use Awk and grep to get the output we want.

This chapter is full of information, which is especially useful if you don't have that much experience with the shell. Take your time, experiment with the commands, and try to understand as much as you can about what we're doing here.

If you're already a Shell Master, you can look directly at the book companion[1] to see the scripts we'll write[2] in these last chapters. Simply come back to the book if you don't understand them.

Enough mumbling. Let's go!

---

[1] https://github.com/Phantas0s/mouseless-book-companion

[2] https://github.com/Phantas0s/mouseless-book-companion/tree/master/part_III/05_user_installer/arch_installer

The Project

I like to have a sub-directory of my home directory where I put everything I build. I call this sub-directory "workspace". Let's create every file and directory we need for this chapter by running the following in the shell:

```
mkdir ~/workspace && ~/workspace/arch_installer
touch ~/workspace/arch_installer/install_sys.sh
cd ~/workspace/arch_installer
```

We'll version our installer using Git and push everything to GitHub, exactly like we did with our dotfiles repository.

First, let's create the repository `arch_installer` on GitHub[1]. Then, let's run the following commands:

```
git init
git remote add origin
    ↪  git@github.com:<your_github_user_name>/arch_installer.git
```

Don't forget to replace `<your_github_user_name>` with... your GitHub user name. While you're writing these glorious scripts, try to commit and push your work to GitHub as often as possible. It's a nice way to backup your progress in case you decide to throw your computer out the window.

Unfortunately, our install scripts will be difficult to test. There are frameworks out there meant to test Bash scripts, but our problem here is that we're doing many operations which have important side effects, like formatting a hard disk or creating a new user. You don't want to do that on your actual system!

As a result, I advise you to have two things open at all time:

- Neovim to write the scripts.
- A terminal running Bash (and not Zsh) to test *most* of the commands you'll write. I'll tell you what to test and what not to test throughout these chapters.

Running bash as a subshell is the easiest way you have to test your commands. Simply run `bash` in any other shell.

For this project, you could also set up a layout file for tmuxp. We saw tmuxp in a previous chapter.

Here's the layout you could create in `$XDG_CONFIG_HOME/tmuxp/arch_installer.yml` :

---

[1] https://github.com/

```
session_name: arch_installer
start_directory: $HOME/workspace/arch_installer

windows:
  - window_name: nvim
    layout: tiled
    panes:
      - nvim
  - window_name: terms
    layout: tiled
    panes:
      -
      - bash
```

The User Interface

Our installation scripts will provide limited flexibility: the user will be able to choose between different options or input text when it's needed. Consequently, we need some kind of interface: we'll use the CLI dialog which can display dialog boxes in a shell.

Let's install it on our system first:

```
sudo pacman -S dialog
```

Now, let's write the first lines of our script `install_sys.sh` :

```
#!/bin/bash

# Never run pacman -Sy on your system!
pacman -Sy dialog
```

We first download the databases of the official repositories with `pacman -Sy` before installing dialog. As we've seen in a previous chapter about package managers, using `pacman -Sy` is rarely a good idea. But here, on our Arch Linux live system, it's not a problem.

To see what dialog looks like, let's try to run the following in Bash:

```
dialog --defaultno --title "Arch Linux Install" --yesno \
"First line. \n\
Second line. \n\n\
Are you sure?" 15 60 || exit
```

You'll see a delightful and old-school dialog box pop up. This is a simple confirmation dialog, but there are many others we'll use. We'll see later how this dialog box works.

Preliminary Configuration

Is It the Good Time?

First, we need to ensure that our time is correct. Let's add the following in `install_sys.sh` :

```
timedatectl set-ntp true
```

Next!

Return Code and Operators

It's time to greet anybody using our script in the most friendly manner. Let's add the following in our file:

```
dialog --defaultno --title "Are you sure?" --yesno \
"This is my personnal arch linux install. \n\n\
It will DESTROY EVERYTHING on one of your hard disk. \n\n\
Don't say YES if you are not sure what you're doing! \n\n\
Do you want to continue?" 15 60 || exit
```

If you wonder what the character `\n` means, it's called a *control character*. It doesn't print anything. Instead, it moves output to the next line.

You can replace the text of the dialog box no matter what your imagination orders you to write. Let's briefly describe the options used:

- `--title` - Display the title of your choosing.
- `--yesno` - Specify the *type* of the dialog box. Here, we want a dialog box type `yesno` .

- `--defaultno` - The choice "No" is selected by default.

If you run the command `man dialog` in your terminal (or `vman dialog` *wink wink*), you'll see every type of dialog you can create near the top of the page. If you search for `--yesno` , you'll see every argument you can pass to this specific type of dialog (text, height and width). As a result, `15 60` represents the height and width of the dialog box, respectively. Using the manual as we just did is the best way to know which arguments you can give to a specific type of dialog box. It serves as a good example to show that the manual can give you precisely the information you want quickly, information for which you could otherwise search for hours on the Internet without any success.

If the user presses the button "Yes" or "No", the dialog box will return an *exit code*. Every command you run in a shell returns an exit code, and you can use it to know if your command succeeded or failed.

An exit code is always a number from 0 to 255, like the number of rubies you can have in the first Zelda game. I suppose they were using one byte to store it.

What do these numbers mean?

- 0 - The command succeeded. It's the equivalent of true. Is it confusing that 0 represents true? Definitely!
- Any other number from 1 to 255 - The command failed.

To see the return code of the last command you've run, you can look at the value of the special shell variable `$?` . For example, you can try this in a shell:

```
date
echo $?
```

The first command `date` was successful, so the second command will output `0` .

What about `|| exit` ? You can use common logical operators in Bash or Zsh, like `||` (the OR operator) and `&&` (the AND operator):

- `<expression_1> || <expression_2>` - If `<expression_1>` has `0` as its exit code, `<expression_2>` is not executed.
- `<expression_1> && <expression_2>` - If `<expression_1>` has something other than `0` as its exit code, `<expression_2>` is not executed.

To go back to our dialog box:

- If the button "Yes" is pressed, the dialog will return the exit code `0` .
- If `No` is pressed, it will return `1` .
- The operator OR `||` is used, so if `No` is pressed, `exit` is executed.

- If `exit` is executed, the subshell running the script is closed and the script stopped.

It might be a bit confusing if you're not used to these operators, but don't worry about it. You'll have your "Aha" moment at one point, I promise. You can also play with them in your shell to understand how they behave.

Output Redirection

Let's now ask what name the users of our script (likely our future selves) want for their new system. Let's add in our file the following:

```
dialog --no-cancel --inputbox "Enter a name for your computer." \
10 60 2> comp
```

Let's try this command in Bash. Looking at the options of the command, we can see that we have a dialog of type `--inputbox` this time. It normally has a cancel button, but we don't want the user to cancel; that's why we hide it with the option `--no-cancel`.

To understand what `2>` means, we need to talk about redirection again. This is a very important topic to understand.

We saw that a command always returns a *return code* or an *exit code*. It can also produce an output, but not always. When you type a command, the output is *redirected* to your current shell by default. For example, `echo "hello"` will output `hello` in your shell.

If you don't want to redirect the output to your shell, you can redirect it to somewhere else using `>`. This symbol will **redirect the standard output** of a given process. We've seen what a process is in a previous chapter, and we saw this idea of I/O redirection while installing Arch Linux in one of the first chapter of this book. The command `echo "hello" > comp` will create the file `comp` (or remove it first if it exists, then create a new one), and the output of your command will be redirected to this file.

In Linux-based systems, data (like output) travel from one point to another using *streams*. Streams are sequences of data made available over time, often created on the fly when you ask for the data. Normally, each process can use a total of 10 streams (from 0 to 9), and the streams 0, 1 and 2 are special:

- The standard input stream (stdin) has the file descriptor **0**.
- The standard output stream (stdout) has the file descriptor **1**.
- The standard error stream (stderr) has the file descriptor **2**.

These streams are represented by special files; to display them:

```
ls -lah /proc/$$/fd
```

What's a file descriptor? It's simply a number assigned by the kernel to an open file.

When we use `>` , we redirect the standard output stream of a process. We can choose what stream we want to redirect to by adding the file descriptor just before the redirect symbol `>` . For example, try to run the following in a terminal:

```
echo "Goblins are charming" > comp
echo "Goblins are charming" 1> comp
```

These two commands are identical: using `>` implies that you're using `1>` . If you want to redirect the standard error stream, you can use `2>` .

Most of the time, a command will output some data using the standard output stream when the command succeeds, and it will use the standard error stream when an error occurs. It allows you to redirect only the error messages of a command if you need to, or only the standard output, or both to different files. Welcome, flexibility, my old friend!

To experiment with that, we can try to run the following command:

```
cat thisfiledoesnotexist
```

The file doesn't exist, so an error will be output in your shell. Now, try:

```
cat thisfiledoesnotexist 2> test
```

Here, we redirect our standard error stream to the file `test` , so the error message is not output in our shell anymore. If you do `cat test` , you'll see the error message. You can delete the file `test` with the command `rm test` .

Back to our scripts, the CLI dialog uses a library called *ncurses* under the hood. It can draw in a terminal without the need to use X. To do so, the standard output stream is used to output the dialog box itself. Since this output stream is busy, what stream is used to output what the user types in the input box?

If you look again at the command we've written in our script to display the dialog box, you should now be able to answer this question.

Any idea?

Yes! The CLI dialog uses the standard error stream to return the content of the input field. We redirect this output into a new file called `comp` by doing `2> comp`. It's quite misleading since the content of the input field is not an error, but standard error and standard output streams work the same. It's not very elegant, I agree, but it works.

UEFI or BIOS, That Is The Question

You might remember that the installation process for Arch Linux is quite different depending on the firmware of your motherboard: `BIOS` or `UEFI`. We need to determine if the computer we're installing our system on uses one or the other.

Let's add this in our script:

```
# Verify boot (UEFI or BIOS)
uefi=0
ls /sys/firmware/efi/efivars 2> /dev/null && uefi=1
```

First, we initialize the variable `uefi` to `0`. The last line will output an error using the standard error stream if the directory `/sys/firmware/efi/efivars` doesn't exist, and return the exit code 1. If this is the case, the motherboard has a BIOS. If it does exist (and the command returns exit code 0), the expression on the right of the AND operator `&&` will be executed, and the value of `uefi` will change to `1`.

In short, if the computer has the UEFI, the variable `uefi` will be equal to `1`; otherwise, it will be equal to `0`.

What's `/dev/null`? It's a black hole in the center of your computer. Everything you redirect to `/dev/null` will be lost forever in the depth of space and time. The standard error stream of `ls` will output an error message we don't really care about, so we throw it away.

Choosing The Hard Disk

What about having a nice dialog box inviting you to choose the hard disk you want to wipe like a savage? We'll use this same hard disk afterward to install our system. We'll see many important concepts from the following lines, so be ready to dive a bit more into Bash scripting:

```
devices_list=($(lsblk -d | awk '{print "/dev/" $1 " " $4 " on"}' \
    | grep -E 'sd|hd|vd|nvme|mmcblk'))

dialog --title "Choose your hard drive" --no-cancel --radiolist \
"Where do you want to install your new system? \n\n\
Select with SPACE, valid with ENTER. \n\n\
WARNING: Everything will be DESTROYED on the hard disk!" \
15 60 4 "${devices_list[@]}" 2> hd


hd=$(cat hd) && rm hd
```

You can try to run these commands directly in Bash to be sure everything's working. Normally, if you run `echo $hd` after validating your choice, you'll see with delight the hard disk you've selected.

Don't be afraid to experiment with these commands to understand how it works, nothing will happen to your poor hard disk. I promise!

As you can see, we now create a type of dialog box called `radiolist`. If you search in the manual (`vman dialog`) for `--radiolist`, you'll see the following:

```
--radiolist text height width list-height  [ tag item status ] ...
```

The last argument is a string containing as many tags, items and statuses as we need, all separated with a space. What are they?

- The *tag* is an ID which differentiates each option. It has to be unique for each of them.
- The *item* is the description of the option.
- The *status* can be `on` or `off` ; the first means that the item is selected, the second means that it's not.

What should be the options for our list? Every hard disk of the computer we're installing the system on. This is the job of the first line of the code snippet. Let's see how it works.

Bash arrays

First, we need to speak about Bash arrays. An array, if you don't know, is a collection of values. In Bash, you can create an array like this:

```
my_array=(1 2 3 4)
```

If you then run `echo $my_array` , it will only output the first element. How do we get the other ones? You can use the *index* of the array for that. We could try the following:

```
echo "$my_array[0]"
echo "$my_array[1]"
```

In theory, the lines above should output the first and second element of the array. Like many other programming languages, the first index of an array is 0. However, if you run the two lines above, you'll end up with some weird output. For example, if you run `echo "$my_array[1]` , it will output `1[1]` . Why?

1. Bash will first interpret `$my_array` , which outputs 1 as we saw above.
2. Bash will think that `[1]` is a simple string; it will output it without interpreting it.

We wanted the value of the index 0 and 1, not this weird output. We need to be more explicit for Bash to interpret *the entire string* `$my_array[1]` as the variable we want to interpret, and not only `$my_array` . To do that, we need to use curly braces as follows:

```
echo "${my_array[1]}"
```

If you try to execute the command above in a Bash shell, the output will be `2` , which is indeed the value of the second element of the array. If you want to display all the values separated with a space, you can use `@` or `*` as follows:

```
echo "${my_array[@]}"
echo "${my_array[*]}"
```

Now, let's come back to this line:

```
devices_list=($(lsblk -d | awk '{print "/dev/" $1 " " $4 " on"}' \
    | grep -E 'sd|hd|vd|nvme|mmcblk'))
```

We saw earlier that we need to use parenthesis to declare an array, which means that mo matter the output of the command `$(lsblk ... 'sd|hd|vd|nvme|mmcblk')` , it will be put into an array and saved in the variable `device_list` .

Inside of the array, we execute a command using `$(<command>)` . We've seen this `$()` construct when we were configuring Zsh. The inside of `$()` will be executed as a command. Without it, Bash would consider it as a string. Then, the standard output of the command will be stored in an array.

Try to execute the command itself:

```
lsblk -d | awk '{print "/dev/" $1 " " $4 " off"}' \
    | grep -E 'sd|hd|vd|nvme|mmcblk'
```

On my computer, this command displays the hard disks I have. You should have something similar on your computer:

```
/dev/sda 465.8G on
/dev/sdb 3.6T on
```

If we look at the first line, the tag for our dialog box would be `/dev/sda` , the item `465.8G` , and the status `on` . The dialog box will output (using the standard error stream) every tag for every option selected separated with a space. The tag is also the name of the hard disk. We can use this name later to know which hard disk we should install Arch Linux on.

The item is just here to indicate to the user how much space there is on each hard disk.

The status looks a bit weird: we have a dialog of type radio button, and normally with this type of dialog you're only authorized to select one option. Yet, it seems that trying to select all of them with the status `on` works! By doing so, the dialog box will only select the first one by default; it looks ugly, but it works.

Let's now analyze the command itself.

Pipes

We saw pipes in a previous chapter. Consider what we have learned in this chapter about output streams (standard and error streams): the pipe redirects the standard output stream from the left side to the standard input stream on the right side.

Let's decompose the first part of our command:

1. `lsblk -d` will output every physical hard disk you have. The argument `-d` won't display the partitions. You can try to run it in Bash to understand what I mean.
2. From this output, we need to extract the information we need: the name and the size of each hard drive. We do that by sending the output of `lsblk` to the input of `awk` .

Awk

Awk is an amazing tool which can do a lot. Like A LOT, in uppercase, because it's a lot. To keep it very brief, it can process rows (lines) and columns of information. This command-line tool works line by line, like many others (grep, for example). Each column on each line is separated by one or more spaces.

That's great, because if you look at the output of `lsblk -d` , it's full of lines and columns. Output of CLIs are often formatted this way, which is why Awk is so damn useful.

The action `{print "/dev/" $1 " " $4 " off"}` is executed on each line of the output. It works like this:

- `$1` is replaced by the first column of the output, `$4` by the fourth column.
- Everything between double quotes is plain text.
- `print` will print the result.

If you run `lsblk -d | awk '{print "/dev/" $1 " " $4 " off"}'` in Bash, you'll end up with something like that:

```
/dev/NAME SIZE off
/dev/sda 465.8G off
/dev/sdb 3.7T off
```

The first line is garbage. We'll ditch it later. You can compare this output with the output of `lsblk -d` to really understand what Awk is doing.

Grep

We used grep before in this book, but let's explain a bit more about how it works here. Grep can filter output using regular expressions or plain text, line by line. Each time a match is found on a line, grep will output the whole line and continue till the end of the input is reached.

I would advise you to use the options `-F` if you want to use a plain text pattern, and `-P` if you want to use regular expressions. Without these options, it's easy to be confused about which metacharacters are available and which are not.

Here, we use the regular expression `sd|hd|vd|nvme|mmcblk` . You can think of `|` as a logical OR. In our case, this means that we want to match every line where one of the pattern `sd` , `hd` , `vd` , `nvme` or `mmcblk` is matched. These weird strings represent different type of hard disk devices you can have on your system.

Try to run the command:

```
lsblk -d | awk '{print "/dev/" $1 " " $4 " off"}' \
    | grep -E 'sd|hd|vd|nvme|mmcblk'
```

You'll see that the first line of our output is filtered out, because it doesn't match any of our patterns. On my system, the output looks like this:

```
/dev/sda 465.8G off
/dev/sdb 3.7T off
```

Hopefully, everything is becoming clear!

Putting Everything Together

Why do we need to put the above output in an array? Let's try to run the following in Bash:

```
devices_list=($(lsblk -d | awk '{print "/dev/" $1 " " $4 " on"}' \
    | grep -E 'sd|hd|vd|nvme|mmcblk'))

echo "${devices_list[@]}"
```

Here's the result of the echo command I've got on my computer:

```
/dev/sda 465.8G on /dev/sdb 3.6T on
```

Everything is now on one line. You don't necessarily need to use an array to do that, but I thought it would be a good occasion to explain what arrays are and how to use them.

This formatting is great because it's exactly how our dialog box expects the tags, items and statuses to be formatted.

Let's back up a bit and look at the whole block of instruction:

```
devices_list=($(lsblk -d | awk '{print "/dev/" $1 " " $4 " on"}' \
    | grep -E 'sd|hd|vd|nvme|mmcblk'))

dialog --title "Choose your hard drive" --no-cancel --radiolist \
"Where do you want to install your new system? \n\n\
Select with SPACE, valid with ENTER. \n\n\
WARNING: Everything will be DESTROYED on the hard disk!" \
15 60 4 "${devices_list[@]}" 2> hd


hd=$(cat hd) && rm hd
```

The two numbers `15` and `60` specify the height and the width of the dialog box, and `4` the height of the option list. When the user of our install script makes a choice, the tag will be returned again via the standard error stream. At that point, we save it into a file named `hd`.

Since it's easier to manipulate variables instead of files, we put the content of the file into the variable `hd` and we delete the file with the command `hd=$(cat hd) && rm hd`.

In a Nutshell

What did we learn in this chapter?

- Every command returns an exit code. The exit code `0` means that executing the command didn't return any error.
- There are three streams you'll often use in the shell: the standard input stream (0), the standard output stream (1), and the standard error stream (2).
- The CLI dialog allows you to create old school dialog boxes everybody loves. It has been scientifically proven.
- You can create variables and arrays in Bash: for example `my_var=0` or `my_array=(1 2 3 4)`.
- Using Awk allows you to manipulate rows and columns (separated with spaces by default) of a given input.
- The backslash `\` allows you to split a command across multiple lines that would otherwise be on one.
- Using grep allows you to filter lines of output using plain text (with the option `-F`) or regular expressions (with the option `-E`).

In the next chapter, we'll write more commands to partition your hard disk and install Arch Linux.

Going Deeper

- Official documentation of dialog[1]
- The Awk Manual[2]
- The GNU Awk User's Guide[3]

---

[1] https://invisible-island.net/dialog/#documentation

[2] https://www.cs.unibo.it/~renzo/doc/awk/nawkA4.pdf

[3] https://www.gnu.org/software/gawk/manual/gawk.html

Partitioning and Installing Arch Linux

We know what hard disk we should use to install our system. That's great!

We'll continue to put together our script to install Arch Linux in this chapter. More precisely, we'll see:

- How to create a dialog where the user can specify the size of the swap partition.
- How to wipe a hard disk.
- How to automatically create partitions with fdisk.
- How to ask the user for the hostname of the current system.
- How to automatically format our partitions with a filesystem.
- How to install Arch Linux.

I won't reexplain everything since we already did all of that manually in the first chapters. Instead, I'll focus on the scripts themselves.

Size of the Partitions

Let's begin like real warriors by adding the following in our script `install_sys.sh` :

```
default_size="8"
dialog --no-cancel --inputbox \
    "You need three partitions: Boot, Root and Swap \n\
    The boot partition will be 512M \n\
    The root partition will be the remaining of the hard disk \n\n\
    Enter below the partition size (in Gb) for the Swap. \n\n\
    If you don't enter anything, it will default to
  ↪ ${default_size}G. \n" \
    20 60 2> swap_size
size=$(cat swap_size) && rm swap_size


[[ $size =~ ^[0-9]+$ ]] || size=$default_size
```

First, we initialize a new variable `default_size` with the value `8` . This is the default size for our swap partition, in gigabytes. Then, we create a dialog box with a text field (type `inputbox`) to let the user change the default size of the partition. We save this size in a file called `swap_size` . Nothing new here, we've already discussed all of that in the previous chapter.

The last line of the script is more interesting. We already saw how to create conditionals in a shell script using square brackets `[]`. The double square bracket `[[]]` extends the functionalities of the single square bracket, but it's not always compatible with old shells. It allows you to use more operators, like matching a string against a regular expression using the operator `=~`, exactly what we use in our script.

The regular expression `^[0-9]+$` will match any number. Consequently, we verify here if the value of the variable `size` is a number. If it's not, what's on the right part of the OR operator `||` is evaluated and the variable size takes the value of the `default_size` variable, `8`. It prevents our future self from typing nonsense and possibly crashing the script.

Come on, we all know we love to type nonsense.

Erasing the Hard Disk

It's time to be a bit more violent: let's destroy everything we have on the hard disk. We'll offer to our user two possibilities: wiping the whole hard disk using `dd` or `shred`. Let's add the following line to our script `install_sys.sh`:

```
dialog --no-cancel \
    --title "!!! DELETE EVERYTHING !!!" \
    --menu "Choose the way you'll wipe your hard disk ($hd)" \
    15 60 4 \
    1 "Use dd (wipe all disk)" \
    2 "Use schred (slow & secure)" \
    3 "No need - my hard disk is empty" 2> eraser

hderaser=$(cat eraser); rm eraser

function eraseDisk() {
    case $1 in
        1) dd if=/dev/zero of="$hd" status=progress 2>&1 \
            | dialog \
            --title "Formatting $hd..." \
            --progressbox --stdout 20 60;;
        2) shred -v "$hd" \
            | dialog \
            --title "Formatting $hd..." \
            --progressbox --stdout 20 60;;
        3) ;;
    esac
}
```

We provide three choices to the user, thanks to the dialog box of type `menu` . This choice is saved to the file `eraser` , the content of which is assigned to the variable `eraser` . You can copy past the code for the dialog box above and try it safely into Bash. It won't wipe your actual hard disk, I promise.

Don't copy and paste in your shell the function `eraseDisk` ! If you did, don't call it, or it will have the effect of a Balrog on Gandalf: fire and shadows.

Speaking of which, we are creating an `eraseDisk` function. The variable `$1` in the function's body contains the value of the first argument passed to that function. Increasing the number will target different arguments depending on their *order*: `$2` represents the second argument passed to the function, `$3` the third, and so on.

We create then a switch case: if `$1` is equal to `1` , the command following `1)` is executed. Note that every case of a switch construct in Bash needs to end with a double semicolon `;;` .

If the user chooses the first option, `dd` will fill the hard disk with zeros. I explain a bit more how dd works in one of the first chapters of this book. The second choice uses `shred` : it's more secure (nobody will be able to recover the data except if the CIA is on the case) but it takes much more time. Since `dd` is already pretty slow, I always stick with it when I need to clean a hard disk.

We can pass arguments to a Bash function by adding them after the function call, separated with space. **Do not call this function on your current system**. Don't ruin your life with one command.

Now, add the following in your script:

```
eraseDisk "$hderaser"
```

We simply pass the choice the user made as first argument of the function.

Creating Partitions

Let's now automatically create partitions using `fdisk` , as we did manually a long time ago.

Boot Partition With BIOS or UEFI

The type of the boot partition is different whether your motherboard's firmware is a BIOS or a UEFI. Let's create a variable to decide what type we need depending on that.

We can add the following to our script:

```
boot_partition_type=1
[[ "$uefi" == 0 ]] && boot_partition_type=4
```

The variable `boot_partition_type` will be set to `4` only if the boot mode is UEFI. Wonderful!

Automating fdisk

Let's now automate the creation of partitions with fdisk. **Don't run the following in one of your shell**, or you might mess up your actual partitions.

I would advise you to copy the following code from the book companion in your script, because the formatting and empty lines between the two `EOF` are critically important. If you want to type them manually, there are two empty lines after the first and second `n`, three of them after the third one.

If you wonder what's the book companion, just click here.

```
1   #g - create non empty GPT partition table
2   #n - create new partition
3   #p - primary partition
4   #e - extended partition
5   #w - write the table to disk and exit
6   partprobe "$hd"
7   fdisk "$hd" << EOF
8   g
9   n
10
11
12  +512M
13  t
14  $boot_partition_type
15  n
16
17
18  +${size}G
19  n
20
21
22
23  w
24  EOF
25  partprobe "$hd"
```

The first lines are comments to explain a bit what's happening here. Very often,
single-letter commands are not the best to convey meaningful information. Imagine
if you had to use single-letter words to communicate! Don't do that at home.

As we saw in this book already, running fdisk displays a prompt where you can manually enter these single-letter commands to do what you want to do. To automate
that, we need to give the good input to fdisk.

We use heredoc to do exactly that. The general syntax is the following:

```
<command> << <delimiter>
    <here_document>
<delimiter>
```

The delimiter often chosen is `EOF` (for e nd o f f ile), but you can use any string you
want. Everything in the `<here_document>` is given to `fdisk` as an input (including
the new lines), thanks to the `<<` , till `EOF` is read.

For example, if you try to run the following in your terminal, you'll see that what you feed to `cat` will be then output by `cat`.

```
cat << EOF
This is a line
This is a new line
Woupi!

EOF
```

What's the role of `partprobe` in this story? It tells the kernel that the partition table changed. We do it before using fdisk in case you changed something manually before, or in case you re-run the script after fdisk failed. We also do it after calling fdisk because we changed the partition table.

Formatting partitions

Now that our partitions are created, we need to format them with the filesystems we want. Again, don't run the next lines in your shell or you might mess up your partitions.

General Case

Let's add the following to our script:

```
mkswap "${hd}2"
swapon "${hd}2"

mkfs.ext4 "${hd}3"
mount "${hd}3" /mnt
```

If you wonder what all of that means, you can come back to this chapter. We assume that `2` and `3` are the partition numbers created via fdisk from an empty hard disk.

Special Case

If the system use a UEFI, we need to format our boot partition and mount it. Let's add the following to our script:

```
if [ "$uefi" = 1 ]; then
    mkfs.fat -F32 "${hd}1"
    mkdir -p /mnt/boot/efi
    mount "${hd}1" /mnt/boot/efi
fi
```

You should be able to understand these few lines by now. If you don't, no worries: it will come with time.

Generating fstab And Installing Arch Linux

It's time for our script to install Arch Linux! I can feel it being full of joy to finally accomplish its main purpose in its life.

Let's add the following to our happy script:

```
pacstrap /mnt base base-devel linux linux-firmware
genfstab -U /mnt >> /mnt/etc/fstab
```

Again, nothing new here. We first install some basic packages, group of packages, and meta-packages, and then we write our mounting points to the file `fstab` .

The Adventure Continue!

We need now to fetch from our GitHub repository the next script we didn't write yet. Let's add the following to our script:

```
# Persist important values for the next script
echo "$uefi" > /mnt/var_uefi
echo "$hd" > /mnt/var_hd
mv comp /mnt/comp

curl https://raw.githubusercontent.com/<your_github_user_name>\
/arch_installer/master/install_chroot.sh > /mnt/install_chroot.sh

arch-chroot /mnt bash install_chroot.sh

rm /mnt/var_uefi
rm /mnt/var_hd
rm /mnt/install_chroot.sh
```

Don't forget to replace `<your_github_user_name>` with the user name of your GitHub account.

What black magic are we doing here? First, we copy the values of the two variables `uefi` and `hd` into two files, and we copy the file `comp` too. We'll need these values in the next script we'll run using `arch-chroot`, and persisting them in files is a good way to pass values from one shell script to another.

The command beginning with `curl` fetch the content from a server (using the HTTP protocol here) and output it. This script doesn't exist yet, but we'll write it in the next chapter.

The line following the call of `curl` execute `arch-chroot` with two arguments:

- `/mnt` – Change the root directory of the live system to the `/mnt` directory.
- `bash install_chroot.sh` – `arch-chroot` will run this command automatically after changing the root directory, in order to run the next script.

The End of the Installer

The script `install_chroot.sh` will call other scripts, too. When the execution of the script is done, the complete installation will be done too. That's why we clean up everything afterward, by deleting every file only useful for installing the system.

Then, we display a farewell message. Add the following to the script `install_sys.sh`:

```
dialog --title "To reboot or not to reboot?" --yesno \
"Congrats! The install is done! \n\n\
Do you want to reboot your computer?" 20 60

response=$?
case $response in
    0) reboot;;
    1) clear;;
esac
```

We use the special Bash variable `$?` to get the return code of the dialog box: `0` if the user chose "Yes" and `1` if the user chose "No".

In a Nutshell

What did we learn in this chapter?

- We can wipe an entire hard disk using dd or shred.
- Using heredoc to pass a specific input can be very practical if you deal with CLIs using their own prompts.

In the next chapter, we'll begin to write a new script we'll execute in the chroot environment.

Going Deeper

- Linux Documentation Project- Here Documents[1]

---

[1] https://tldp.org/LDP/abs/html/here-docs.html

Creating Users and Passwords

It's time to create our new script:

```
touch ~/workspace/arch_installer/install_chroot.sh
```

This script will run in the context of `arch-chroot`, which means that it will use the new root directory we've set.

What will we see in this chapter?

- How to reuse the variables we've saved in files at the end of the previous chapter.
- How to automatically install the bootloader GRUB.
- How to automatically set the clock, the timezone, and the locale.
- How to create new users and change the password of existing ones using a homemade function.

Are you ready to dive even deeper into shell scripting? I hope, because let's face it: it's your destiny.

Getting Back the Block Devices and the Boot Mode

First and foremost, we need our shebang at the beginning of our script, as always:

```
#!/bin/bash
```

Next, we need to reuse the variables we saved at the end of the previous script. Just add the following lines to `install_chroot.sh`:

```
uefi=$(cat /var_uefi); hd=$(cat /var_hd)
```

In case you forgot: using `;` allows you to tell the shell interpreter that what follows should be on a new line. As a result, the line above is equivalent to:

```
uefi=$(cat /var_uefi)
hd=$(cat /var_hd)
```

We now have our block device (the hard disk) and the firmware of our motherboard (BIOS or UEFI) back.

Naming Your Newborn System

We need to name our system. Just add the following command:

```
cat /comp > /etc/hostname && rm /comp
```

That was easy!

Keyboard Layout

If you changed the keyboard layout during your first installation of Arch Linux, you also need to change it in your installer. Add the following to your file:

```
loadkeys <your_keymap>
echo "KEYMAP=<your_keymap>" >> /etc/vconsole.conf
```

You can replace `<your_keymap>` with the layout you've defined in the file `/etc/vconsole.conf`.

Installing The Bootloader GRUB

We've changed our root directory and the CLI dialog is not installed on this new filesystem, so let's add to the script:

```
pacman --noconfirm -S dialog
```

Next, let's install GRUB by adding these lines:

```
pacman -S --noconfirm grub

if [ "$uefi" = 1 ]; then
    pacman -S --noconfirm efibootmgr
    grub-install --target=x86_64-efi \
        --bootloader-id=GRUB \
        --efi-directory=/boot/efi
else
    grub-install "$hd"
fi


grub-mkconfig -o /boot/grub/grub.cfg
```

As you can see, the GRUB installation is a bit different if we have a UEFI: we need to tell good old GRUB about the mount point of our boot partition.

Clock and Timezone

Time is important, so let's define our timezone. Let's add these lines to the script:

```
# Set hardware clock from system clock
hwclock --systohc

timedatectl set-timezone "<your_timezone>"
```

Don't forget to replace `<your_timezone>` with... your timezone. If you're not sure what your timezone is, you can get it on your system by running `timedatectl` without any arguments.

To list all timezones available, you can run `timedatectl list-timezones` in your shell.

Configuring the Locales

Now that our timezone is set, we need to configure our locales. Let's add the following in the script:

```
echo "<your_locale>" >> /etc/locale.gen
locale-gen
echo "LANG=<your_locale>" > /etc/locale.conf
```

Again, you need to replace `<your_locale>` with whichever locale you want. You can display the locale you have on your system with the command:

```
localectl status
```

Here's the output I have on my system:

```
System Locale: LANG=en_US.UTF-8
    VC Keymap: n/a
    X11 Layout: n/a
```

I'm French, living in Berlin, but I like my computer to speak American English. As a result, I have in my install script the following:

```
echo "en_US.UTF-8 UTF-8" >> /etc/locale.gen
locale-gen
echo "LANG=en_US.UTF-8" > /etc/locale.conf
```

If you're not sure what to write in the file `/etc/locale.gen` , you can run in a terminal `grep <country_code> /etc/locale.gen` , as we did already a long time ago. I would advise you to choose `UTF-8` if it's available.

Root Password and User Creation

This chapter till now was pretty easy (and boring). It's time for interesting bash scripting.

We need to ask the user running our installation scripts to choose a password for the root user. As we saw, it's risky to use this user by default because it has too much power. We don't want to destroy our beautiful system or allowing a creepy hacker to steal all our funny cat pictures, do we?

The following function will allow you to create as many users as you want and to choose a password for them. The function itself can take zero or one argument. Let's add it to your script:

```
function config_user() {
    if [ -z "$1" ]; then
        dialog --no-cancel --inputbox "Please enter your user name."
          ↪ \
            10 60 2> name
    else
        echo "$1" > name
    fi

    dialog --no-cancel --passwordbox "Enter your password." \
        10 60 2> pass1
    dialog --no-cancel --passwordbox "Confirm your password." \
        10 60 2> pass2

    while [ "$(cat pass1)" != "$(cat pass2)" ]
    do
        dialog --no-cancel --passwordbox \
            "The passwords do not match.\n\nEnter your password
              ↪  again." \
            10 60 2> pass1
        dialog --no-cancel --passwordbox \
            "Retype your password." \
            10 60 2> pass2
    done
    name=$(cat name) && rm name
    pass1=$(cat pass1) && rm pass1 pass2

    # Create user if doesn't exist
    if [[ ! "$(id -u "$name" 2> /dev/null)" ]]; then
        useradd -m -g wheel -s /bin/bash "$name"
    fi

    # Add password to user
    echo "$name:$pass1" | chpasswd
}

dialog --title "Root password" \
    --msgbox "It's time to add a password for the root user" \
    10 60
config_user root

dialog --title "Add user" \
    --msgbox "Let's create another user." \
    10 60
config_user
```

Let's break this down to understand what this code is doing:

```
if [ -z "$1" ]; then
    dialog --no-cancel --inputbox "Please enter your user name." \
        10 60 2> name
else
    echo "$1" > name
fi
```

As we saw earlier, `$1` is the value of the first argument passed to the function `config_user`. The *conditional operator* `-z` verifies if the variable is empty.

- If that's the case, we didn't pass any argument when calling the function. Therefore, we want to create a new user; so we ask for a user name using a dialog input box.
- If we want to modify the password of an existing user, or creating a user with a specific name, we can directly pass the user name to the function.

In both cases, the user name is saved in a file called `name`.

We then have the following commands:

```
dialog --no-cancel --passwordbox "Enter your password." \
    10 60 2> pass1
dialog --no-cancel --passwordbox "Confirm your password." \
    10 60 2> pass2

while [ "$(cat pass1)" != "$(cat pass2)" ]
do
    dialog --no-cancel --passwordbox \
        "The passwords do not match.\n\nEnter your password again." \
        10 60 2> pass1
    dialog --no-cancel --passwordbox \
        "Retype your password." \
        10 60 2> pass2
done
name=$(cat name) && rm name
pass1=$(cat pass1) && rm pass1 pass2
```

Two new dialog boxes are created. The first allows us to add a password for the user, the second one to confirm the password, and both input fields are saved in two different files. We use a loop `while` here to verify that the two passwords are the same. If not, the while loop goes on forever till the two passwords match.

We then create the variables `name` and `pass1` taking the content of the files we've created. We delete the useless files afterward.

Next, we have this code:

```
# Create user if doesn't exist
if [[ ! "$(id -u "$name" 2> /dev/null)" ]]; then
    useradd -m -g wheel -s /bin/bash "$name"
fi

# Add password to user
echo "$name:$pass1" | chpasswd
```

The condition `"$(id -u "$name" 2> /dev/null)"` verify that the user does exist. To really understand how it works, you can try to pass the following in your Bash shell:

```
id -u root
```

This command will return `0` because the user root exists; if you try to run `echo $?`, you'll see that the exit code is `0`, too. Now, you can try to run this in Bash:

```
id -u thisUserDoesntExists
```

Since the user `thisUserDoesntExists` doesn't exist, an error will be output via the standard error stream, and the exit code will be `1`, which means that there's an error somewhere. To go back to the conditional in our script, we throw away the error message because we don't really care about it, by doing `2> /dev/null`.

Now, we want to execute the inside of the `if` statement if the user doesn't exist. However, our conditional is true if the user does exist; that's why we need to add a bang `!` to inverse the exit code. If it's `0`, it will be considered as false, and if it's something else, it will be true.

That's all for the conditional. What about the following line?

```
useradd -m -g wheel -s /bin/bash "$name"
```

We've seen `useradd` in a previous chapter. If the user doesn't exist, this command will create it (with its home directory), add it to the group `wheel`, and set its default shell to Bash (for now).

What about the last lines of the functions?

```
# Add password to user
echo "$name:$pass1" | chpasswd
```

This is a convenient way to set up passwords for users. It takes an input which is of format `<user_name>:<password>` . Simple and effective.

That's all! We've covered the entire function. What about these last lines?

```
dialog --title "Root password" \
    --msgbox "It's time to add a password for the root user" \
    10 60
config_user root

dialog --title "Add user" \
    --msgbox "Let's create another user." \
    10 60
config_user
```

The function `config_user` is called two times. The first call creates the root password: the user root does already exist so it's not created. The second call create a new user, displaying an input box during installation to enter its name.

Arch Linux Is Now Fully Configured

A big part of our installation is done! We can then install all the applications we need. We'll create another script for that.

But before let's add the following in our current script `install_chroot.sh` :

```
echo "$name" > /tmp/user_name

dialog --title "Continue installation" --yesno \
"Do you want to install all your apps and your dotfiles?" \
10 60 \
&& curl https://raw.githubusercontent.com/<your_github_user_name>\
/arch_installer/master/install_apps.sh > /tmp/install_apps.sh \
&& bash /tmp/install_apps.sh
```

First, we save the user name we've created in a file to use it in the next script. Then, we ask if the user wants to install all the applications we need and the dotfiles we've already created throughout the book.

If we answer `yes` to this sweet dialog box, the next script will be downloaded thanks to cURL. Don't forget to replace `<your_github_user_name>` with the user name of your GitHub account. Finally, we call the script.

If the user answers "No", the script stops. Since the whole purpose of `arch-chroot` is to run the script, it stops too. In that case, the last part of the first script `install_sys.sh` is executed and the farewell dialog box is displayed.

In a Nutshell

What did we learn in this chapter?

- The installation of Grub is different depending on the firmware of your motherboard.
- How to automatically configure timezones and locales using a Bash script.
- How to create a more complex function to create users or update their passwords.

In the next chapter, we'll write another script to begin to install all the applications you need on your system.

Going Deeper

- Bash conditional expressions[1]
- `man id`
- `man useradd`

---

[1] https://www.gnu.org/software/bash/manual/html_node/Bash-Conditional-Expressions.html

Installing The Tools

Now that Arch Linux can be installed and configured using our beautiful installation scripts, it's time to automatically fetch and install all the applications we need.

We'll introduce a bit of flexibility here. Our needs can change as well as the software we want to use.

In this chapter we'll see:

- How to create a CSV containing all the apps we'd like to install using Neovim and how to parse it using Bash.
- How to install every application in this CSV.
- How to automatically add our new user to the wheel group (with the permission to run sudo).

We're close to our goal: courage and determination!

The List of Applications

It's time to create another new script. Run the following in your shell:

```
nvim ~/workspace/arch_installer/install_apps.sh
```

Then, let's add the following:

```
#!/bin/bash

name=$(cat /tmp/user_name)

apps_path="/tmp/apps.csv"
curl https://raw.githubusercontent.com/<your_github_user_name>\
/arch_installer/master/apps.csv > $apps_path
```

First we get back the user name we created in the last chapter and store it in the variable `name`. We'll use this variable later in the script. Second, we download a mysterious file called `apps.csv`. As always, replace `<your_github_user_name>` with your real GitHub user name.

The file `apps.csv` will contain all the applications we want to install on our new system. To create it, you can execute the Neovim command `:new apps.csv` directly in the editor. Neovim will open a new split window and create a new file `apps.csv` in the working directory. Remember: you can run `:pwd` to display the p ath of your w orking d irectory in Neovim.

This is where the Neovim plugin `chrisbra/csv.vim` we've installed in a previous chapter will come in handy. It will display the file in a more readable way, without modifying it.

Let's copy and paste the following lines in our file `apps.csv` :

```
essential,xorg,X server
essential,xorg-xinit,Display server boot
essential,man,Manual
essential,man-pages,Manual pages
network,openssh,Remote login tool for SSH protocol
network,networkmanager,Network manager
tools,rsync,Synchronizing files across computers
tools,arandr,xrandr GUI
tools,xsel,Manipulate the X selection
tools,fzf,Command line fuzzy finder
tools,scrot,Screenshot software
tools,udiskie,Automount devices
tools,lxappearance,Theme switcher for GTK+
tools,xcape,Configure modifier keys to act as other keys
tools,ripgrep,Faster alternative to grep
tools,htop,Interactive process viewer
tmux,tmux,Terminal multiplexer
tmux,tmuxp,Configure tmux session + windows + panes via config files
notifier,dunst,Notification system
notifier,libnotify,Notifier
git,git,Version control system
git,diff-so-fancy,Human readable git diff
i3,i3-wm,i3 window tile manager
i3,i3status,i3 status bar
i3,i3lock,i3 lock monitor
i3,dmenu,Dynamic menu for X
i3,feh,X11 image viewer
i3,arc-gtk-theme,Desktop themes
zsh,zsh,Unix shell (Z-Shell)
zsh,zsh-completions,Additional completions for Zsh
zsh,zsh-syntax-highlighting,Syntax highlighting for ZSH
neovim,neovim,Editor... and much more
neovim,python-neovim,Python for neovim
neovim,python2-neovim,Python2 for neovim (AUR)
neovim,ruby-neovim,Ruby for neovim (AUR)
neovim,nodejs-neovim,Nodejs for neovim (AUR)
js,nodejs,Nodejs (for coc.vim)
js,yarn,Dependency manager (for coc.vim)
urxvt,rxvt-unicode,Terminal Urxvt
urxvt,urxvt-tabbedex-mina86-git,Improved tabs for Urxvt (AUR)
firefox,firefox,Browser Firefox
qutebrowser,qutebrowser,Qutebrowser
lynx,lynx,Text-based browser
```

What does each column represent?

- The first column is the group ID.
- The second column is the *exact name* of the package we want to install.
- The third column is the description of the package (for information only).

Everything we've installed manually from the beginning of this book is included here. Feel free to add or delete anything you want.

Groups of Applications

Why do we need a group ID as first column of our CSV? I find it very handy to let our future selves choose the applications we want to install. We won't have the granularity to choose exactly what package we want, but we'll have the opportunity to choose the groups of packages we need as defined in our `apps.csv` file. To do so, let's copy the following in the script `install_apps.sh` :

```
dialog --title "Welcome!" \
    --msgbox "Welcome to the installation script for your apps and
    ↪  dotfiles!" \
    10 60

apps=("essential" "Essentials" on
      "network" "Network" on
      "tools" "Nice tools to have (highly recommended)" on
      "tmux" "Tmux" on
      "notifier" "Notification tools" on
      "git" "Git & git tools" on
      "i3" "i3 wm" on
      "zsh" "The Z-Shell (zsh)" on
      "neovim" "Neovim" on
      "urxvt" "URxvt" on
      "firefox" "Firefox (browser)" off
      "js" "JavaScript tooling" off
      "qutebrowser" "Qutebrowser (browser)" off
      "lynx" "Lynx (browser)" off)

dialog --checklist \
"You can now choose what group of application you want to install.
↪  \n\n\
You can select an option with SPACE and valid your choices with
↪  ENTER." \
0 0 0 \
"${apps[@]}" 2> app_choices

choices=$(cat app_choices) && rm app_choices
```

Here we create a new Bash array `apps` . We build it based on these three elements:

1. A group ID matching the ones in our CSV file `apps.csv` . It's important not to misspell them!
2. A name to display.
3. The default status (`on` or `off`) for each package group. Every package belonging in a group with status `on` will be installed. We can change it manually during the installation.

If you remember our dialog box of type `radiolist` , we needed a tag, an item and a status for each option. We try to do the same here, but for another type of dialog box, a `checklist` . The only difference: the user can select more than one option.

On the last two lines we save every group ID the user selected (the groups with the status `on`) in a file `app_choices` . We then copy the value of the file into a variable, as we did many times before.

You can try to run in Bash the commands above to understand how it works. For example, if the user doesn't change the default selection, the content of the variable `$choices` will be:

```
essential network tools tmux notifier git i3 zsh neovim urxvt
```

We know what we want to install. Great! But it's not over. We still need to:

1. Parse the CSV.
2. Find the group IDs in the CSV which are equal to the group IDs we've selected in our dialog box.
3. Install every application in these groups.

Parsing the CSV

To get what we want from the CSV, we need to create a regular expression to extract the package names from the second column.

Let's copy the following into your script `install_apps.sh`:

```
selection="^$(echo $choices | sed -e 's/ /,|^/g'),"
lines=$(grep -E "$selection" "$apps_path")
count=$(echo "$lines" | wc -l)
packages=$(echo "$lines" | awk -F, {'print $2'})

echo "$selection" "$lines" "$count" >> "/tmp/packages"
```

Let's analyze this line by line:

```
selection="^$(echo $choices | sed -e 's/ /,|^/g'),"
```

We build here a regular expression (or regex) based on the observation that each group ID is at the very beginning of each line in the CSV. We also notice that a group ID end when we encounter the first comma `,` of each line. We get the value of the variable `choices` (the choices made by the user thanks to the dialog box), and we pass it as input to the CLI `sed` we've seen in a previous chapter. `sed` will replace every space with the characters `,|^`.

For example, if the variable `choice` has the following value:

```
essential network tools tmux git i3 zsh neovim urxvt
```

The variable `selection` will have therefore this value:

```
^essential,|^network,|^tools,|^tmux,|^git,|^i3,|^zsh,|^neovim,|^urxvt,
```

The value of `selection` is a regular expression. The characters `^` and `|` are called meta-characters. These characters have a meaning when they are used as argument to some CLIs. More precisely, the caret `^` means "beginning of the line", and the pipe `|` is a logical OR in this context.

Let's now look at the second line:

```
lines=$(grep -E "$selection" "$apps_path")
```

We create here a new variable `lines` , based on the value of the variable `apps_path` we've defined at the beginning of the script. We pass the whole content of the CSV file to grep as input, and grep will output every line matched by our regular expression.

To really understand what this means, let's look at the first group ID from the variable `selection` : `^essential,` . The CLI grep will output every line beginning (`^`) with the string `essential,` . Since we use an OR `|` , grep will try to match every line beginning with `network` , every line beginning with `tools,` , and so on. As a result, the content of our CSV minus the lines not matching our regular expression will be saved in the variable `lines` .

Let's look now at the third line:

```
count=$(echo "$lines" | wc -l)
```

We use the CLI `wc` (for w ord c ount) with the option `-l` to count the number of lines we have. It gives us how many applications we need to install; we'll simply display this information for the user.

What about the fourth line?

```
packages=$(echo "$lines" | awk -F, {'print $2'})
```

We use Awk again but, this time, we use it with the option `-F` followed by a comma `,` . This means that we want to separate the different columns of our input using a comma `,` , and not with a space (the default, as we saw in a previous chapter). The variable `packages` will contain the second column of every line in `lines` . In other words, we'll end up with the list of packages we want to install.

The last line output the result of all these variables in a temporary file.

```
echo "$selection" "$lines" "$count" >> "/tmp/packages"
```

This temporary file can be useful if you have a problem and you need to debug what's happening. Once again, I encourage you to try all of these commands in Bash to understand how it works.

Updating the System

Now that we have the packages we want to install, we just have to loop through them and install them one by one. But before doing that, let's update the whole system by adding the following in our script:

```
pacman -Syu --noconfirm
```

Now it's time to populate our empty system will all these juicy packages!

Installing the Packages

We'll use Pacman to install the different packages. We can't install the AUR packages yet for two reasons:

1. We need to install the package manager Yay to install AUR packages.
2. An AUR package should never be installed by the user root. In our script, right now, we are the all powerful root.

For now, let's add this line in our script `install_apps.sh` :

```
rm -f /tmp/aur_queue
```

If Pacman can't find the package we want to install, we assume it's available in the AUR. We need to defer the installation by writing the package name in the file `/tmp/aur_queue` . We'll use this file in our next script to install these packages.

Before doing that, we need to make sure that the file `/tmp/aur_queue` doesn't exist already. That's why we delete it using `rm` . Without the option `-f` (for `f` orce), rm would output an error if the file doesn't exist.

Let's add an amazing message in our script:

```
dialog --title "Let's go!" --msgbox \
"The system will now install everything you need.\n\n\
It will take some time.\n\n " \
13 60
```

Then, copy the following lines in the same script:

```
c=0
echo "$packages" | while read -r line; do
    c=$(( "$c" + 1 ))

    dialog --title "Arch Linux Installation" --infobox \
    "Downloading and installing program $c out of $count: $line..." \
    8 70

    ((pacman --noconfirm --needed -S "$line" > /tmp/arch_install
     ↪  2>&1) \
    || echo "$line" >> /tmp/aur_queue) \
    || echo "$line" >> /tmp/arch_install_failed

    if [ "$line" = "zsh" ]; then
        # Set Zsh as default terminal for our user
        chsh -s "$(which zsh)" "$name"
    fi

    if [ "$line" = "networkmanager" ]; then
        systemctl enable NetworkManager.service
    fi
done
```

As always, let's go through the different commands, beginning by this one:

```
echo "$packages" | while read -r line; do
done
```

We iterate through every package here using a while loop, which begins with the keyword `while` and end with `done`. We give as input (using a pipe) the content of the variable `packages` to `while read -r line`. It will store every line of `packages` in a new variable, `line`. This `line` variable will have the package name as value. We can then use this name in the body of the loop itself.

The option `-r` is only useful if your input has backslashes, but I would advise to always use it with `read` because it's always better to be safe than sorry.

The awkward line `c=$(( $c + 1 ))` show you how to do arithmetic with Bash scripts. Quite horrible, isn't it? The variable `c` represents the number of packages installed, to display how many packages we've installed and how many still need to be installed.

Next, we display a dialog box with some useful information with the following commands:

```
dialog --title "Arch Linux Installation" --infobox \
"Downloading and installing program $c out of $count: $line..." 8 70
```

Nothing new here. After that, we finally install the packages themselves with the lines:

```
((pacman --noconfirm --needed -S "$line" > /tmp/app_install 2>&1) \
|| echo "$1" >> /tmp/aur_queue) \
|| echo "$1" >> /tmp/arch_install_failed ;
```

The line `pacman --noconfirm --needed -S "$line"` installs the package. We know that the option `--confirm`, and `--needed` only install a package if it's not installed on the system already (or not up-to-date).

The symbol `>` indicate that we redirect the standard output stream of pacman into the file `/tmp/app_install`, in case something goes wrong.

We have not encountered yet `2>&1`. We can use `&` to indicate that we want to redirect a stream to another stream. If we would have written `2>1`, we would have redirected the standard error stream (with file descriptor 2) into the file with name "1". What we do instead is redirecting the standard error stream to the standard output stream, which is itself redirected to the file `/tmp/app_install`, thanks to the character `&`.

In short, any output from Pacman (errors or not) will be redirected to `/tmp/app_install`.

It's very likely that one day you'll encounter something very similar in another shell script:

```
pacman --noconfirm --needed -S "$line" &> /tmp/app_install`.
```

If you do, don't panic: `&>` is just a handy alias for `2>&1`.

You'll notice that all of this is surrounded with parentheses. If any command has an exit code different from 0 (meaning something went wrong), we will consider the package causing the failure is available via the AUR. Therefore, we write the package name into the file `/tmp/aur_queue`.

If pacman itself fails, we write to another file to indicate that the package will never be installed. Again, pretty useful if you want to debug something which went wrong afterward.

Finally, the last lines run some commands depending on the package we install:

```
if [ "$line" = "zsh" ]; then
    # Set Zsh as default terminal for our user
    chsh -s "$(which zsh)" "$name"
fi

if [ "$line" = "networkmanager" ]; then
    # Enable the service NetworkManager for systemd.
    systemctl enable NetworkManager.service
fi
```

If we're installing Zsh, we set the default shell for our user at the same time. If we install the network manager, we make sure systemd will run the service at boot time, for us to then be able to access The Great Internet and argue on Reddit for hours.

Permission For Power: sudo

You remember that we needed to use `visudo` to add our new user to the `sudo` group? Well, this time, we won't. We'll just add the line we want to the file `/etc/sudoers` :

```
echo "%wheel ALL=(ALL) ALL" >> /etc/sudoers
```

I admit it's a bit dirty (it's always better to use `visudo`) but it works. That's the most important.

Invoking The Last Installer Script

We can now call the next and final script `install_user.sh` that we haven't written yet. Let's add the following in our script (don't forget to replace `<your_github_user_name>`):

```
curl https://raw.githubusercontent.com/<your_github_user_name>\
/arch_installer/master/install_user.sh > /tmp/install_user.sh;

# Switch user and run the final script
sudo -u "$name" sh /tmp/install_user.sh
```

Thanks to `sudo -u` , this new script will be run by the user we've created in the last chapter.

That's all for this script!

In a Nutshell

We went through quite a lot in this chapter:

- We can filter out the packages we don't want to install by creating a regular expression and use it with grep.
- To install these packages, we go through every single one of them using a while loop.

In the next chapter, we'll see how to install the packages available in the AUR.

Going Deeper

I think you went deep enough!

The User Installer

This is it! In this chapter we'll write the last script for our installer. The end is near my friend.

In this chapter we'll see:

- How to install the applications which are available on the Arch User Repository (AUR).
- How to download and install our dotfiles.

Let's first create a new script:

```
nvim ~/workspace/arch_installer/install_user.sh
```

Courage! We're almost there! I can already see the light!

Usual Linux Directories

Many Linux distributions comes with two "well known" directories[1]: `~/Documents` and `~/Downloads` . They are used by many applications so let's create them. Just add the following at the beginning of the script:

```
#!/bin/bash

mkdir -p "/home/$(whoami)/Documents"
mkdir -p "/home/$(whoami)/Downloads"
```

If your dream is to finally understand who you are, the command `whoami` will help you in a profound way. It will return the name of the current user, which is the name of the user's home directory too. Deep, I know.

Keyboard Layout

If you don't use the US keyboard layout, you need to change it for X by adding this command in your file:

---

[1] https://wiki.archlinux.org/index.php/XDG_user_directories

```
localectl --no-convert set-x11-keymap <country_code>
```

You need to change `<country_code>` by the one you want, for example "fr".

Installing Packages From the AUR

Let's create a new function in our script by adding these lines:

```
aur_install() {
    curl -O
      ↪   "https://aur.archlinux.org/cgit/aur.git/snapshot/$1.tar.gz"
      ↪ \
    && tar -xvf "$1.tar.gz" \
    && cd "$1" \
    && makepkg --noconfirm -si \
    && cd - \
    && rm -rf "$1" "$1.tar.gz" ;
}
```

This function needs to be called with one argument: the name of the package we want to install from the Arch User Repository (AUR). We already went through this process when we installed the package manager Yay; this is the automated version.

What's happening in `aur_install` ?

1. We download a snapshot of the repository.
2. We decompress it.
3. We use the script `makepkg` to build the package, with `-s` to s ynchronize its dependencies, and `-i` to i nstall the package with Pacman afterward.
4. The last line delete the temporary files.

Next, let's add the following function accepting one or more arguments:

```
aur_check() {
    qm=$(pacman -Qm | awk '{print $1}')
    for arg in "$@"
    do
        if [[ "$qm" != *"$arg"* ]]; then
            yay --noconfirm -S "$arg" &>> /tmp/aur_install \
                || aur_install "$arg" &>> /tmp/aur_install
        fi
    done
}
```

The command `pacman -Qm` outputs the packages installed which are *not* in the databases of packages from the official repositories. These packages need to be installed manually, or with an AUR helper like Yay. The output of `pacman -Qm` gives back the name of the package in the first column and its version in the second. We pipe this output to Awk to only get the packages' name.

Then, we loop on the special variable `$@`, which is an array of every argument passed to the function. At each iteration of the loop, a package name is stored in the variable `arg`. The conditional `$qm != *"$arg"*` verifies that if one of the arguments passed to the function is not in the list of packages installed (but not present in the official repositories), we install it.

Let's now look at the following line:

```
yay --noconfirm -S "$arg" &>> /tmp/aur_install \
    || aur_install "$arg" &>> /tmp/aur_install
```

What happens here is:

1. The command `yay --noconfirm -S $arg` is interpreted. We try here to install the package given as an argument to the function.
2. `&>>` redirects the standard output and the standard error streams to the file `/tmp/aur_install`.
3. If Yay fails, we use the function `aur_install` to install the package.

Everything's good so far! Now, let's add the following in our script:

```
cd /tmp
dialog --infobox "Installing \"Yay\", an AUR helper..." 10 60
aur_check yay

count=$(wc -l < /tmp/aur_queue)
c=0

cat /tmp/aur_queue | while read -r line
do
    c=$(( "$c" + 1 ))
    dialog --infobox \
    "AUR install - Downloading and installing program $c out of
    ↵ $count: $line..." \
    10 60
    aur_check "$line"
done
```

We first install Yay directly using our function `aur_check`, and then we iterate
through our file `/tmp/aur_queue` where we've written every package Pacman
couldn't install.

Installing the Dotfiles

It's time to install the dotfiles we've been crafting with love throughout the book.
Let's add the following to our script:

```
DOTFILES="/home/$(whoami)/dotfiles"
if [ ! -d "$DOTFILES" ]; then
    git clone
    ↵ https://github.com/<your_github_user_name>/dotfiles.git \
    "$DOTFILES" >/dev/null
fi

source "$DOTFILES/zsh/.zshenv"
cd "$DOTFILES" && bash install.sh
```

I know it's getting a bit old, but I'll repeat it anyway: don't forget to replace
`<your_github_user_name>`.

The conditional `-d "$DOTFILES"` is true (return the exit code 0) if the d irectory
stored in the variable `DOTFILES` exists. We negate this expression with a bang `!` to

execute the body of the conditional if the directory doesn't exist. Then, we download our dotfiles.

Next, we source our file `.zshenv` to get all the environment variables we need to install all our dotfiles.

When the script ends, `arch_chroot` ends too, and we come back to our script `install_sys.sh`. It displays a last dialog box and... the installation is done!

The One Command To Invoke The Installer

The easiest way to test our scripts is to use a virtual machine. We can install virtualbox for that:

```
sudo pacman -S virtualbox
```

When you boot the Arch Linux live system from your USB key, you first need to connect to the Internet. You'll find everything you need in one of the first chapter of the book.

Then you can type and run the following command in a shell:

```
curl -LO https://raw.githubusercontent.com/<your_github_user_name>\
    /arch_installer/master/install_sys.sh
```

This command will download your first script. To run it:

```
bash install_sys.sh
```

When you'll install all your applications using Pacman, you can change tty with the keystroke `CTRL+ALT+F2`, for example. To go back to the installation, hit `CTRL+ALT+F1`.

When you're on another tty, you can look at the output of Pacman while all your software is being installed, with the command:

```
tail -f /tmp/arch_install
```

Kind of neat, isn't it?

In a Nutshell

What did we learn in this chapter?

- Many applications use the directory `~/Documents` and `~/Downloads` by default. Using them is the easiest way to keep your sanity.
- To install our AUR packages, we need to be sure they're not installed on our system, they're not present in the official repository, and they can be fetched from the AUR.
- To install our dotfiles, we need to download them, source all the environment variables we need, and run the dotfiles installer we wrote.
- To install your own system after booting on the Arch Linux live system (from a USB key, for example), you need first to connect to the Internet, second to download and run the first script `install_sys.sh` .

This is the end of the adventure! But an adventure should always lead to a treasure. We'll discover it in the next chapter!

Going Deeper

- Official AUR home[1]
- Arch Wiki – Arch User Repository[2]
- Arch Wiki – XDG user directories[3]

---

[1] https://aur.archlinux.org/

[2] https://wiki.archlinux.org/index.php/Arch_User_Repository

[3] https://wiki.archlinux.org/index.php/XDG_user_directories

Part IV - Customizing Your Environment

Alternative Tools

The adventure is over. In front of you lays a treasure every mouseless developer dreams about: free alternative tools you can explore at your heart's content.

The knowledge and the experience you've accumulated throughout the book will allow you to skim the documentation of these tools with ease, configure them with a graceful dexterity, and integrate them in the little world you've crafted with love, the love of a Mouseless God (or Goddess).

Linux Distribution

If you want to toss Arch Linux for another distro, here's a small selection which might answer your needs:

- Manjaro[1]

You like the benefits of Arch Linux but you don't want to be involved in the installation process? You should take a look at Manjaro. It's based on Arch and propose many different installations.

- EndeavourOS[2]

EndeavourOS is based on Arch Linux too. It's pretty new but it's already considered as the spiritual successor of another beloved but discontinued distro, Antergos.

Like Manjaro, it offers different ways to install Arch Linux, even an offline one. Handy if you can't configure Internet before installing everything.

- Lubuntu[3]

You still want a very light OS but you don't like this concept of rolling distribution? You don't want to install everything manually or use scripts to install your whole system? Lubuntu should please you.

It's shipped with LXDE/LXQT, a very light desktop. Additionally, It's easy to install i3 on side: Lubuntu will let you choose the desktop environment you want at each login. Perfect to get used to tiling window managers.

Lubuntu is based on Debian, Ubuntu, and LXQT.

---

[1] https://manjaro.org/

[2] https://endeavouros.com/

[3] https://lubuntu.net/

- Debian[1]

Debian is a popular Linux distro used on many desktops and servers. It's considered very stable and secure, and it's the base for many other distros too. A solid choice.

- openSUSE[2]

With openSUSE you have the choice between rolling or regular releases. If you're frustrated with Arch Linux or just curious to look at a similar distro, it's an alternative you should try.

An Alternative to X

As we saw, the display server X11 is around for a long time, and it comes with some technical and security issues. Wayland[3] is an attempt to provide a new display server for Linux-based systems trying to fix all these issues.

Because many GUIs (including desktops and tiling windows managers) rely on X, it's a bit more difficult to find some application fully compatible with Wayland. It has a layer of compatibility with applications relying on X, but not all will work as you would expect. If you want more adventures in the Abyss of the Eternal Configuration, you should definitely give it a try.

Tiling Window Manager

- xmonad[4]

You might fall in love with xmonad if you're already a haskell lover: you can program this tiling window manager using your favorite language.

I don't know the ways of Haskell myself (it's on my list), so I never really tried it; however, it has good reputation and you can apparently automate everything heavily. Who doesn't like that?

- dwm[5]

---

[1] https://www.debian.org/

[2] https://www.opensuse.org/

[3] https://wayland.freedesktop.org/

[4] https://xmonad.org/

[5] https://dwm.suckless.org/

If you think i3 is too bloated, you should try dwm. It's a very minimal tiling window manager with less than 2000 lines of code. To configure it you need to modify the code of the application itself.

- AwesomeWM[1]

If you want a mix between i3 and xmonad without Haskell, you should try AwesomeWM. You can program it using Lua and it comes with many functionalities out of the box, like desktop notifications or a system tray for example.

- Sway[2]

If you decided to drop X for Wayland, you might be sad to learn that i3 won't work very well. I'm here to cheer you up : Sway is an attempt to bring an i3-like window tiling manager under your new and shiny display server.

Shells

You want an alternative to Zsh? Bash is the obvious one. Beyond that, here's a couple of shells you might like. You can find many others on the Internet, but I don't think they bring much more on the table.

- Fish[3]

Zsh has the reputation to be complicated to configure by yourself and pretty bloated. That's why many prefer using Fish. You might also prefer its simpler completion system.

- nushell[4]

This is a nice attempt to create a more modern shell. It has many interesting functionalities you should check out, like the ability to output tables you can manipulate easily instead of lists of strings like more traditional shell.

Terminal Emulators

I love URxvt for its speed, but I agree that it's far from being perfect. There are many alternatives you can check out but I think these three stand out.

---

[1] https://awesomewm.org/

[2] https://swaywm.org/

[3] https://fishshell.com/

[4] https://www.nushell.sh/

- st (Simple Terminal)[1]

The simple terminal is even simpler than URxvt. If you want something extremely light, you should definitely consider this one.

- kitty[2]

kitty is part of a new generation of terminal using the GPU to squeeze out some good performance. It can tile multiple windows making tmux almost unnecessary. You can also extend it with small terminal scripts named... kitty. Speaking of which, let's admit it: this terminal has a cute name.

- Alacritty[3]

Alacritty, like kitty, is a GPU-accelerated terminal. It tries to be as tiny and fast as st or URxvt, while displaying characters and glyphs as accurately as possible.

Editors

There are too many editors out there for my poor brain to know them all. I'll focus here on editors you can run in your shell.

Non-Modal Editors

Neovim makes you sick? You hate these useless NORMAL and INSERT modes? That's your right, and I respect it. Here are some non-modal alternatives:

- GNU nano[4]

Should I really describe nano? It's simple:

1. If you cultivate an infinite hate for Vim, you'll like nano.
2. If you like Vim, you'll try to burn nano to the ground.

- GNU emacs[5]

---

[1] https://st.suckless.org/

[2] https://sw.kovidgoyal.net/kitty/

[3] https://github.com/alacritty/alacritty

[4] https://www.nano-editor.org/

[5] https://www.gnu.org/software/emacs/

Neovim has not enough functionalities? You want an ~~editor~~ OS on top of your OS you can configure endlessly using a nice dialect of Lisp? You should try emacs in that case.

There is a bloody war between the Adepts of emacs and the Monk of Vim going on for decades. Personally, I know on what side of the fence I am. Do you?

- ne (nice editor)[1]

If you think Vim or emacs are too complicated, you should try ne. It's a very simple and lightweight editor.

- micro[2]

Another simple and lightweight editor you can configure using Lua. It has nice defaults too.

- Tilde[3]

This editor offers you a nice TUI (Terminal User Interface) which tries to mimic a GUI in a terminal. Why not?

Modal Editors

You want a modal editor but you know that your hate for Neovim will continue to burn for all eternity? You can try these alternatives then:

- Vim[4]

Vim is the grandfather of Neovim. It's *almost* identical to Neovim at the time I'm writing these lines. The main difference is the philosophy: Neovim is more community driven and Vim is tightly managed by its main authors and contributors.

Both editors will diverge more and more as time goes by. For example, Neovim will integrate directly the support for LSP and allow you to write your configuration and your customized functions using Lua. Vim has another roadmap.

- Kakoune[5]

Kakoune tries to be more visual than Vim or Neovim: you can see each step of the changes you're making while typing keystrokes.

---

[1] https://github.com/vigna/ne

[2] https://micro-editor.github.io/

[3] https://os.ghalkes.nl/tilde/

[4] https://vim.org

[5] https://kakoune.org/

- amp[1]

This editor tries to give you only what you need. As such, it has no plug-ins and zero configuration.

Terminal Multiplexer

Many find tmux bloated, and I can't blame them: it has many functionalities indeed. If you search lighter alternatives, these two might answer your needs:

- GNU screen[2]

GNU screen is around for a long time. It has less functionalities compared to tmux.

- dtach[3]

If you think that screen is still too bloated, you should look at dtach. It's very minimal and care only about creating, attaching, and detaching sessions.

In a Nutshell

Keep in mind that I only described a fraction of what's available out there. The possibilities are infinite!

If you have other nice suggestions, don't hesitate to reach out. I'm always happy to discover new tools and new ways of getting things done.

In the next chapter we'll virtually hug, cry a bit, and say goodbye to each other.

---

[1] https://amp.rs/

[2] https://www.gnu.org/software/screen/

[3] https://github.com/crigler/dtach

Inspiring Communities

If you're here because you've just finished this book, I would like to congratulate you. You've made it, you've built your own Mouseless Development Environment. I hope it was useful and you've enjoyed it!

I would like to thank you for picking this book. I've put a lot of time and energy into this project, and I hope it shows. I would also like to apologize for any mistakes I've made while describing the Mouseless Development Environment. Sorry. I'll do my best to catch them, but, you know, I'm human. I think...

Feel free to contact me about any mistake you've spotted, feedback, question, or any cool stuff you've stumbled upon this morning while browsing the Internet:

- I'm on Twitter[1], trying to deliver as much value as I can one tweet at a time. My content there is mostly for developers.
- I've a blog[2] where I publish articles related to mouseless tools from time to time.
- You can send me an email at `matthieu.cneude@yahoo.fr` . I know, I might be the only one left on this planet using Yahoo as email provider. It's mainly to feel different.

All the tools I describe in this book are free. It would be great to support these projects if you can. This kind of support often comes in the form of either money or time, please check the websites for these tools to see how to best contribute to their individual projects. If you don't have the capacity to do that, tell your friends and relatives how cool they are. The more exposure these tools get the better. Even a small amount can go a long way.

Farewell, and see you soon for new and exciting adventures!

Going Deeper

Here are some communities where you can find new tools and ideas to improve your system:

- Arch Linux[3]
- Reddit - Command-line[4]

---

[1] https://twitter.com/Cneude_Matthieu

[2] https://thevaluable.dev/

[3] https://bbs.archlinux.org/

[4] https://www.reddit.com/r/commandline/

- Reddit – Unix porn (nothing offensive there)[1]
- Reddit – Neovim[2]
- Reddit – Zsh[3]
- Reddit – tmux[4]

---

[1] https://www.reddit.com/r/unixporn/
[2] https://www.reddit.com/r/neovim/
[3] https://www.reddit.com/r/zsh/
[4] https://www.reddit.com/r/tmux/

Annexes

i3 Cheatsheet

General

WIN+ENTER	Open a new terminal
WIN+SHIFT+q	Quit the focused window
WIN+d	Open the dmenu launcher
WIN+SHIFT+c	Reload i3's configuration
WIN+SHIFT+r	Restart i3
WIN+BACKSPACE	Lock, shutdown, or reboot menu
WIN+CTRL+SHIFT+l	Lock the system
WIN+x	Open the dmenu screen management
WIN+z	Remap CAPS LOCK to CTRL and ESC

Moving Around

WIN+[hjkl]	Focus window: left (h), down (j), up (k), right (l)
WIN+SHIFT+[hjkl]	Move window: left (h), down (j), up (k), right (l)
WIN+r	Switch to resize mode (then WIN+[hjkl] to resize)
WIN+CTRL+h	Split container horizontally
WIN+CTRL+v	Split container vertically
WIN+SHIFT+<number>	Move container to workspace <number>

Container Layout

WIN+e	Switch to split layout (default)
WIN+s	Switch to stacked layout
WIN+w	Switch to tabbed layout

Scratchpad

`WIN+SHIFT+t`	Scratchpad tmux
`WIN+SHIFT+p`	Scratchpad htop

URxvt Cheatsheet

Copy & Paste

CTRL+ALT+c	Copy
CTRL+ALT+v	Paste

Tabs

CTRL+SHIFT+n	Open a new tab
CTRL+SHIFT+r	Rename tab
CTRL+SHIFT+k	Select next tab
CTRL+SHIFT+j	Select previous tab
CTRL+SHIFT+h	Move tab to the left
CTRL+SHIFT+l	Move tab to the right

Clearing Shell

CTRL+g	Clear shell's output

Neovim Cheatsheet

Basic Horizontal Motions

`[hjkl]`	Move cursor: left (h), down (j), up (k), right (l)
`w`	Move to the next word
`b`	Move backward to the previous word
`0`	Move to the beginning of the current line
`^`	Move to the first non-blank character on the current line
`$`	Move to the end of the current line

Basic Vertical Motions

`1 SHIFT+g or gg`	Move to the first line of the current buffer
`SHIFT+g`	Move to the last line of the current buffer
`<number> SHIFT+g`	Move at line `<number>`
`%`	Move to the matching bracket (if the cursor is on bracket)

From NORMAL to INSERT mode and back

`i`	Switch to INSERT mode before the character under the cursor
`a`	Switch to INSERT mode after the character under the cursor
`A`	Switch to INSERT mode after the end of the current line
`o`	Open a new line below the current one, and switch to INSERT mode
`O`	Open a new line above the current one, and switch to INSERT mode
`ESC`	Switch back to NORMAL mode

Scrolling

`CTRL+u`	Move half a screen upward
`CTRL+d`	Move half a screen downward

Undo and Redo

```
u         Undo
CTRL+r    Redo
```

Operators (need to be followed with a motion)

```
d    Delete
c    Change
y    Yank (copy)
```

Examples of Text Objects

```
diw    Delete Inside Word
ciw    Change Inside Word
caw    Change A Word
ci'    Change Inside '
```

Creating and Navigating Windows

CTRL+[hjkl]	Navigate windows: left (h), down (j), up (k), right (l)
CTRL+w v	Split vertically the current window
CTRL+w h	Split horizontally the current window
CTRL+w n	Split horizontally the current window, and open a new buffer
CTRL+w ^	Split the current window with the alternate buffer

Resizing and Moving Windows

CTRL+W r	Rotate the windows
CTRL+W x	Exchange the focused window with the next window

CTRL+W [-+]	Decrease (-) or increase (+) window's height
CTRL+W [<>]	Decrease (<) or increase (>) window's width
CTRL+W =	Resize windows equally for them to fit the screen

Writing Buffers and Closing Windows

:w	Write the current buffer into the file
:q	Quit the current window, close Neovim if there is no more window open
:q!	Quit the current window, and ignore the buffer's modifications
:qa	Quit all the windows (add ! to ignore buffers' modifications)
:wqa	Quit and write all the windows

tmux Cheatsheet

General

`CTRL+SPACE`	Prefix key
`PREFIX r`	Reload tmux configuration

Panes

`CTRL+[hjkl]`	Navigate panes
`PREFIX h`	Split window horizontally
`PREFIX v`	Split window vertically
`PREFIX ALT+ARROW KEYS`	Resize panes

Windows

`PREFIX w`	Create a new window
`PREFIX n`	Rename the current window
`ALT+[kj]`	Go to: next window (k), previous window (j)

Copy Mode

`PREFIX [`	Enter copy mode
`[hjkl]`	Navigate the shell (in copy mode)
`CTRL+[ud]`	Move half a page: up (u), down (d) (in copy mode)
`/`	Search (in copy mode)
`v`	Selection (in copy mode)
`y`	Copy selection (in copy mode)

Plugins

`PREFIX SHIFT+i`	Install the plugins declared in tmux.conf
`PREFIX /`	Regex search (copycat)
`PREFIX CTRL+g`	Select files from Git status output (copycat)
`PREFIX CTRL+u`	Select URLs from shell output (copycat)
`PREFIX CTRL+i`	Select IPs from shell output (copycat)
`PREFIX TAB`	Select and copy output with fzf (extrakto)

www.ingramcontent.com/pod-product-compliance
Lightning Source LLC
LaVergne TN
LVHW060607200726
843509LV00004B/200